THE FABULOUS FLYING MRS MILLER

Carol Baxter is the author of many highly acclaimed books about fascinating people, including *An Irresistible Temptation*, *Captain Thunderbolt and His Lady*, *Black Widow* and *The Peculiar Case of the Electric Constable*, published in the United Kingdom and around the world. She lives in Sydney and is a fellow of the Society of Genealogists.

Jessie 'Chubbie' Miller: the picture that Bill Lancaster
treasured most. (Getty Images)

Other books by Carol Baxter
An Irresistible Temptation
Breaking the Bank
Captain Thunderbolt and His Lady
The Peculiar Case of the Electric Constable
Black Widow

THE Fabulous Flying MRS MILLER

A true story of adventure, danger, romance and derring-do

CAROL BAXTER

SCRIBE

Scribe Publications
2 John St, Clerkenwell, London, WC1N 2ES, United Kingdom
3754 Pleasant Ave, Suite 100, Minneapolis, Minnesota 55409 USA

Published by Scribe 2019
Reprinted 2019

Maps by Janet Hunt
Set in Minion Pro by Midland Typesetters, Australia

Scribe Publications is committed to the sustainable use of natural
resources and the use of paper products made responsibly from those
resources.

9781947534773 (US edition)
9781911617921 (UK edition)
9781925693614 (ebook)

A catalogue record for this book is available from the British Library.

scribepublications.com
scribepublications.co.uk

To the fabulous Chubbie Miller, for your consideration in leaving so many personal accounts describing your activities, thoughts, feelings and conversations.
A reader's delight. A writer's dream.

Contents

FAMOUS WOMAN FLYER ARRESTED

Mrs Keith Miller, internationally known aviatrix, was taken to the county jail here today and held for investigation by State Attorney's investigators. Jail attendants said they understood she was held in connection with the shooting of an airline pilot.

Harold Farkas, United Press

Prologue

Nobody could have foreseen such an unprecedented response.

From all over Britain, people converged on London's Croydon Airport, lugging picnic baskets brimming with pies and buns and sugary cakes, and pulling out cards and novels to while away the hours. By mid afternoon on Sunday, 29 May 1927, every approach was clogged with vehicles and pedestrians, a honking, cursing muddle. Trams and buses pushed through the crowds. Trains disgorged thousands more to join the eager multitudes. At 3.30 pm, when the long-awaited plane commenced its journey across the English Channel towards Croydon, 25,000 spectators already thronged the aerodrome's perimeters.

Airport authorities watched apprehensively as wooden fences bent under the pressure. Still the people kept coming: 50,000, 100,000 . . .

At 5.52 pm, the control tower's klaxon sounded its discordant warning. All eyes turned towards the horizon where a clump of dark dots had appeared. A moment later, a drone could be heard as if a swarm of bees buzzed towards the aerodrome. Soon, the dots transformed into an honour guard of three large biplanes at the front and three smaller ones at the back. Between them, Lilliputian-like, flew a sleek monoplane.

At the sight of the monoplane, the spectators' mood changed. A sigh of satisfaction, of awe, erupted from thousands. Then they swept across the airfield, trampling wooden fences, knocking down iron barriers, surging through the police cordons, determined to reach the runway where the plane was about to land.

Officials, policemen, pressmen and photographers screamed 'Get back! Get back!' Airmen jumped into automobiles to try to herd the mob like sheep. If they failed to corral them, the pilot would have to abandon the official British welcome and land elsewhere in ignominious obscurity—not the celebration planned for the newly crowned King of Aviation.

As the monoplane circled the aerodrome, a strip of ground cleared amid the throngs of people and vehicles, allowing the pilot to swoop down and roll to a stop. The cockpit opened and a smiling man stood up and waved to the cheering crowd. America's Captain Charles Lindbergh had just reached England in the *Spirit of St Louis* after his epic Atlantic crossing from New York to Paris, the flight that would launch the Golden Age of Aviation.

Never before had the entire world worshipped a human as if he were a god. In the words of a biographer, it was as if the man had walked upon water rather than flown over it.

The world's extraordinary response to Lindbergh's achievement was an epiphany to anyone who had ever dreamed of success or craved a more exciting life. One such person was in London that day, a petite, vivacious, twenty-five-year-old Australian housewife, with bobbed dark hair and mischievous brown eyes. In the years to come, she would move into Lindbergh's aviation circle. Indeed, her name would also be splashed across the world's newspapers although, in her instance, partly through fame and partly through infamy. Yet Lindbergh's flight didn't directly trigger the transformation in her life that began a few weeks later. Instead, it was something so small, so mundane, so ridiculously prosaic, as a pat of butter.

Part One
HOPES

Chapter One

If she'd been asked before her holiday to imagine a word to describe London, it wouldn't have been 'freedom'.

Her late father had long urged her to visit his home country. His England was a world of dainty whitewashed cottages nestling around spires that thrust resolutely towards the heavens, of church fetes and church dances and church picnics, where the vicar was loved almost as much as his god. It was a world of moral rectitude and righteousness, of class and, most importantly, tradition. Everyone had their place and—as long as they accepted it—all was right with the world.

The lure for her had been different, touristy more than anything. The chance to drink tea beside the Thames as it slipped through the greatest city in the western world. To stroll across the romantic London Bridge. To ogle the crown jewels that boasted the nation's wealth and importance.

Yet it was the atmosphere of flapper London that proved so unexpected, so at odds with her father's fond memories of a Victorian England. The 'bright young things' who dashed around London in their loose glittery dresses and daring knee-high skirts had not only abandoned the Victorian constraints of corset and crinoline, of piety and prudery, they had embraced the sensual. Their adventurous flamboyance expressed an intoxicating independence, an uncaging of body and soul. This freedom represented the dawn of a new era, with London as its centre, the quintessence of modernity.

It couldn't have been more different to the insular world she had come from, the world that would drag her back when her six-month holiday had ticked away.

She was born Jessie Maude Beveridge on 13 September 1901 in what, by comparison, was the middle of nowhere: the town of Southern Cross, sitting on Western Australia's flat red earth, 230 miles from Perth at the terminus of a railway line. The town was named after the constellation that twinkles above the southern continent and guided two prospectors to strike gold there in 1888. Its name suggested an otherworldliness for its inhabitants, that they were beings of both the Earth and the stars. But while most of its early residents never had the chance to rise above the Earth's clutches, for 'Chubbie'—as she was nicknamed in childhood—life would be different. Not only would she take to the skies, the name 'Southern Cross' itself would play a strangely significant role in shaping her destiny.

Her birth in Southern Cross proved as serendipitous as the gold discovery. Those glittering specks lured business operators to set up shop alongside its dusty roads, among them her father, Charles Stanley Beveridge, a Commercial Bank manager. The pious son of an English vicar, Charles met her mother, Ethelwyn Maude Lavinia Hall, who was the equally devout daughter of an Australian clergyman, when she visited Southern Cross to attend a wedding. Their marriage was a match made in heaven, so to speak. But for Chubbie, all that stultifying spirituality would propel her from the nest as soon as her fledgling wings could carry her.

Late in 1906, her family packed their trunks and headed to Broken Hill, New South Wales, another hot dry mining town in Australia's sunburnt outback where her father established another Commercial Bank branch. There she found her own spiritual solace: the piano. As music filled her soul, she dreamed of becoming a concert pianist. Her parents' ambitions for her were more traditional: marriage and motherhood. And she had been brought up to respect and obey.

When the Great War began, she dutifully knitted socks and mittens for the soldiers. She would have preferred playing the piano or being outside in the sunshine: swimming, playing tennis or riding any horse given to her, whatever its temperament. Her adventurous spirit wasn't suited to the role of a submissive daughter—or, in the future, wife. Nor was her sense of humour or her tendency to say what she thought. To fit in, she needed to curb her hasty, unrestrained ways, to learn tact and reticence.

In 1915, her family relocated to Timaru in New Zealand's South Island—prettier but much colder than outback Australia—where her father established yet another bank branch and she attended the Craighead Diocesan School for Girls. There, her musical abilities were celebrated in gold letters on the school's honour board, an achievement that for most of her peers would have been their only award in the inexorable progression towards marriage and motherhood.

Two years later, her family moved back across the Tasman to Australia's second-largest city, the bustling metropolis of Melbourne. Desperate to escape the family home, she took the only step towards freedom allowed in her parents' narrow world.

His name was George Keith Miller, although everyone called him Keith, and he was a twenty-two-year-old journalist for Melbourne's *Herald*. They were married on 3 December 1919, just two months after her eighteenth birthday. Looking back, she could see that they were mere babes playing at being adults. Still, marriage offered her more control over her life: no more strict rules, no more prayers and piety, no more church.

As the 1920s dawned, her first baby was born prematurely at six months and lived for only five hours. Her second and third miscarried. The doctors said she wasn't the right build for child-bearing, so her hopes of having a family died with them. Then her father succumbed to cancer in 1924 and her brother Tommy to kidney disease in September 1926, aged only twenty. She and Tommy had been soulmates, lying on the hearth rug together on chilly winter nights, making plans to travel the world. His death was the final soul-destroying loss in a half-decade of heartbreak.

Her husband couldn't provide the consolation she needed. Their personalities and characters were so different they had already drifted apart. She was finding it increasingly difficult to hide the truth from herself, to admit that she had married the wrong man and was stuck with him forever. They jogged along together, making the best of things, and probably would have kept on doing so if Tommy's death hadn't acted as a catalyst.

When she received a letter from her father's sister inviting her to England, she decided that a six-month holiday was the medicine she needed. She asked Keith to join her. But while she still yearned to travel the world, Keith was content to sit by the fire. He said no.

She thought about travelling there on her own, but didn't know how to finance such a journey. Her despair deepened.

Over the previous few years, a feeling of discontentment and purposelessness had festered inside her as she realised that the role of wife and mother—the role she had been nurtured to fill—was no longer open to her. What was she to do with the rest of her life? It was obvious that the postwar world was different to that of her childhood. The war had allowed middle-class women to enter the workforce and, try as the conservatives might, this genie refused to be shoved back inside the domestic bottle. Women like herself were no longer valued only as wives and mothers. They could work and earn money rather than wait for handouts from their parents and husbands.

The chance to earn her holiday cash came only a short time after Tommy's death, when she attended Melbourne's Royal Show. For a lark, she stepped up to demonstrate an electric suction cleaner and proved so able she was hired by the company and sent into rural Victoria to sell their products. Before long, she had earned enough money to pay for her fare.

As summer slipped into the autumn of 1927, she kissed and hugged her loved ones and climbed the gangway of the ship that would take her to England. With a blast of its horn and an answering yelp from the tugboats, it pulled away from the dock and headed down the Yarra River. As she stood on the deck waving goodbye, she wasn't to know she was farewelling her old life forever.

Melbourne had seemed the epitome of modernity until she saw London's sophistication and elegance and found herself swept up in its giddy atmosphere of endless possibilities. She spent six weeks at her aunt's Hampstead home then, with a recently arrived Australian friend, she rented a furnished bedsit in Baker Street, the street made famous by the Sherlock Holmes mysteries.

As she and her friend clomped up the stairs one day, they encountered a young man descending towards them. He paused and asked them a question. Only with hindsight would Chubbie realise that a fork in the road had appeared in that moment—and might not have reappeared if they had given a different answer. He asked if they could lend him some butter. And they said, 'Yes'.

He knocked at their door a few days later and held out a replacement butter pat and a hand of greeting. His name was George, he said, and he was an artist living on the floor above them. Would they like to come up and see his paintings?

As he opened his door, the heady odour of paint and turpentine wafted towards them. They gazed around his large airy apartment, furnished with nothing but a small sleeping divan, a table and chair, and a scattering of cushions for his guests. His art was clearly his passion. It was everywhere—lining the walls, squatting on easels, stacked in corners. Moving around the room, they inspected his work and murmured their approval. Their sincerity transformed the hand of greeting into one of friendship.

They spent many hours with George over the next few weeks. He treated them with affectionate amusement, laughing at the things they said and did, asking fondly if all Australian girls were as naïve. In the big smoke of Melbourne, they would have resented such teasing, being convinced they were thoroughly modern women. In this bohemian city, though, far from the apron-strings of pursed-lipped family members, their eyes had been opened to their own innocence and unsophistication. Chubbie, especially, could only laugh sheepishly and ruefully admit the truth of his gentle taunts. He would understand if he knew about her pious parents and strict upbringing.

One day he announced that he was having a party and they were invited. Could they help him decorate his apartment by purchasing some items at Woolworths? Delighted to help—their first London party!—they dug into their savings and bought the requested lampshades, cushions and cheap glasses. They also agreed to use their apartment as a powder room and cloakroom for his female guests.

A few days before the party, a fist hammered at their door. George stood outside looking distraught. He said that fifty people had accepted his invitation including Layton and Johnstone—yes, the black American vocal and piano duo who had taken London's elite clubs by storm. Other famous musicians were coming as well so he had rented a grand piano from the piano manufacturer's showroom downstairs but the company required a £15 deposit and he was temporarily short of cash. Could they help him out?

Chubbie dug into her savings again.

On the big night, they donned their best evening frocks and waited at their front door to assist George's guests. They gazed star-struck at the exquisitely dressed women and then followed their perfume trail up to George's apartment. There, through the cigarette fug, they saw people talking and laughing and shrieking out greetings to newly arrived friends. It was intoxicating. Layton sat down at the magnificent piano and stretched his elegant fingers across the ivory and ebony keys. When Johnstone's rich voice joined in, Chubbie felt a sense of joy flood through her, washing away the pain of her years of heartbreak. It was time to live life to the full again.

The only discordant note in the wondrous evening was that Great War veteran Captain William Newton Lancaster—or 'Bill', as everyone called him—was besieging her. He was a few years older than her, a nice-looking man of middling height, balding, as so many were, with a friendly manner and an infectious laugh. George had introduced him as a Royal Air Force reservist who was about to fly solo from London to Australia. He introduced her as a recently arrived Australian. At the word 'Australian', Bill's eyes had lit up. Thereafter, he hadn't left her alone.

He told her that no one had yet flown a light aircraft from Britain to her homeland and he wanted to be the first. Sure, the Smith brothers had piloted the pioneer flight back in 1919 but they had flown a much larger Vickers Viking, a heavy aircraft designed for war-time service as a bomber. While theirs had a been a risky flight, it was substantially less so than his own endeavour would be. Then he plagued her with interminable questions about landing fields and weather conditions, questions that she had little chance of answering correctly as she had lived a cloistered domestic existence far from his flight path.

As she looked longingly at the musicians and other guests, he started talking about his route. He droned on and on—he evidently planned many stops between England and Australia—but the noise prevented her from hearing him clearly. At last, he admitted defeat and asked if she would have tea with him the following afternoon at the Authors' Club in Whitehall. Relieved to be free from his pestering, she agreed to meet him and returned to mingling with London's artistes.

In the distinguished tranquillity of the Authors' Club the following day, Bill described his plans again and showed her a map of his route. Although she couldn't provide much useful information, she now listened with interest. Bill said that his choice of plane was a two-seat Avro Avian biplane, an aircraft with parallel upper and lower wings or planes, as they were called, hence the term biplane. It was classified as light because its maximum take-off weight was less than 12,000 pounds, and it was designed and built for aeroplane clubs and private owners. Of course, it would need modifications for the long haul to Australia: larger fuel tanks, for example. However, he would be able to maintain it himself during the journey, which was critical. Many of the landing fields on his route would be nothing more than that—fields.

As she listened, she noticed a serious omission. Nothing concrete seemed to have been done: no plane had been ordered, no maps purchased or permits obtained, no sponsorship locked in. She asked him point blank when he was leaving London. The sorry story trickled out. He didn't have the money and his father wouldn't help him because he thought it a crazy idea.

By this time, she had had her own crazy idea. She had realised that Bill was a dreamer who lacked the practicality to put his ideas into action—a minion used to taking orders rather than the master who gave them. He needed a partner, someone who could listen to his plans, put his ideas on paper, make lists of what needed to be done, and implement them. Not only did she know such a person, she had heard him mention that he was planning to fly a two-seat aircraft.

'If I can raise the money,' she began tentatively, 'can I come with you? I have to go back to Australia and I would much sooner fly back than go by boat.'

Bill looked startled. Then he tossed a seemingly endless list of objections at her: the extra weight and its effect on petrol consumption; the dangers of plane travel; the risks they faced in politically unstable countries; the arduous conditions in an open cockpit biplane; and the obvious additional problem of her being a woman. He ended by saying that he would, however, accept any donations towards his flight fund if she was willing to offer them.

'No go, no money,' she told him firmly.

Stalemate.

They eyed each other. Bill was the first to waver. Chubbie wasn't surprised. He was smart enough to recognise that he had little to lose. If she succeeded in raising the money, his dream would come to fruition. If she didn't, he was no worse off. The only problem might be the threat to his sense of masculinity when his RAF mates discovered he was contemplating taking a *woman* on his flight.

When Bill opened his mouth, his tone was one of extreme reluctance. But he said that critical word: 'Yes'.

Soon afterwards they went to Stanfords, the travel emporium in Charing Cross Road. Although Bill had already planned his route to Australia, he needed to purchase strip maps and employ an experienced navigator to mark his courses and distances. They entered a large sunny room smelling of ink and crisp new paper. Maps of every imaginable form filled the room, mostly loose sheets of paper, but they could also see wall-mounted linen maps and spinning globes. Atlases and surveys, guidebooks and travel memoirs lined the polished shelves. It was an international traveller's Aladdin's Cave, a delicious taste of their adventures to come.

As Bill explained his requirements, he described their route. He intended to follow the exhaust trail of Dennis Rooke, who had recently attempted to fly the first light plane to Australia but had been forced to abandon the endeavour in India.

Just hearing the place names made Chubbie's blood fizz with excitement. She had already memorised the route. From Croydon aerodrome they would cross the Channel and head to romantic Paris. Then they would fly above the castles and vineyards and farming lands of France and Italy and over the Mediterranean to the sandy wastes of Libya. From there they would follow the Imperial Airways route that hugged the North African coast until it reached the land of the Pharaohs. They would cross the biblical lands of the Middle East to India then travel through the exotic Far East to Port Darwin on the northern Australian coast.

Bill had told her that Rooke's wasn't the shortest route to Australia. That honour fell to the Great Circle route, which crossed central Europe, south-east Russia, Afghanistan and the Khyber Pass to India. His friend Bert Hinkler, an Australian aviator, was soon to tackle the Great Circle route in an attempt to beat the England-to-India record. But most aviators thought it too hazardous because of its high mountains and dangerous weather conditions. Bill wasn't attempting to set a speed record—his intention was to prove that light planes provided a reliable means of travel over long distances—so he was happy to follow Rooke's safer course. At least Rooke had successfully reached India, where the two routes joined.

Stanfords said that the marked-up maps would cost £40. When Chubbie pulled out the money and handed it over, it acted as the seal

The Flight of the Red Rose

Croydon
Lympne Abbeville
Paris
Lyons
Marseilles
Pisa
Rome
Naples
Catania
Malta
Tripoli
Khoms
Sirte
Benghazi
Sollum
Aboukir
Cairo
Suez
Shaibah
Busayrah
Basra
Ramadi
Rutbah Wells
Baghdad
Persian Gulf
Bushire
Bunpaur Abbas
Karachi
Charpasni
Jodhpur
Agra
Allahabad
Ganges River
Patna
Calcutta
Akyab
Rangoon
Tavoy
Moungmagan Beach
Victoria Point
Penang Taiping
Kuala Lumpur Singapore
Batavia
Surabaya
Bima
Atambua
Darwin

Mediterranean Sea
R. of the Euphrates
INDIAN OCEAN

Legend:
— Flightpath
■ Proposed stopover
○ Actual landing point

for their verbal contract. Afterwards, as she held the precious paper receipt, she felt as if she was holding the ticket to a new life.

She sent cables to her husband and mother saying, 'Flying back with a well-known aviator. See you soon.' The return cables were almost identical and unsurprising: 'Return by boat immediately. Have cabled fare.'

She was delighted. More money. She had already brought funds from Australia to cover her return journey. And she still had her emergency fund, cash she hadn't needed to spend because of Keith's allowance. Now she had two more fares to add to the flight's treasury. She sent them pleading letters, explaining that she would never again have such an opportunity. In the end, to her astonishment, they agreed to her plans.

After collecting their maps, Bill took her to meet his parents. His father, Edward, was a retired engineer while his mother, Maud, was a strong-minded eccentric whom Bill adored. Maud had written a successful book for housewives, *Electric Cooking, Heating, Cleaning, etc.,* which had brought her financial independence. This pragmatic streak was counterbalanced by a passionate interest in spiritualism. She spent most of her time assisting the Mission of Flowers charitable organisation. She donned a nun's veil and called herself Sister Red Rose, a tribute to their family name of Lancaster and its historical allegiances.

Bill's parents were shaken—indeed scandalised—when he told them about their plans. Was their son, a married man with two children, really travelling halfway around the world with another woman? And what did his wife think?

Chubbie had already learnt by this time that Bill had a wife and two young daughters. Bill called her Kiki, although she was actually Annie Maud, yet another woman named after Lord Tennyson's Maud, the heroine of his wildly popular 1855 poem. Bill said that Kiki wasn't concerned, that she hoped the trip would rid him of his wanderlust and allow him to settle down. Chubbie later organised to meet Kiki so she could be sure of his wife's approval before the flight commenced.

Meanwhile, for Bill's parents, the fact that Chubbie was heading home to her husband made the venture slightly more palatable. And they were impressed when they saw the maps. Still, Maud told her twenty-nine-year-old son that she would consent to his flight only if he used his plane to distribute religious tracts over heathen countries. Bill explained that he couldn't carry such a weighty bundle so they agreed she would dispatch the tracts in advance and he would distribute them during his journey. Although nothing eventually came of her plans, when Bill and Chubbie needed more money in the final weeks of their preparations, it was Maud who came to their rescue.

Chubbie was amazed at the costs of such an expedition. It seemed to eat all their cash. As she later explained to her female supporters, it was like a dressmaker's bill: you estimated that a frock would cost a certain amount to be made and then discovered, when the bill came in, that you'd forgotten those little extras like buttons and fabric lining.

For an international flight, maps weren't their only additional expense. They had to purchase passports and pay for landing permits and leave deposits for telegrams that would alert other governments of their imminent arrival. They also had to buy flying kit. Fortunately, Burberrys gave them a fifty per cent discount on their flying gear.

Their largest expense was the Avro Avian, which was advertised as costing £750. A.V. Roe & Co. gave them a big discount on it, however, recognising the publicity value of their flight. Nonetheless, they still had to hand over a considerable sum of money.

To obtain the necessary funds, Chubbie had contacted those who previously promised support for Bill's flight. Most now offered excuses instead of money. So she tramped London's streets buttonholing wealthy Australian businessmen—including rich cattle king Sir Sidney Kidman—and others with an Australian connection, begging for sponsorship. She approached London's *Daily Express*, which agreed to provide funds in return for cabled reports. Her husband's newspaper and the Australian *Sun* newspaper chain signed up for the same arrangement. Obtaining a few pounds here and the occasional fifty there, she scraped up just enough money to cover the basic costs of their flight.

As she discussed the venture with potential sponsors, she discovered the key to opening their wallets: while people were politely interested in Bill's planned flight, they were fascinated to learn that she, a woman, was to accompany him. No woman had ever flown such a long distance before, either as a pilot or as a passenger, so if they reached Australia her participation alone would put their names in the record books. It wasn't long before she saw the irony. While Bill had been reluctant to accept her proposition, preferring her money to her companion-ship, it turned out that it was her involvement that served as the money magnet. Without her, his flight would never have got off the ground.

In addition to obtaining money, she kept the press abreast of their plans. Bill's friend Bert Hinkler, who had long wanted to fly to Australia, never sought publicity; however, as the wife of a journalist, Chubbie fully appreciated its value.

The press announced their imminent flight in August 1927 and published updates over the next few weeks as she and Bill provided new press releases. The newspapers added their own headlines, most focusing on her own participation—'Flight to Australia: First Lady Passenger' and 'Woman's Flight to Australia' among them. The press knew what would draw their readers' attention.

As the clock ticked down towards their planned departure date—25 September—they attended meetings with petrol and oil companies, who agreed to ship free fuel supplies to the stops along the route and offered bonuses in the event of a successful journey. Every day she went through her lists, crossing off one item after another. Her many tasks included making sure they had all the necessary landing permits—landing in a country without a permit could land them in a prison cell, particularly in places that were hostile to the British.

Bill had initially planned for two planes to make the flight, the second carrying two RAF pilots. If something went wrong with one of the planes—a distinct possibility on such a long haul—the other plane could conduct a rescue mission or obtain the necessary parts or assistance. However, the cost of two planes proved prohibitive and the RAF authorities refused to grant leave to the other pilots. By mid September they were down to one plane and a much riskier journey. Still, it wasn't enough to deter Chubbie, even though she had never been up in an aeroplane.

She had admitted early on to her lack of aviation experience, saying that her motivation for accompanying him was that the trip sounded like a great lark. But the closer they came to their departure date, the more Bill realised that it would be best if he didn't begin a 12,000-mile trip with a passenger who had no real comprehension of what was involved. She might suffer air-sickness or vertigo, or such terror that she endangered herself and everyone around her.

'Look here,' he said to her, 'you had better have a flight somewhere. Learn a bit about it so you don't go putting your foot through the wing.' He approached his friend Neville Stack, who with Bernard Leete had flown the first light plane to India, and asked if he would take her up for a spin.

Chubbie looked around at Croydon's vast aerodrome with its office buildings, hangars, fuel bowsers and aircraft of every imaginable size and type, from large imposing passenger planes to feisty little single seaters. Distant planes hummed as they waited to take off, then the sound rose to a roar as they sped past. Noise and activity surrounded her while petrol fumes made the air shimmer in the sunlight. And men were everywhere—in pilots' uniforms, mechanics' overalls, business suits. The only women she could see were airline passengers or busy office girls.

She climbed onto the wing of the RAF biplane and over the cockpit edge, settling herself into her own circular roofless compartment. Soon the propeller spun and the engine growled, surprisingly loud at such a close proximity. The plane vibrated around her. Then it bumped across the field and turned into the wind. The gentle buffeting from the propeller-driven air-stream became a confronting turbulence as the plane picked up speed. The roar was almost deafening. Finally the plane lifted off the ground, leaving her feeling strangely heavy and weightless at the same time.

As they soared into the sky, she peered over the side. The city below them reduced in size as if she were peering through the wrong end of binoculars. The higher they flew, the more it resembled a doll's village. The nearby countryside looked like a crazed chequerboard of greens and yellows, browns and greys. Gossamer-like roads criss-crossed the terrain. Trains trailed puffs of smoke but their whistles couldn't be heard above the brain-numbing drone of the engine.

She felt not a qualm, not a hint of air-sickness, just pure joy. She couldn't wait to commence their grand adventure.

Chapter Two

Bill hadn't really expected Chubbie to succeed where he had failed. A woman? A housewife? Of course, female business success wasn't completely unknown to him because of his mother's accomplishments. However, his mother was surely the exception rather than the rule and his engineer father had played a crucial role in her achievements. So he was astonished when the pint-sized Australian managed to line up sponsors and generate press attention. And he was delighted when their filling coffers signalled that his dream flight might actually take to the air.

Compared with Chubbie's previously humdrum existence, his own life had been eventful—until recent years. Born in Birmingham on 14 February 1898, he had been a thrill-seeking boy who needed to be kept physically active. He had just turned sixteen when his parents dispatched him to Australia to gain experience on the land. He headed to the Riverina district of New South Wales, a vast expanse of grass-covered plains, where he worked as a jackaroo and learnt how to manage a pastoral station. The work was tough: long days mustering livestock and mending fences, nights sleeping under the stars around a campfire.

Any pretensions to British snobbery were soon booted out of him. His brother, Jack, joined him there two years later. Jack had worked as a Westinghouse Electrical Company apprentice, so they established an electrician business in Hay. The physical, practical and problem-solving skills Bill learnt during his two years in Australia would prove an invaluable source of knowledge when he later became a pilot.

Six months after Bill was exiled to the antipodes, the Great War began. Like most adventure-seeking lads, he saw war as the stuff of dreams and legends. In his imaginary world, it was a real-life tale of heroes and villains, of good battling evil, of glory and self-sacrifice in a noble cause.

In mid 1916, just after Jack turned seventeen, they headed to Sydney and enlisted in the Australian Imperial Forces, lying about their ages so that Jack appeared eligible for war service. As drivers in the Field Company Engineers, they sailed for England in November 1916. During the voyage, Bill ingloriously contracted mumps and was hospitalised in Cape Town for a month.

Reaching England in February 1917, he joined Jack at the Perham Down training camp near Salisbury. When they saw fighter planes wheeling and swooping across Britain's skies—and English lasses fluttering their eyelashes at the swaggering flyboys—they volunteered to join the Australian Flying Corps. On 1 November, after four and a half months' training, they officially joined the corps and were seconded to 80 Squadron, Royal Flying Corps, to support the Allies in the ongoing war.

Bill knew that he was never considered more than a fair pilot to his instructors. Nonetheless, they appreciated his courage and fearlessness. These two attributes were especially useful for wartime pilots who faced death every time they climbed into a cockpit—more because of their own plane's shortcomings than the skills of their adversaries.

His first job was to ferry fighting planes across to France. It ended in January 1918 when he crashed in a blinding English snowstorm. Admitted to hospital with concussion, he suffered ongoing neurological problems: headaches, nightmares, tremors, stammered speech. 'Will never be of any use flying again,' was the medical board's dismissive opinion six months later. As there were no available ground positions with the Australian Flying Corps in the United Kingdom, and as he wanted to remain near his family rather than return to Australia, his service was terminated on 14 October. A month later, the war ended.

His father pulled some strings and obtained a temporary RAF commission for him. He spent the next year at an aviation depot in London. Demobilised in February 1920, he walked away with his war-widow bride, Kiki, the honorary rank of captain, and an opportunity to undertake a two-year university degree. He chose dentistry.

Boredom soon set in. After his years in the military, student life lacked the Boy's Own adventurousness he was used to—the thrill, the camaraderie, the feeling that, in protecting the nation, they had a higher purpose in life. More importantly, dental students with little money couldn't afford to fly. And he lived to fly. He applied to rejoin the RAF and was granted a short service commission from April 1921.

Volunteering for the forces on India's North-West Frontier, he was sent to 31 Squadron, which policed the rebellious Afghanistan and Waziristan border regions. By early 1923 he was back in England where he was on sick leave for a few months. The remainder of his commission was spent performing administrative duties at RAF training schools, first at Halton in Buckinghamshire and later at Manston in Kent.

During these training school years, he developed quite a reputation, although not because of his piloting skills. With a view to a post-RAF future, he and his father purchased an automotive garage at Wendover, not far from the Halton base. Naming it the Red Rose Garage, they installed a manager until Bill was available to run it.

With his easy access to automobiles, he became the person everyone wanted to know when a trip to London was proposed. But after they alighted from the hair-raising ride, he was the last person anyone ever wanted to travel with again. Always game, he accepted a challenge to ride a bucking bronco at an international rodeo at Wembley Station where he used his Australian outback riding skills to great success. This spawned his nickname, 'Bronco Bill'. And when the RAF finally adopted parachutes in 1925, he was among those who volunteered to demonstrate them.

His daredevil attitude to life wasn't suited to the civilian world. When he was transferred to the RAF reserves in April 1926, boredom again set in. He wanted to be back in the air. As Bill dreamed and schemed, Lindbergh conquered the Atlantic and the aviation world changed forever.

As Chubbie and Bill continued their preparations, the *Manchester Guardian*'s aviation journalist professed himself glad the deteriorating weather had halted the 'insensate craving' for flying the Atlantic that had developed over the previous few months. Instead, with summer coming in the southern hemisphere, legitimate air tourists would soon be out in their Moths and Avians, showing the world that the aeroplane was a practical, reliable and pleasurable means of travel. The flights to the dominions were generating the most interest, he reported, among them Mrs Miller's.

The Australian press was also intrigued by their venture. Melbourne's *Table Talk* advised that two great flights to Australia were again drawing the world's attention to their southern continent. From England, Captain Lancaster and Mrs Keith Miller were attempting to match Sir Alan Cobham's feat, except that Cobham had flown a large powerful seaplane whereas they were flying a small 'land' plane. And from America came the news that Charles Kingsford Smith and his companions would soon cross the Pacific in the *Southern Cross*, an epoch-making endeavour if they survived the journey.

Other aviation experts expressed mixed feelings about the flight of the *Red Rose*—the name Bill had chosen for the plane—or ignored it altogether. *The Aeroplane*'s editor was tactful: 'For some reason or another, this particular flight does not seem to be taken very seriously by those who have seen the preparations for it being made at Croydon.' In truth, Croydon's aviators were treating the whole exercise as a joke and laying bets that Bill wouldn't get much further than France. He was considered little more than an amateur because he had sat at a desk throughout most of his RAF service. By contrast, Charles Kingsford Smith and Bert Hinkler were already acclaimed pilots when they set their sights on the record books.

The experts wondered if Bill even had the skills to undertake such a hazardous journey. The most serious threat came from the lengthy water expanses he would have to cross in his single-engine Avian. The last stretch across the Torres Strait to Australia was the most dangerous. Some experts maintained that any ocean flying in a single-engine plane was nothing but a foolish stunt. Others thought that the sturdy Cirrus engine should carry it successfully to its destination. *The Aeroplane* concluded: 'For the good of British aviation in general one may hope that the attempt will meet with better success than is generally predicted.'

Then there was the issue of Bill's female passenger. Was it just a publicity stunt? The general consensus was that a female passenger on a record-breaking flight was nothing but a dead weight. Whether Chubbie would prove a help or hindrance, only time would tell.

Meanwhile, the press made the occasional reference to Hinkler's dreams of a flight to Australia. 'When Bert Hinkler does start off in his Avian for his native Queensland (which he is sure to do with the utmost secrecy),' wrote the *Manchester Guardian*, 'we shall be very much surprised if he does not lower all records for speedy travel.'

Bill knew about Bert's plan. He wasn't worried. His aviator friend had struggled for a decade to finance his own Australian flight. Surely, the odds of him miraculously finding funds overnight were slim. Besides, Bert was busy. Recently, he had garnered accolades when he flew 1200 miles non-stop from Croydon to Riga, Latvia, in thirteen hours. Currently, he was preparing his Great Circle flight to India. By the time he finished that trip and acquired enough money to pursue his Australian dream, the *Red Rose* would have completed its five-to-six-week journey. Bert might later make a faster flight but he wouldn't win the acclaim for the first light-plane flight to Australia.

And in these days of aviation glory seeking, few remembered those who came in second.

Chapter Three

Chubbie's father would have rolled in his grave if he had known she would spend most of her English holiday preparing to fly home to Australia in a flimsy open-cockpit aeroplane with an unknown married man. Of course, it wasn't how she had imagined spending her holiday either. Still, it meant that her trip was ending with more fanfare than she could have expected if she had departed as she had arrived: alone on a ship. She and Bill were the guests of honour at a farewell party hosted by the nation's pre-eminent aviation official, Air Vice Marshal Sir Sefton Brancker, Britain's Director of Civil Aviation.

Sir Sefton was a visionary who saw the potential benefits of civilian air services between Britain and its dominions. An ardent advocate of long-distance flights, he was among those who supported the *Red Rose*'s venture and had offered advice and assistance to ensure its success. He had written letters of support to Australia's Prime Minister, Governor-General, and Controller of Civil Aviation, letters that Bill and Chubbie would carry with them. And as the date of the *Red Rose*'s departure drew near, he organised to hold the farewell party at the prestigious Murray's Night Club in Soho.

There, among the glitz and glamour of cabaret London, as they twirled under the chandeliers to the jittery beat of the latest dance tunes, Chubbie had her last taste of the exhilarations of 1920s London. The vibrant city—indeed the entire world—would be vastly different by the time she returned.

When she chatted to their host, he asked about her luggage. It was a subject she'd been too busy to think about until a short time before. Restricted to only a few pounds, she had bought a small leather pouch and had stuffed it with a single change of lightweight underwear, a clean shirt and pair of shorts, a small comb and mirror, a box of powder, and a sponge bag containing a tube of toothpaste, a toothbrush and a small cake of soap. Sir Sefton told her that it was essential she pack an evening dress—a chiffon frock, perhaps—and a pair of evening shoes. While Britannia no longer ruled the waves, its imperial presence still dotted the globe. Social events would be organised at some of their stopping places and she would feel mortified if she had nothing to wear but her shorts or flying gear.

Heeding his advice, she raced into town the next morning and bought a black ninon-and-lace evening frock and a pair of black satin shoes, both weighing barely anything at all. She stashed these and a pair of silk stockings in her bag. She would silently thank Sir Sefton every time she had occasion to wear them in the weeks that followed.

Near midnight on Thursday, 13 October, Chubbie and Bill motored down to Croydon, where they were staying overnight to ensure an early departure. Bill's wife and five-year-old daughter, Patricia, accompanied them, while the baby, Nina, was left in the care of others.

When they threw back the curtains on Friday morning, they were hoping to see a blue sky or at least high, unobtrusive clouds. Instead, the pilot's bane greeted them. A thick gauze-like fog cloaked everything—buildings, trees, even the usual sounds of the morning—as if a giant eraser had swooped in overnight and obliterated their surroundings.

Chubbie pulled on her flying gear: a striped sweater, knickerbockers, thick stockings and sturdy brogues. As she stuffed her toiletries back into her bag, she hoped that the next time she tugged them out she would be across the Channel in France.

When they reached Croydon airport, they gave the *Red Rose* a final once-over, trusting that the weather would have improved by the time they were finished. A large continental airliner took off but returned a short time later, forced back by the fog blanketing southern England and the Channel. As it landed, airport officials hoisted the forbidding red flag. No more planes would be permitted to depart until the weather conditions improved.

Chubbie and Bill tried not to chafe at this new delay. Last-minute hitches had already forced them to reschedule their departure date a few times, preventing Sir Sefton and Australia's High Commissioner, Sir Granville Ryrie, from attending. The High Commissioners' wife, however, had said she would still christen the Avian although she would delay her arrival until she was certain of their departure.

As the hours ticked by and the red flag remained stubbornly in place, Chubbie and Bill and their well-wishers retired to a nearby hotel for lunch. Bill's parents accompanied them, his mother dressed in an outlandish purple costume with a red cross on her cap. Maud had looked at the tiny silver plane squatting insect-like on the airfield and had registered the danger of her son's flight. Tugging at his sleeve, she begged him not to go. When she failed to dissuade him, she passed him her little silver St Christopher medallion for luck.

Joining the party at the pub were Australian holidaymakers and expatriates whom Chubbie had befriended during her six-month holiday. Bill's RAF buddies accompanied them, among them Bert Hinkler.

A good sport, he was hiding his disappointment that Bill had beaten him—to the starting blocks, at least. As they both knew, the *Red Rose* had a long trying trip ahead of it and anything could happen along the way. Departure celebrations and press attention didn't take out the record. Landing in Australia did. Until that happened, the record remained anyone's for the taking.

Tempted by the mouth-watering aromas of hot pies and roast dinners, they all feasted and celebrated, toasting Chubbie's and Bill's health with champagne. Bundles of telegrams were brought out and read, some from British well-wishers, others from Australian friends. Chubbie's husband wished them every success in their journey. A group of her Melbourne friends invited them to lunch at the Quamby, a women's club in Melbourne, at their earliest convenience. Chubbie cabled back, 'You bet we will.'

When they returned to the airfield, the red flag was gone.

Photographers swarmed around them, snapping pictures, while newsmen pestered them with questions. Asked about her decision to make the flight, Chubbie declared, with publicity-conscious fervour more than truthfulness, 'I am an Australian and have always wished to be the first woman to fly from London to Australia.' She laughed off the journalists' remarks about risks and hardships, and said that she couldn't wait to get started.

Naturally there were the inevitable questions about her luggage. When she showed it to the journalists, one quipped, 'This is probably the smallest amount of luggage ever taken by a woman on a journey of this length.' She had set a record even before the *Red Rose* took off.

Bill talked about the route and reiterated that it wasn't a stunt flight, that his aim was to show the feasibility of flying to Australia in a light plane. He said that he would only fly in fair weather, even though this would slow them down, because he didn't want to risk compromising the success of the flight. Asked about his female companion, he said she was cool and capable and had a fine air sense. In fact, she seemed such a natural flier that he had fitted the plane with dual controls so she could take over when he was tired.

At 2.20 pm, the High Commissioner's wife swept in with her daughter and handed Bill two letters. One was from her husband to Australia's Prime Minister. The other commended the fliers to all the world's nations on behalf of the Australian Government. She scattered rose petals over the plane and christened it the *Red Rose*. They were ready to go.

Chubbie accepted a bunch of white heather for luck. With a final beaming smile and cheery wave, she climbed onto the lower wing and into the open front cockpit. Only the top half of her head could be seen above the cockpit rim.

As Bill prepared to climb into his own cockpit, Kiki gave him an affectionate goodbye kiss and then left with their daughter, saying that she preferred not to see him taking off. Every aviator's wife would have heard about Lindbergh's terrifying take-off from New York for his historic flight, when his fuel-overladen plane cleared the power wires at the end of the runway by mere inches.

Chubbie and Bill donned ear protectors to minimise the engine's drone, then pulled down and adjusted their goggles. As a member of the groundcrew pulled the propeller, the engine roared to life with a throaty growl.

At 2.37 pm, as twenty-five photographers and cinematographers captured the historic moment, the *Red Rose* rolled across the field, increasing speed until it lifted off smoothly. The crowd roared its approval.

As it climbed into the white sky, a giant Fokker came in to land. No one watching the take-off would forget the image of the two juxtaposed planes, a mosquito dwarfed by an eagle. Few could help but wonder whether such a minuscule machine could really travel 12,000 miles across half the globe to Australia.

The *Red Rose* circled the aerodrome twice as a farewell. Flanked by two other planes, it turned south-east and disappeared over the horizon.

The aftermath was anti-climactic. Instead of heading straight to the Channel and soaring across it to commence their adventure, they had to stop at Lympne aerodrome for customs clearance.

There, Bill telephoned his father to discuss the one item that hadn't yet been finalised: insurance. The insurance companies had also doubted that such a tiny plane could reach Australia without serious damage.

'To hell with them,' Bill seethed when his father told him that none of the insurance companies had weakened. 'We'll go uninsured.'

His pragmatic engineer father argued that they mustn't travel without insurance.

'If we don't leave now, we never will,' was Bill's simple response.

Unmentioned was the humiliation—the jokes, the teasing—if they scuttled back to London after all the celebrations.

Around 4 pm, they took off from Lympne and steered towards the English Channel. They were determined to spend the night in France, even though they had only an hour to fly there. However, the aviator's witching hour was approaching. Sunset. It was best not to be airborne after darkness had fallen.

Chapter Four

Heavy fog wrapped around them. By dead reckoning alone, they knew they had crossed England's shoreline, the demarcation zone between land's relative safety and the lethal sea. Yet a Channel crossing without a water sighting lacked any sense of magic. It wasn't the exciting start to their journey Chubbie had been dreaming about.

Before they left Croydon, they had been advised to rethink their overnight stop as they wouldn't make Paris before nightfall. Abbeville was a reachable alternative, a market town and regular stopping point on the London-to-Paris commercial route. But Bill hadn't had time to recalculate his compass settings. As the weakening light warned that dusk was approaching, he pulled out his book of strip maps for the region and turned to the relevant page. Reading maps while flying in an open cockpit plane was a tricky exercise. Over the engine's drone, he yelled to Chubbie, 'You take her.'

Chubbie turned around in her tiny cockpit and gaped at him. Did he really want her to fly the plane? Already? Realising that he did, she detached her joystick from the cockpit's side clip and slotted it into its socket, securing it with its pin. Grasping the knob firmly with both hands as if she would have to fight it for control, she pulled it towards her. The nose lifted and the plane shot up sharply into the fog-laden sky.

'Put her down, you clot!' Bill screamed.

She shoved the joystick forward and the nose dropped—too far. Gradually, by moving the stick forwards and backwards, she managed level flight. She turned her head to see Bill's reaction. He wasn't looking. Face down, with his head under the cockpit rim, he was examining his maps.

She kept flying, making joystick adjustments when air pockets bumped them around. Bill had told the press she was a 'natural' and his lack of concern served as a confidence booster for her. As she felt the freedom of soaring weightlessly through the sky combined with the sense of power at being in control of such an extraordinary vehicle, a change swept through her. By the time Bill had taken control again, flying had taken over her soul.

Luck continued to elude them. They crossed paths with the setting sun before they reached Abbeville. Ahead, all they could see were the soft white lights of a large town, as if the plane had turned upside down and they were gazing at a star-filled constellation in an otherwise dark sky. But none of the lights lay in distinctive parallel lines. Abbeville wasn't expecting them and hadn't turned on its airfield lights.

Chubbie already knew from Bill's preparations that night landings were to be avoided at all costs. The *Red Rose* had no lights on its panel, no night-flying instruments and no landing lights to illuminate the path ahead or to show the ground below. A crash-landing was a serious possibility—a disastrous way to commence their adventure, a deadly way, perhaps. Yet Bill seemed strangely unfazed. He looked over the cockpit rim on one side and then the other until he spotted a suitable field. As if his eyes could see through the darkness, he touched down on the bumpy ground and taxied safely to a stop.

She was impressed.

England's relations with France over the last hundred years had been a study in ambivalence: enemies to begin with, allies at the end, with intervening periods of wary contempt. French customs officials at Paris's Le Bourget airport cast suspicious gazes over Chubbie and Bill when they landed there the next morning. Learning of the flight's destination, their looks of wariness changed to astonishment. They asked to see the pair's luggage. Eyebrows rose even higher. A 12,000-mile trip to Australia, of all places, with a female passenger and virtually no luggage? They stared at Chubbie in amazement.

French Imperial Airways pilots gathered around them, intrigued by the tiny British plane. Bill took one of the pilots up for a short demonstration joy ride and the French pilots reciprocated by taking them out to celebrate. Surrounded by air rich with the aromas of coffee and pastries, with the majestic Eiffel Tower stark against the skyline, the two visiting fliers had a Parisian evening to remember, one that ended with them paddling barefoot in the cool fountain waters outside the Folies Bergère.

It was the type of merriment Chubbie had imagined when she proposed joining the flight.

Fog again for the third day in a row. Chubbie decided that she and Bill must be fog magnets. By 10 am, visibility had improved enough for them to take off. Soon afterwards though, fog engulfed them again. It was eerie and disconcerting, almost claustrophobic, and its chilly dampness clung to them in their unprotected cockpits.

Bill increased his altitude to ensure they cleared the cloud-sheathed mountains. Unable to climb above the fog layer, he maintained his course by compass alone. As long as its needle remained true, and the wind didn't push them into areas where the mountain peaks pierced the heavens, and engine trouble didn't force them down, they might yet outfly the fog layer.

Near Dijon, a rain-burst lashed the plane. Water droplets ricocheted off the propeller. Although their faces were largely protected by their windscreens, the rainwater sluiced into their open cockpits, leaving them cold, sodden and miserable. Bill dropped lower and lower, down to the dangerously low altitude of 100 feet, still unable to see the ground clearly and hoping it wouldn't rise up suddenly to become a hill or mountain. By the time the clouds thinned over Dijon, he had flown nearly blind for two-and-a-half exhausting hours. They landed for lunch and a breather before taking off again for Lyons, their stop for the night. To their surprise and delight, word of their adventure had spread and a crowd had gathered at Lyons to welcome them.

Day four and the weather continued to test Chubbie's optimism. As they flew from Lyons to Marseilles down the picturesque Rhône Valley, violent cross-winds assaulted them. The wind howled through the wings and struts, slamming against the plane from one direction then another, throwing it around so violently, so terrifyingly, she wondered if its nuts and bolts could withstand the strain.

They couldn't.

The strut bolts on the port side sheared. As the Avian lurched up and down in one particularly rough air pocket, the flying wires between the upper and lower wings slackened. These bolts and wires held the two wings together and gave the *Red Rose* its rigid wing structure and inherent strength. Any weakening allowed the two wings to move independently, creating strain on the remaining struts and wires. Unless the wind eased soon, the plane might be pulled apart.

As she clung to the side of her cockpit, the plane suddenly plummeted. The freefall shot her from her seat and slammed her into the centre section between the cockpits. Only the sturdiness of her seatbelt and buckle kept her from being thrown from the plane. They kept falling—100 feet . . . 200 . . . 300.

Their freefall ended as suddenly as it had begun, as if a parachute had miraculously bloomed in the sky above them. She dropped down into her seat again with an almighty whack. Looking around her with relief, she tugged thankfully at her seatbelt, a timely reminder of the importance of a secure buckle.

Eventually, the cross-winds eased. As they neared the Mediterranean seaport of Marseilles, the sun peeped from behind the clouds. For the first time she could see patches of blue sky, a hopeful omen after four days of depressing greyness.

They hadn't planned to stop for the night at Marseilles but they needed time to repair the plane. In the past, Bill would have alighted and walked off, leaving the repairs and maintenance in the hands of the RAF mechanics. Now the two of them were solely responsible for the daily service, a task that usually took about four hours.

Chubbie's main jobs were to clean the plugs and to filter the petrol to prevent water entering the fuel tanks. Filtering petrol was a ghastly job. Once she found something to stand on, she would pour fuel from a can through a chamois leather into the tanks. It didn't always make it. She usually wore bright red petrol burns on her skin for hours afterwards, more so when the weather was windy.

Bill had initially seemed surprised at her willingness to help, as if he had expected her to stomp her foot and say 'No!'—that she had paid her passage and refused to get her hands dirty. When he realised she wasn't just taking control of the joystick for a lark, that she wanted

35

to learn everything about piloting and maintaining a plane and was willing to do whatever was needed, dirty or otherwise, his attitude towards her began to change.

Men had always been drawn to her bubbly effervescence. On this trip, though, when they encountered her intelligence and pragmatism, her courage and adventurousness, many men began to look at her differently. Bill was among them. During the preparations for their flight, when he saw her transforming his dream into reality, his look of respect had seemed to turn inward, as if he were seeing a movie reel of what the future could hold. Now, as each day of their journey passed, as she filtered the horrid petrol and climbed back into the cockpit despite more fog and rain and wind, and as she survived each life-threatening experience without screaming that this wasn't the holiday she had expected, that she wanted to go home—in anything but a plane!—she glimpsed another look in his eyes. It was unexpected.

She helped him re-bolt and tighten the strut screws. In the previous few days, it had become increasingly obvious why long-distance pilots needed planes that could be easily maintained and why the pilots themselves required more than just basic mechanical skills. It would have cost too much money to pay for assistance everywhere they landed. Moreover, if Bill was correct, in many of their future landing places there wouldn't be any mechanics to pay, whatever the cost.

Bill used the turnbuckles to 'true up' the rigging. This involved tightening and loosening the wires until the paired wings returned to the correct rigging angle, a critical part of the plane's aeronautical design. As they worked, French aviators came to assist them, offering an international helping hand and a spirit of friendship.

Afterwards, these newfound French friends took them into Marseilles to see the sights. They ate at a peasant restaurant where hens strutted between the tables and climbed over their feet. Chubbie was ravenous, as always. Bill refused to carry stores on the plane, telling her that every ounce mattered, that the plane needed fuel more than her stomach. The restaurant staff brought sardines and onions with thick hunks of bread and cheese and vinegar-like French wine. It was their final chance to savour French food and culture. The next day, they would pass into Mussolini's Italy.

Chubbie had known that the foul weather wouldn't miraculously improve when they crossed the invisible border, but she hadn't expected it to deteriorate. The fog was now so thick she couldn't see the plane's nose. It masked the mountains that swept all the way down to the shore-line. Bill was forced to fly at 200 feet above the grey Mediterranean waters, always keeping the shoreline in sight so they could ditch into shallow water and swim to safety if anything went seriously wrong. When they reached Pisa, he mischievously circled the town's leaning landmark, astonishing the tourists tramping the unbarricaded ledges.

Blinding rain replaced fog on the leg to Rome, again forcing them out from the shoreline. As Chubbie hugged her soaking body in a futile attempt to keep out the cold, she wondered if she would have to fly all the way back to Australia before she saw much sunlight. She hadn't expected such appalling weather. It was only halfway through autumn.

When she had lain in her bed imagining their trip, her thoughts had focused on the sights and exciting experiences she would have in the places they were to visit. Six days of flying had taught her that their airborne experiences were the most dramatic. In fact, the tales she could now tell would deter most people from climbing into a cockpit. Yet, strangely, she herself wasn't deterred. Indeed, she was having so much fun she wondered how she could ever return to the boredom of married domesticity.

Rome bore an ancient splendour, with the bridges spanning the Tiber looking like clips cutting a silver ribbon into segments. Naples, the next day, had a different magnificence: the looming presence of Mount Vesuvius as a backdrop.

Upon landing at Naples, they received a warm welcome from the local airmen, as warm as the welcomes at Pisa and Rome. Two years previously, Italy's most famous aviator, Francesco de Pinedo, had flown a seaplane from Italy to Australia and had been treated with such kindness that the Italians were keen to reciprocate. They were even happier to be of assistance when the Australian was a pretty young woman.

Shortly before they were due to depart the next morning, she was sitting in the rear cockpit hand-pumping petrol when she caught her knuckles on the plane's interior wall. Blood dripped over her hand. When she showed her new friends, they flocked to her aid with a bottle of iodine.

A moment later, Italo Balbo came striding towards them. Soon to become Mussolini's heir apparent, Balbo was a National Fascist Party Blackshirt and Secretary of State for Air. He was endeavouring to build up Italy's air force, not only because of his own enthusiasm for aviation but because his empire-building leader saw it as a means of achieving his planned conquests.

When Balbo reached the *Red Rose*, he shook Bill's hand and offered him every success in his venture. He turned to Chubbie. Before she realised what he was about to do, he gallantly bent over her hand and kissed it. When he raised his head, blood and iodine stained his mouth. Aghast, she stared into the eyes of this powerful Blackshirt, who had the ear of a dictator renowned for his acts of brutality.

Balbo smiled.

'The age of chivalry is not dead,' she would later write with great relief in her journal.

At Catania, Sicily, a special messenger arrived with a note from Mussolini, offering his best wishes for a successful trip. They stashed it among their luggage. They already had the words 'Viva Mussolini' splashed across the Avian, written by Italian airmen who worshipped *Il Duce*. They hoped these advertisements for Italy's ruthless dictator wouldn't create problems for them once they left Italy.

The lonely British outpost of Malta, rising defiantly from the Mediterranean Sea, was their last European stopping point. They stayed for two nights, allowing themselves enough time to thoroughly overhaul their plane before the lengthy sea crossing ahead.

The weather had finally turned in their favour when they took to the air at 9 am on Monday, 24 October. Three RAF seaplanes followed them as they began their journey over the Mediterranean's sparkling waters. Two cruisers were also positioned at different locations along their flight path to render assistance in the event of trouble. The *Red Rose* chugged steadily through miles of clear sky as the rising sun wrapped them in its crisp light and welcome warmth. Around midday, without experiencing even the slightest hint of trouble, they crossed the Mediterranean's southern shore into Libya.

After flying 2000 miles, they had left the relative familiarity and safety of Europe for the hazards of North Africa. They had always known that if disaster was to befall them it would most likely happen after they left Europe. However, their conversations with Italy's airmen had left them even more concerned about the next legs of their journey. Inclement weather and engine trouble would be the least of the perils they might face.

Chapter Five

Politically, Libya was a sporadically erupting volcano. For centuries, conquering armies had tramped across its sands. In 1911, its most recent conquerors, the Italians, had used planes to drop bombs on its former occupiers, the Ottoman Turks, with brutal efficiency. It was the first nation to turn aircraft into weapons of war. Italy renamed Libya 'Italian North Africa' and began transplanting its own citizens—Italian-speaking Christians—onto territory Libyans saw as the land of Islam. The Italian occupying forces also ruthlessly slaughtered and subjugated the native population, particularly after Mussolini's ascension in 1922. Thus, the *Red Rose* was flying into territory in which a plane itself was a symbol of an unwanted conqueror's power and brutality, while its crew— white and Christian—were considered infidels by the increasingly wrathful Islamists.

Italy's airmen had warned Chubbie and Bill about unrest in Libya, saying, 'If you have to make a forced landing anywhere along the coast, you are in for a bad time. So, whatever else you do, take our advice and fly with the Union Jack on your machine.'

Appreciating the advice, Chubbie and Bill had searched Malta's shops and purchased a little silk automobile flag, which they tied to one of their plane's struts. If any disgruntled Libyans came within shooting range, they would hopefully see the distinctive red, white and blue British flag and hold their fire.

The Italians had also told them they would be welcome at Italian airfields, which were positioned on military bases dotted along the Mediterranean coastline. One was at Tripoli, their first North African stopover.

Tripoli's airmen mobbed them, handing Chubbie a flower bouquet so large it dwarfed her diminutive frame. They organised an afternoon tea dance, with delicious cakes and lively music. She danced and flirted with the smitten airmen, enjoying herself tremendously except for the mortification of having to entertain the men in her dirty breeches.

That evening, they dined with the British Consul, who had grave concerns about the political situation. The Italians were building a road from Benghazi to Tripoli, which had infuriated the Libyans. A skirmish had broken out—directly under the *Red Rose*'s flightpath— so stray bullets posed another threat.

Chubbie already knew about the danger of deliberate potshots. When Alan Cobham had flown to Australia two years previously, an angry desert Bedouin had fired a shot at his plane which, by an unbelievable stroke of bad luck, had killed his engineer. That the *Red Rose* might find itself flying over a battle zone was a peril she hadn't previously considered.

The next morning, Bill turned east to follow the Imperial Airways route along the North African coast, climbing high to keep away from danger. He and Chubbie felt apprehensive about landing in Khoms (Al-Khums), seventy-five miles from Tripoli, where they were to collect fuel and oil supplies. As it happened, the Libyans welcomed them as warmly as their conquerors had.

From Khoms, Bill's plan was to fly directly to Benghazi, however a strong headwind forced him to re-examine his maps. He decided instead to stop at Sirte, another coastal Italian air force base some 160 miles from Khoms.

As they flew over ochre desert, over seas of sand and scimitar-shaped dunes, they spotted a huddle of tents and congregating Libyans. From high in the sky, they looked like toys in a children's sandpit. Bill stuck his head over the side to inspect them more closely. Seeing four sharp puffs of smoke, he pulled his head back in, relieved he had maintained his high altitude.

The headwind turned into a forty-five-mile-an-hour gale. It picked up the sand and whirled it around them like a maelstrom. In their unprotected cockpits, the fine granules—more dust than sand at this height—worked their way into their teeth and ears and hair and down the backs of their clothes, chafing like sandpaper. They dismissed the personal discomfort as annoying but not dangerous. More worrying was the thought of granules working their way into the carburettor. If the engine failed, they would be forced down onto Libyan soil away from the safety of an air base.

Willing the engine to continue humming steadily, they battled through the sandstorm. When Bill calculated they were two hours overdue, he decided that the headwind couldn't have slowed them down that much, and that the sandstorm must have blinded them. He turned around and headed back the way they had come. Spotting a village, he prayed for a favourable welcome and dropped down to ask for directions. It turned out that they hadn't missed Sirte after all.

They still had another hour to travel. They reached the base just as dusk was falling.

For the first time, they faced a language barrier. Even Chubbie's schoolgirl French was of no use. As they struggled to explain themselves to the military officers staring suspiciously at them, they remembered the Italian newspapers they had stashed in their luggage, which carried the front page reports of their exploits. They pulled them out and offered them as a letter of introduction.

Suspicion turned into delight and effusive greetings. The Sirte commander's only concern was how to accommodate Chubbie in an all-male base while maintaining his countrymen's reputation for chivalry and kindliness. He ended up accommodating her in the gaol while Bill was invited to share his own quarters.

In the evening the officers presented them with a delicious dinner and opened the base's last two bottles of champagne in celebration. Afterwards, they sat on the balcony smoking Italian cigarettes.

As the evening progressed, Chubbie noticed that the Italian commander, a bachelor, was becoming increasingly flirtatious and affectionate. He handed her a memento, an aerial photograph of the base. She glanced at it then did a double take. It wasn't a scenic shot. It was a military view, depicting underground storage areas around the base's perimeter, areas that housed parked planes and oil and petrol dumps.

Later that evening, as she tucked the photograph into her luggage, her realisation that she possessed a valuable piece of military information made her feel a part of world events in a way she never had before. Married life in Melbourne had been like a cocoon. She had cooked and cleaned and lunched with friends. She hadn't had to worry about anything happening elsewhere in the world, particularly events on the other side of the globe. And when she had started the flight, the plane had seemed like another cocoon, a propeller-driven wall between herself and the political events in the countries she passed through. That feeling had been reinforced by the friendliness of men like Mussolini and Balbo. Even knowledge of the guerrilla warfare being waged on the terrain below hadn't generated any sense of a personal connection with the region's political turmoil, merely annoyance that it might threaten their trip's success and their own safety.

But holding that photograph was like an epiphany, a recognition that, like it or not, she was as much a part of world events as anyone else. And, with that picture she had a chance to make a difference. She wouldn't keep it as a memento. When they reached Benghazi, she would pass it to the British authorities for military use.

Around 4 am, three of the commander's men knocked on her door. With tears in their eyes, they asked if she would return the photograph. They said that if anyone discovered he had given it to her, he would be shot.

As she collected the photograph, she tried to imprint its image in her memory. When she later passed her information to the British authorities at Benghazi on 26 October, no one seemed interested. They couldn't foresee that there would be two battles waged at Sirte fourteen years later, when the British would pit their might against their Italian enemies.

The leg from Benghazi would take them away from the dangers of Libya and into Egypt, the oldest nation state in the world. Egypt had recently gained independence after half a century of British rule, although Britain still maintained a haughty presence, much to the frustration of the nationalists. They were angry that government officials, military officers and business leaders were mainly foreigners, with locals serving as underlings. The nationalists had dramatically expressed their frustration three years earlier by assassinating the army's commander-in-chief, Sir Lee Stack, in Cairo's streets. British rule, however, had largely been untroubled so Chubbie and Bill weren't worried about the political tensions. They were more relieved to be landing in a partly English-speaking country again.

After fighting strong winds for most of their journey, they reached Sollum (El Salloum) on the coastal border between Libya and Egypt. The ash-coloured terrain looked as if a huge hand had scooped earth from the barren, flat-topped cliffs that ringed the town, leaving level ground hugging the sickle-shaped bay. They flew over the town—as grey and barren as the cliffs—looking for the airfield or anywhere else to land.

When Bill failed to find a suitable landing place, he remembered that the Italians had given him some smoke bombs for just such a contingency. Candle-shaped objects, they exploded when lit and emitted billowing smoke. He could use them to gain the locals' attention and obtain directions to the airfield. With the delight of a schoolboy playing with firecrackers, he lit one and tossed it over the side.

Never had a landscape changed so quickly. One moment there was no sign of life in Sollum. The next, people were running in all directions, like ants scurrying away from a disturbed sandhill. They looked up in horror as if the *Red Rose* had dropped a real bomb on them.

Bill headed down and circled the town, signalling that he needed somewhere to land. He was directed to the official landing field, which proved to be so poorly constructed that rocks—invisible from the air—had been left embedded in the ground. As he touched down and bumped along the rough field, the rocks broke the tailskid, the support for the aircraft's tail when it was on the ground. The *Red Rose* had suffered its first injury.

They jumped out and inspected the damage, seeing with relief that the fuselage was intact. The purpose of the trip, from Bill's perspective at least, was to prove that a light plane was a safe vehicle for long-distance travel, so it was frustrating that an airfield in what was recently a British dominion should be the first to let them down.

A wave of Egyptians surrounded them. A smartly uniformed officer asked in perfect English who they were. Bill apologised for the smoke bomb and then, a little wistfully, mentioned that they were starving, having eaten nothing since the previous evening. They were in luck. Instead of being offered a simple meal, they were invited to a banquet to honour Major-General Sir Charlton Spinks, who was in Sollum to conduct the annual troop inspection.

General Spinks gave up his own bed for Chubbie while Bill was accommodated in one of the officers' houses. After washing and changing, they were driven to a large marquee redolent with the mouth-watering aromas of roast meat and spices. When Chubbie stepped inside, she again sent her silent thanks to Sir Sefton Brancker for recommending that she pack an evening frock.

The next day they followed Egypt's coastline to Aboukir (Abu Qir), which sat on a peninsula fourteen miles north-east of Alexander the Great's eponymous city. Shortly after they landed, a fleet of four RAF flying boats roared across Aboukir's skies and alighted on its protected seaplane port. These 'air battleships' had boat-like fuselages that served as self-contained homes for their four-man crews. They were on a mission to show the flag in the farthest parts of the British Empire and were planning to circumnavigate Australia before basing themselves in Singapore.

Chubbie and Bill spent the evening with the flying boat crews, delighted that they were among their own again. They compared schedules and expressed the hope they would cross paths on their journeys to Australia. The *Red Rose* was heading to Cairo the next day but would have many more stops before it reached its destination.

The press were also monitoring the flying boats' progress, often referring to the two Australia-bound expeditions in the same column. With the *Red Rose* and the flying boats heading east and Charles Kingsford Smith planning to fly west, the Australian newspapers speculated that their country would experience a marked change in its attitude towards aviation along with a much-needed stimulus to its aviation industry.

Back in England, British newspapers reported that Bert Hinkler appeared to have abandoned his own proposed flight to Australia. Bert's friends laughed at the news. The man was Australian. Flying to Australia wasn't just about taking out the record. It was about his sense of who he was, his sense of what he had achieved with his life. It would be foolish to think he had forsaken his dream simply because he wasn't talking about it. Importantly, he hated fanfare, so the public might not learn of his intentions until he took off on his adventure.

Another threat loomed from a different direction. Dennis Rooke, the plucky airman who had crashed in India on his first attempt at the Australian light plane record, told the press that he was considering another Australian flight. If he did make a second attempt, he would probably follow a different route.

Chubbie and Bill's international well-wishers knew that the *Red Rose* had been maintaining a good pace. Nevertheless, it was critical that they keep it up if they were to take out the light plane record. With other pilots contemplating much speedier journeys to the antipodes, any delay might prove disastrous.

Chapter Six

'Bad idea,' said the commanding officer at Cairo's Heliopolis aerodrome after Chubbie and Bill mentioned their planned departure the following day with their usual food and water supplies: none. 'It's a terrible bit of desert there by the Dead Sea.' He ordered them to wait until Monday so they could accompany a Baghdad-bound plane.

Early on Monday, 31 October, they followed a RAF Vickers Vernon, which carried five officers and two RAF policemen, on the longest leg of their journey so far, 800 miles to Baghdad. Bill wasn't concerned about undertaking such an extended flight. They had already flown more than 3000 miles in seventeen days with the tailskid breakage their only problem. Protected by their escort, they could afford to put the Avro Avian through its paces.

As they flew east in the wake of the Vernon, Chubbie peered down at the terrain. Seeing the sun's gentle morning rays burnishing the sand with a gilded beauty, she felt for the first time the desert's mystery and fascination. But this feeling didn't last long. Soon the sun was scorching them again, inescapable and unforgiving.

Ahead, they could see a desolate lake, the aptly named Dead Sea, which was so toxically saline that it killed everything in its vicinity. The lake was only nine miles at its widest point, a ten-minute crossing at their cruising speed. But they were battling a forty-mile-an-hour headwind that slowed their forward velocity until they barely made any headway at all.

As they crept across the lake, mile by struggling mile, the *Red Rose* hit an air-pocket and dropped like a stone. Chubbie's stomach churned with the sickening weightlessness of a freefall descent. The air-pocket seemed endless as they fell through 300 feet, 400 feet, 500 feet. The Dead Sea, which had seemed so small beneath them, loomed ominously close. Then, as suddenly as it began, the plane stopped falling. Bill was in control again, although still fighting the headwind. It took thirty minutes to complete the crossing.

The eastern bank was surrounded by equally desolate-looking hills rising sharply from the lake. In the lee of the hills, the thermals tossed them around like a cork on waves. Bill pulled the joystick back and tried to climb high enough to clear the hills. Weighed down by their fuel load, the plane struggled. They willed it upwards, glad that this time they had a rescue escort.

After slipping over the hilltop, they flew for another half hour until the Vernon signalled they were to land at Ziza (Zizya/Al Jiza), twenty miles south of Amman, Jordan. Both planes needed to refuel after the strong headwind. And since the wind wasn't easing, the officers decided to remain there overnight.

Ziza was a dismal place, nothing more than a rest house and a fuel pump, the last place Chubbie would choose to spend the night. With only a small amount of water between them, she and Bill had to freshen up using the same minuscule dishful. At least they had something else to drink. After depositing their passengers, the RAF pilots had flown on to Amman and brought back beer supplies.

Chubbie and Bill shared the officers' rations, a delicious stew of bully beef and onions served on rusty tin lids, with an old tin mug as the community cup. One of the officers dug out his ukulele and strummed cheerfully for the rest of the evening.

The contrast to the pomp and ceremony of the Sollum dinner only four days earlier left Chubbie shaking her head in bemusement. The formal dinner had been more pretentious than pleasurable, the type of social gathering where one lived in fear of choosing the wrong knives or forks from the vast array lined up around their plates. In this tiny desert hut, as she and the men shared simple cutlery and makeshift crockery, she felt a sense of contentment and camaraderie, as if this new world of adventurous spontaneity was where she truly belonged.

With 500 miles still to travel, they set off early the next morning. Again they slammed into a merciless headwind. This time it picked up loose sand from the Syrian Desert and swirled it around them.

It was almost impossible for them to talk while airborne because of the deafening engine drone so they mostly communicated by passing notes between the two cockpits through an open hatchway under Chubbie's seat. As the plane lumbered through the sandstorm, Bill knocked on his windscreen, which lay between the two cockpits, to indicate he was passing her a note.

'What are you doing with your feet?' he had written. 'Are you thumping them on the floor?'

'No,' was her response.

'Something's wrong,' he messaged back.

Then she smelt smoke.

Their light plane—like most others—was made of wood, and of linen covered with dope-glue, and had as much fire-resistance as a piece of deadwood in an incinerator. A fire could cause catastrophic damage to the plane or life-threatening problems for the crew before they had time to find a safe landing spot. A fire in a waterless plane flying over a waterless desert inhabited by potentially hostile Arabs had to be one of the greatest dangers of all.

Bill flew on, indicating that he hoped to nurse the plane as far as the RAF desert post at Rutbah Wells (Ar Rutba). There they would have a better chance of fixing the problem and continuing their journey. The post had a wireless station in addition to a fuel dump, which would be helpful if they needed to alert others to their predicament.

The smoke continued to drift out rather than billow and they reached Rutbah Wells without seeing any flames. When Bill examined the engine, he discovered that the driving sprocket of the impulse starter magneto had sheared and was smouldering. He doused it and left the engine to cool down before trying to fix the problem.

The RAF officers shared their lunch of bully beef and biscuits and then everyone trudged back to the *Red Rose*, fighting the gale-force winds that were trying to blow them and the plane away. Bill attempted to start the engine. It wouldn't kick over. Rain-bursts soon soaked them but he kept trying. Still nothing. The RAF crew offered to wait with them; however, they were already overdue so Bill thanked them and sent them on their way.

The local Imperial Airways mechanic offered to help. As the three of them worked on the engine, four armoured cars swept in from the desert. They bore RAF patrol officers who planned to stay overnight in Rutbah's solid stone fort. The men asked Chubbie and Bill to join them there. Rutbah Wells lay on the main road between Damascus and Baghdad and was a regular stopping point for travellers, including the nomadic tribes who bedded down in the rickety black goatskin tents that dotted the landscape.

The wind and rain had cleared by dinnertime so they all perched on kerosene tins beside a campfire and ate stewed gazelle off a single shared plate. Wild animals howled in the darkness beyond the campfire's glow. Chubbie was grateful for the campfire's protection as well as its warmth; the temperature had dropped as rapidly as Melbourne's when chilly southerlies swept through the city late on a scorching summer day. It was the only similarity to the world of her past.

When she went to bed, the *Red Rose* was on the landing ground outside Rutbah Wells in the care of an Arab guard. During the night, another gale blew up. Fearing that the plane might fly off on its own, she went out to check on it. As she stumbled through the darkness, a voice called out to her. Unable to understand the language, she kept moving towards the plane. Then out of the darkness, the muzzle of a rifle appeared, pointing directly at her face.

Shocked, she stood there gawping. Then she realised that the guard must have been demanding that she halt and identify herself. With shaking hands, she attempted to light a match in the strong wind. After flickering for a moment, it offered enough light for him to recognise her as one of the fliers. He apologised—well, she assumed it was an apology—and escorted her to the plane. As he helped her secure it, rain started to bucket down and the wind intensified. Increasingly concerned about damage to the plane, Chubbie decided to move it into the fort for protection. The guard helped her fold back the wings and wheel it into the fort. It passed through the entrance with only three inches to spare.

All the next day, she and Bill worked on the engine. Only once did they hear its welcome growl before it spluttered into silence again.

Chubbie was awed by Bill's patience. She had already seen his courage and fearlessness in the face of danger and his skill as a pilot. Now, as they tried the same thing over and over again, and as they failed over and over again, she saw no tantrums, no floods of swearwords, no kicking or shouting or stomping. Just the quiet confidence of a man who knew what needed to be done and who had the patience to keep doing it, knowing that at some point or other things would go his way.

It didn't happen that day. At 5 pm, as the light waned, they packed up their tools for the night.

The following morning, after much difficulty and with the assistance of a hand-cranked starting magneto, the engine roared to life around 11 am. Worried about further engine trouble but accepting that they couldn't fix the problem until they reached a RAF depot, they thanked their helper and set off to fly the remaining 165 miles to Baghdad.

The engine cut out five times during their flight. The fifth time, when it refused to start again, Bill glided towards the desert floor. Just before the wheels touched down, the engine kicked into life again so he kept it running while he inspected the machine. When he set off, the engine continued running erratically, forcing them down again at Ramadi. At last, after four hours of sporadic flying, they landed in the pouring rain at Hinaidi aerodrome, the British RAF station near Baghdad.

As Bill and the RAF mechanics worked on the engine, rain pummelled the hangar roof. Outside the hangar door, the water rose. By the time the engine fired and ran smoothly, the aerodrome was flooded.

It took five days for the water to dissipate.

Each day, Chubbie and Bill hopefully inspected the runway, then gave up and went sightseeing. While the golden minarets glowing in the setting sun were stunning, Chubbie was otherwise unimpressed with Iraq's fabled city. She remarked in her journal that a few centuries before—and under sunnier skies—the city might have been a place of wonderment. But now it seemed like a faded tapestry with only specks remaining of its original vibrant colour. The Tigris, which elsewhere looked like an angry snake squirming across the countryside, was here just a muddy, sluggish stream. Even the palm trees seemed to have wilted. To realise that the Arabian Nights' magnificence was now little more than trampled drabness made her feel as if her joy in the fairy tale had been destroyed.

At last, on Tuesday, 8 November, the twenty-fifth day of what was intended to be only a forty-day trip, they took to the sky to begin the 280-mile run to Basra. As Chubbie gazed at the miserable villages and sullen rivers beneath them, Bill sighed with frustration. Magneto trouble again. He landed at Nasiriyah, two-thirds of the way to Basra, but found the landing area worryingly soft after the recent heavy rains. Afraid of being bogged, he took off again and flew a short distance to Ur of the Chaldees, once thought to be the birthplace of biblical Abraham. The terrain was as flat as an ancient coin worn smooth through handling. Centuries of sand had hidden nature's contours and man-made constructions except for the ruins of this ancient city.

Soon after they landed, two RAF planes arrived from the Shaibah RAF base near Basra to conduct a tour of inspection of the Ur junction. Bill told them about the *Red Rose*'s journey and troubles. The officers reported that they were heading back to Shaibah the next day and could take the magnetos to their base and return them repaired the same day. When the officers returned though, they brought back a message from Shaibah's commanding officer saying that he himself would bring the magnetos and escort them to Basra.

In the brief time it took the officers to convey this message, someone stole their book of Indian maps from the *Red Rose*. Not only had the maps cost a small fortune, it would be impossible for Bill to fly beyond Persia without their guidance.

The local authorities imprisoned most of the villagers—including the nimble-fingered children—in the hope of identifying the thief and recovering the maps. But everyone remained button-lipped.

Bill left Chubbie alone to guard the *Red Rose* while he went to send a message to Baghdad's commanding officer asking for new maps. Chubbie stood outside the plane with an automatic pistol positioned ostentatiously on her hip. The locals surrounded her and the plane, squatting on their haunches, staring at her. She stared back. It was the first time she had ever experienced such a deep-seated anger, almost a malevolence. She knew that it wasn't aimed so much at her as a person as at what she represented, but it was unsettling, frightening.

Soon afterwards, Shaibah's commanding officer arrived with the two magnetos. As the men stood in the boiling sun trying to start the engine, Chubbie mused that the spectres of bad weather and engine trouble had slipped onto the flight and were showing no signs of leaving.

The men struggled to install the repaired magnetos. It was well into the following day before the *Red Rose* was able to take off again.

When they reached Shaibah, Bill cabled the Avro company for replacement magnetos, unwilling to risk any further problems with such an important part of the engine. The *Red Rose* would be stuck there until the parts arrived.

Chapter Seven

Basra's customs officials were displeased. Glaring at Chubbie and Bill, they announced that the *Red Rose* and its crew should have cleared customs at Baghdad. Then they tossed around words like 'broken the law' and 'arrest' and 'gaol'.

Bill apologised profusely and described their engine problems, saying that in the stress and confusion he had forgotten about clearing customs. Chubbie remained quiet, aware that as a passenger and as a woman her opinion lacked any value. Silently, though, she fumed that the whole thing was absurd, that little things like customs clearances were trivialities compared to the life-threatening dangers they had experienced.

Fortunately, Shaibah's commanding officer had driven them the twenty miles into Basra. His authoritative presence and firsthand knowledge of their engine problems kept them out of gaol. Afterwards, he dropped Chubbie at the British Consul in Basra and took Bill back to Shaibah, where the RAF flying boats they had crossed paths with in Egypt had just arrived.

Chubbie spent the following days sightseeing and socialising. She thought Basra a remarkable place, a hub of industry and activity, with the usual stench of sewage warring with the delicious aroma of spices. The twenty miles separating them meant she saw little of Bill although they managed to keep in touch by telephone.

Shortly before the magneto parts were due, more bad luck befell them: a cholera outbreak. Quarantine regulations demanded a city-wide lock-down and prevented anyone from leaving for seven days. And when the magneto parts finally arrived, they were missing a critical component. Bill had to cable for further replacements, which would take another eight days to reach them.

Meanwhile, trouble was brewing on the southern Iraq border. An Iraqi frontier police post at Busiyah (Al Busayyah), seventy-five miles north of the border, was attacked by a Wahhabi tribe from central Arabia leaving fifty dead including twenty Iraqi policemen. A Wahhabi sheik reportedly had five thousand men ready for another attack. As tension gripped Basra, RAF planes were sent out to scout the district. Meanwhile, the base's officers were placed on active service and told to keep their rifles and ammunition with them at all times in case of an emergency.

Bill and Chubbie were deeply concerned. Although their new magnetos hadn't arrived, Bill decided to escape Basra on a single magneto after quarantine was lifted on 21 November. But before they could set off, tragedy struck the RAF base. A bomb-laden plane plummeted to the ground just after take-off and exploded in flames, incinerating the crew. Then came the devastating news that Bert Hinkler had died during his attempt at the Great Circle route. Feeling like tragedy was surrounding them, Bill changed his mind about leaving. He would heed the omens and wait until his plane was fully functional.

Frustrated by the continued delays, they were delighted when the Royal Navy's HMS *Enterprise* anchored in the middle of the river. The navy officers entertained them as if they were royalty. In the ruggedly masculine environment, where each man was attempting to prove his virility to the single pretty woman in their midst, someone threw out a challenge to swim from the ship across the shark-infested river to the shore. Bill accepted, much to Chubbie's horror. It was as if he wanted to impress her the most. Luckily for both of them, the world's press didn't get to craft appropriately alliterative headlines: 'Ace aviator eaten' or 'Feeding frenzy finishes flier'.

While they waited at Basra, Bill discussed his flight plans with his RAF colleagues. When he said that he planned to take the quick route across the Persian Gulf to Persia (Iran), the RAF pilots advised him to take the longer coastline route, explaining that the gulf was filled with sharks so they would have little chance of surviving a ditching. Bill refused to listen. He had swum through the supposedly shark-filled river without a problem and, apart from the now-repaired magneto issues, the engine had been working perfectly. Having travelled only a thousand miles in a month, he was determined to get cracking.

On 26 November, they set off on their 300-mile south-east leg to Bushire (Bushehr). Crossing the shoreline, they saw dozens of sharks drifting through the sluggish waters of the Persian Gulf. They gazed at them curiously—and with a twinge of alarm, a feeling they tried to suppress because it would be hours before they reached the eastern shore. Then their alarm turned to horror. Their brand new magneto was malfunctioning.

Bill immediately turned east towards the coastline to reduce their time over the water. Chubbie talked to the engine, alternately ordering it to keep going and pleading with it not to stop. Both kept a look-out for suitable places to land. There weren't any. Even when they reached the shore, the coastline was too rugged. And ditching near the shoreline wasn't much of an alternative. The sharks' distinctive silhouettes were visible in the shallow coastal waters as well.

Onwards they flew as the engine continued spluttering. But at least it kept running. By the time they reached Bushire, Chubbie felt as if terror had drained her of all her energy and courage.

Somehow they and their machine had survived yet another potential disaster. Surely, though, this balance of bad luck followed by fortuitous good luck couldn't last. Either their luck had to improve or one of their problems would end calamitously. It was only a matter of time.

People at the airfield commented on the dreadful noise coming from the engine as the *Red Rose* came in to land—the aviation equivalent of nails scraping across a blackboard. When they inspected the engine they discovered that, after only four hours of flying, the new magneto had stripped the distributing gear.

Bill contacted Shaibah's commanding officer who said he would try to find new magnetos and send them by air. As they commenced another interminable wait at the British Consul's residence, Chubbie wondered why they had experienced so much magneto trouble. Bill speculated that the abrupt change from cold and wet Europe to the African heat was responsible.

After fretting for a while at this new delay, Bill decided that he'd had enough. He would try to craft his own distributing wheel. He and Chubbie extracted the magnetos and took them to a Persian workshop that had a lathe. With the Persians' assistance, they made tools to cut a new wheel. After ten attempts over four days, trying a variety of materials, they produced a brass one. It was only moderately 'true' but it would at least get them on their way again.

Meanwhile, their trip across the Persian Gulf had proved to be more than just a nightmare-inducing near-disaster. It was a relationship watershed. And conveniently, their British Consul host went on leave a short time after their arrival, leaving them alone in his residence.

It wasn't only the lust that commonly follows a near-death experience that spurred their new intimacy. Their victories and vicissitudes over the previous six weeks had exposed their characters, warts and all. And each of them had come to appreciate—indeed to love—what they saw in the other.

They knew that the world would label their love 'adultery' and that many would believe there was a price to pay for such a sin. Whatever the label, whatever the judgement, it was clear they had reached a turning point in their lives.

Chapter Eight

Relying on a makeshift repair wasn't ideal at the best of times, let alone when flying across the unforgiving Middle East. However, Bill was increasingly worried about their delays. The news of Bert Hinkler's death had been premature. The Australian aviator was apparently back in England making who-knew-what plans. As Bert owned his own Avro Avian, he might suddenly decide to throw his goggles into the ring and attempt to beat them to Australia. And it was feasible that he could do so. He had recently flown 1200 miles in thirteen hours, compared with their own 1000 miles in a month. If he set off now and maintained that daily pace, he could catch up with them in little more than a week—particularly if their own appalling luck continued. It would be best if they didn't give him any reason to try for the record.

When they reached cruising height after leaving Bushire on 2 December, a tailwind sped them on their way to Bandar Abbas. They hoped it was a sign that their bad luck had changed at last.

While the flying conditions had improved, the terrain beneath them remained hostile. Rugged pinkish-purple mountains rose straight up from the shore, offering not a sliver of flat land for a safe set down if the magneto failed. Thankfully their engine kept purring—no grinding, no cutting out. When they checked it on their arrival at Bandar Abbas, they were pleased to discover that their makeshift wheel had stood up to the stresses.

The next day they had another excellent flight, arriving at nightfall at Charbar (Chābahār) on the Gulf of Oman. The telegraph officer was one of only four Europeans in the village and was happy to accommodate them—indeed, all aviators. Their exciting stories provided a welcome break in his tedious existence.

When they woke, the wind had changed direction. They would be battling yet another headwind on their 400-mile flight to Karachi.

As they attempted to take off, their tailskid broke. After aborting the take-off, they lifted the tailskid and wheeled the plane off the airstrip to inspect it. The fuselage seemed undamaged so they decided to continue. After experiencing so many problems and so much fear, they were developing an attitude of 'what will be, will be'.

They followed the Persian coastline again, looking down on quaint villages nestling under towering cliffs to the north and the Gulf of Oman to the south. The headwind didn't ease. Instead, it grew stronger.

As if they had tempted fate by speculating about their change of luck, they flew into heavy clouds. Then a violent sandstorm enveloped them, preventing them from seeing more than a few feet in front of them. Bill was not only blinded, he was disoriented. He couldn't see water or coastline or mountains. He wasn't even sure if he was flying the right way up. He shut down the engine and let the plane glide, knowing that the Earth's gravitational pull would provide the answer. As they drifted downwards, he and Chubbie desperately hoped that they were still flying above the sea and hadn't drifted over the nearby mountains.

The clouds and sandstorm continued to smother them, forcing Bill to make the same dangerous move over and over again. When the cloud layer thinned, they were thankful to see water beneath them. They flew east by compass alone without seeing any land for hours.

Worried about their fuel supply, Bill tried to set down at Pasni, India (now Pakistan), only to see that the aerodrome was flooded. He landed safely at a nearby beach and sent a request for fuel to the aerodrome via an English-speaking local.

The entire population turned out to watch their perilous take-off. The plane faced the gulf as Bill spun the propeller. Climbing onboard, he gunned the engine and raced down the beach's short steep slope towards the water. If he couldn't build up enough speed to lift off, the plane would plough into the sea, with devastating consequences. As the propeller began to slice the water, the wheels lifted off the beach. They were airborne.

Every mile from Pasni to Karachi was a battle with the elements. Thick sandstorms banked around them as if determined to prevent them from completing their journey. The sand scratching their eyes and slipping beneath their clothes made them feel as if they were back in Africa again.

Darkness was falling by the time they arrived at Karachi. A welcoming line of flares greeted them. It turned out that the airport authorities had almost closed up shop but had decided to light the flares, just in case. Despite Bill's worries about the broken tailskid, he managed a perfect wheels-only landing.

In the day's dramas, they had forgotten about the makeshift distributing wheel. When they checked it, they were appalled to discover so much wear and tear that they would have remained airborne for another thirty minutes only. It meant further delays while repairs were undertaken at the nearby RAF depot.

The good news was that they had reached the halfway point, having travelled nearly 6000 miles. Admittedly, they had only flown ninety-two hours in fifty-one travelling days and should have already reached

Australia. However, as the undaunted Chubbie told the press, 'Our tail is still up.'

Their Karachi sojourn felt like a reunion when the RAF flying boats and the HMS *Enterprise* joined them there. With a week at least in Karachi and a busy social calendar, Chubbie paid a tailor to run up a white China-silk tennis frock. She also bought a white felt hat, which Bill later used to wrap tools, much to her annoyance.

Another expatriate society; another gossip hub. They knew they had to be careful. No looks. No touches. Nothing to give away that they were no longer just business partners. The consequences of such a revelation didn't bear thinking about.

Fortunately, Karachi and its inhabitants had their minds focused on other things. The city was preparing for a visit from His Majesty the Amir of Afghanistan. Like Turkey's Mustafa Kemal Atatürk, Amanullah Khan was a social and religious moderate. He had gained Afghanistan's independence from British rule in 1919 and had set out to modernise his country, establishing schools for boys and girls and overturning the strict dress codes for women. He had even established a small air force with donated Soviet planes. He was to visit Karachi while on a trip to Europe and Great Britain and had expressed a wish to meet Chubbie and Bill and to inspect the Avian.

On the day of his visit, Bill flew the *Red Rose* to the Imperial Airways aerodrome, where they waited for the Amir to arrive. Like a mother wanting her child to impress, Chubbie tried to visualise the *Red Rose* from a stranger's perspective. She decided that it looked a little wilted after its many trials.

The hours passed. They were feeling hungry and fed up when a group of fifty people headed towards them, led by a man who could only be the Amir. Chubbie suddenly felt terrified. She had no idea what she was supposed to do or say. She had never met royalty before. Housewives from Melbourne rarely did.

The Amir stopped in front of them and held out his hand. In perfect French, he said, 'How do you do.' He was so gentlemanly, so gracious, that her panic subsided. He stayed for about twenty minutes, questioning them and examining the plane, intrigued by its folding wings. He asked if she liked flying and whether she was herself a pilot. After signing their logbook and shaking their hands again, he congratulated them and wished them all the best for the remainder of their journey.

While the Amir was in Europe, reactionary opposition to his moderate rule increased. He was forced to abdicate a year later and few of his modernist reforms were maintained.

On Wednesday, 14 December, they saluted the *Enterprise* and the other ships in the bay and began the 400-mile journey to Jodhpur. The *Red Rose* had been thoroughly overhauled by the depot mechanics, so they were no longer concerned about engine problems. They were also rich—well, richer than they'd been at any other time in their journey. Sir Charles Wakefield of Castrol Oil had sent them £50. A.V. Roe & Co. had sent them a similar amount, perhaps grateful for Bill's cable expressing his conviction that only an Avro Avian could have survived their ordeals. After paying their expenses, they had £75 between them.

The engine purred, the sun shone, the clouds and wind and sand and other weather annoyances kept their distance. Chubbie's optimism grew.

At Jodhpur's aerodrome they were met by a representative of the Maharajah, the state's ruling prince. Taken to his home for the night, they were awed by the opulence: his palace, surrounded by a lake; his glittering state jewels; his 110 cars, including thirteen Rolls-Royces. Like a greedy boy, he told them that he now wanted an aeroplane.

Agra, their next destination, could be seen long before they reached the city—dominated by the Taj Mahal's gleaming magnificence. Bill dropped down until they were flying directly above and around the mausoleum. Chubbie thought it the loveliest sight she had ever seen, both then in the sun's glow and later when they wandered through the building in the silvery moonlight.

After a dawn departure they headed towards Allahabad some 265 miles away. Conditions were perfect, with a crisp morning breeze tempering the sun's gentle warmth. Bill flew east-south-east until they reached the mighty Ganges River, a mile wide in some parts, then followed it towards Allahabad, which was situated on the confluence of the Ganges and Yamuna rivers.

At the sight of hundreds of crocodiles sunning themselves on the river's mudflats, Bill dropped to ten feet so they had a close-up view of the river monsters. Some slid into the river as soon as the plane appeared while others lay there lethargically, ignoring the gnat buzzing over them. They could see why the crocodiles flourished there. Their feeding ground included hundreds of dead bodies that floated along the holy river's surface.

Hawks and vultures flying above the river headed towards them. Bill steered away from them as if he were avoiding anti-aircraft flak. After everything they had survived, it would be humiliating to be brought down by an inquisitive bird.

They remained in Allahabad—the 'city of God'—for two nights so they could attend a dance then flew to Patna where they stopped for the night. The following day, Monday, 19 December, was the beginning of Christmas week. They had planned to celebrate the festive season in Australia; however, even the most optimistic of new itineraries wouldn't get them there until early in the new year.

As Bill hurtled down Patna's strip to commence their 300-mile journey to Calcutta, he realised he couldn't move his joystick far enough to take off.

The *Red Rose* could be controlled from either cockpit by the simple expedient of inserting a joystick into the appropriate slot. When both joysticks were in place, they moved in unison so control could easily be handed from one pilot to the other. Since Basra, though, Chubbie's joystick had had limited functionality. They had been forced to install extra fuel tanks in the front cockpit to assist with the long Far East hauls, and this restricted the front joystick's manoeuvrability. Chubbie was supposed to remove her stick before they took off, but on this particular morning, she had clearly forgotten to do so.

As Bill jiggled his joystick, he saw a huge pile of road-metal looming towards them. This ugly sculpture of leftover stone, cinders and tar warned him that the end of the runway was fast approaching. He tried pulling his joystick back, but it barely moved. The front stick must have jammed when he had pushed his own stick forward. It was now too late to slow down. It was too late to change direction. It was too late to do anything but close his eyes and hope they cleared the deadly obstacle.

If sheer willpower alone ever lifted a plane off the ground, this was the moment. The *Red Rose* cleared the heap by only two feet.

Safely aloft, Chubbie received a note from Bill asking that she remove her joystick. She replied, 'You'll have to climb while I get it out.' To climb, he had to pull his own joystick towards him which would help release hers.

After climbing for a while, he obviously thought she'd had enough time to remove it because he levelled out. But she wasn't finished. And now his change in direction jammed her stick between the fuel tank and the instrument panel.

The plane suddenly dived towards the ground. Her jammed stick was preventing Bill from manoeuvring his own stick and he had lost control. Unless she could release her joystick, they would continue to dive until they slammed into the ground.

As she tugged and tugged, Bill pummelled her on the head screaming, 'Get that stick out! Get that stick out! I'm rigid. I can't move my stick.'

She screamed back that her joystick was stuck. The plane continued its dive. They both went silent as the ground rushed towards them.

With terror-induced strength, she fisted her hands together and whacked the joystick sideways, a dangerous move in any situation. But her drastic action was enough to release the jam.

Bill pulled his stick back. With only forty feet to spare, the Avian flattened out and started climbing.

Calcutta was easy to spot because of the city's pall of smoke, pumped from the jute-producing factories that were one of the city's major industries. They landed at Dum Dum aerodrome around 2 pm on 19 December, where Bernard Leete met them. Aviators Leete and Neville Stack—the man who had taken Chubbie for her first flight—had jointly flown the first light plane to India.

Knowing how thirsty they would be, Leete had brought bottles of iced beer and glasses. After two joystick-induced near disasters, Chubbie thought that beer had never tasted so delicious.

The beers weren't just a much-needed refreshment; they were a celebration. The *Red Rose* now held the world record for the longest distance travelled by a passenger-carrying light aeroplane. And Chubbie had gained the world record for the longest flight ever undertaken by a woman. Bill said to the press, 'It is fitting that the world's record for women should be held by an Australian. It is a wonderful achievement considering the light plane used.'

Tasmania's *Examiner* responded, 'Australia will crown her bravery with an immense welcome.'

A third record was also at their fingertips. 'If we reach Rangoon,' Bill told the press, 'we will hold the world record for the longest flight in a light aeroplane.' The previous record had been set only two weeks before their departure by an 8000-mile flight from London to Cape Town.

And if they made it to Australia, anyone attempting to beat their record would pretty much have to circle the globe, an unlikely flight in a light plane because of the long stretches of ocean. Chubbie and Bill would have their names in the history books forever.

If they made it to Australia.

Chapter Nine

They were broke. And it was Bill's fault.

They had stayed two nights in Calcutta, fascinated by this huge, noisy, industrial city. Human voices provided a constant background hum, punctuated by rickshaw honks and tram bell trills and the mournful bellows of the water buffalo lumbering along its main streets. The only quiet was in the mosques and temples that seemed strangely out of place among the city bustle.

On the morning of their departure, Leete was among the large crowd that farewelled them. He told Chubbie that while she had attended to her own preparations and packing, Bill had had a whole tribe of people endeavouring to put on his shoes and meet his every need. She would later grumble: 'No doubt that was why he didn't do any thinking for himself and left behind our most needed possessions.'

Leaving India, they inched their way across the Bay of Bengal towards Burma, seeing nothing but water for hours. Once they reached Burma's coastline, they followed it south over a mix of hilly and irrigated country to the town of Akyab (Sittwe). Fuel was easy to obtain because Akyab sat at the mouth of an estuary where three navigable rivers converged. After the *Red Rose*'s tanks had been filled, Bill reached into his pocket for their money. Pulling out an empty hand, he turned to Chubbie and asked, 'Have you got the money?'

'No, you insisted on keeping it yourself.'

Then he remembered. He had placed all their money—£58—and his mother's precious St Christopher medallion under his Calcutta pillow and had forgotten to collect them. Not only were they broke, they had lost their good luck charm.

Chubbie berated him for a while then decided it was no good moaning. If they were stranded, so be it. They'd been in worse trouble before. She had the grand total of ten rupees in her purse, but it wasn't enough to reimburse the now frantic old man who was pestering them for payment. Bill tried to explain what had happened and signed a chit for the fuel, assuring him that payment would soon come. He then used five of the precious rupees to send telegrams to the hotel manager, to Bernard Leete and to the Calcutta Police Commissioner to advise them of the loss.

He made the mistake of listing his room number. When the authorities reached his room, the money was gone.

The weather the next day was clear and bright, perfect for flying. They cheered up as they crossed some of the loveliest landscape they had seen during their journey. Sea as blue as the Côte D'Azur. Emerald islands. Pristine white beaches.

Strong winds buffeted them as they crossed the Arakan Mountains, but their sturdy plane again came through unscathed. They followed the Irrawaddy River south above tiger-filled jungle to Bassein Creek, where they turned east. Shortly after 1 pm, they spotted Rangoon a few miles away.

Chubbie was just thinking that she knew little about the city, except that they were to land at the racecourse and had been told to visit a stunning pagoda, when she heard some loud bangs from the engine. It began to screech. Then the plane started shaking violently. Clinging to her cockpit, she screamed to Bill, 'What's happening?'

As Bill listened to the engine and felt the vibrations increase, he suspected that a piston or cylinder had broken. Whatever the cause, if the vibrations continued, the engine would be shaken loose. He must shut it down.

The *Red Rose* had been flying over the sea at 2000 feet when the trouble began. He delayed shutting down the engine until he had turned towards land. They were now at the mercy of the air currents as he attempted a 'dead stick', or powerless, landing. At least he had enough altitude to allow him some control over where they set down. At 1000 feet he would have been forced to ditch into the sea.

He looked over the side, searching for a suitable landing place. He needed to avoid the city's busy streets, full of people, vehicles and animals. He also needed to avoid the fields where adults and children laboured. The only flat unpopulated stretch within gliding range was an absinthe-green field, a rice paddy seemingly, to the east of Rangoon on land separated from the city by a river.

He steered towards it. In the almost surreal silence, he controlled the plane's descent and lined up for the final glide. Then he remembered the fuel tank sitting on the cockpit floor in front of Chubbie. If the plane nosed into the ground or slammed into hidden rocks under the green surface, the tank could be pushed back onto her legs and crush them. He screamed at her, 'Hold your legs up! I think we are going to crash!'

Without the engine's loud drone, Chubbie could easily hear him screaming at her to lift up her legs. She could even understand what he was saying. Yet her legs remained glued to the cockpit floor as if she had lost all connection between thought and action. Instead, her brain buzzed with horrible possibilities. Would the *Red Rose* remain upright or plough nose first into the ground and somersault? Would the undercarriage stay intact or collapse and slam the fuselage into whatever lay underneath the surface? Would she die?

As the ground came closer and closer, she braced for the inevitable impact.

The plane glided onto the paddy field. As it touched down, it settled in an upright position and continued to roll forward, its speed decreasing as the crops and muddy ground snagged at its wheels. Soon it came to a smooth, undramatic, trouble-free halt.

For a moment she sat there unable to believe their luck. Then she stood and twisted around to face Bill. As they shook their heads in wonder and pumped hands furiously, Bill said, 'We have the luck of a fat priest.'

While luck played a considerable part, Chubbie knew that his presence of mind and calm control of the plane had saved their lives. They would later learn that Bill had chosen the perfect spot to land, a section of the paddy field where the reaped rice lay in heaps. It had cushioned their landing, protecting the *Red Rose* from the serious damage it would otherwise have suffered.

One moment they were alone. The next, people swarmed towards them from every direction. Some were Burmese. Some Indian. All were fascinated by the sight of the downed plane. And they looked astonished when they saw Chubbie clamber from one of the cockpits.

A local English-speaking man appeared and told them they had landed in an area that was surprisingly difficult to access despite its seeming proximity to Rangoon. The only transport to the city was by launch and the only telephone was at the railway station, a two-mile walk away.

It was around 1.15 pm when they landed and the afternoon heat was already unbearable. They decided that Bill would accompany the man to find the telephone, leaving Chubbie to guard the plane. She soon regretted the decision. The Burmese were so intrigued by the plane they kept climbing over it and boring their fingers through its fabric, trying to work out what it was made of and how it worked. She—a tiny unknown white woman who didn't speak their language—clearly had no authority in their eyes. They ignored her beseeching gestures and looks, her angry frowns and threatening fists.

For two and a half hours, in heat so scorching that steam rose off the paddy fields, she raced around the plane pushing them away. While she was on one side, a flank attack would be made from the other, as if they were conducting a well-planned military assault. They all seemed to think it a great joke to watch her running a marathon around the plane, which motivated them to keep clambering over it and poking it, just to see her reaction. As they continued to do so, she feared that the plane would be damaged beyond repair by the time Bill returned.

The English-speaking man had left two of his overseers to help Chubbie but they were as inquisitive as the rest of the locals. She tried to tell herself to be grateful that the Burmese hadn't acquired the souveniring habit or they would have, bit by bit, walked away with the entire plane. She was at her wit's end when an English couple named Tait appeared with iced soda water. They were as welcome as Bernard Leete had been with his beer.

When Bill returned, the Taits placed a guard on the plane and guided them to their home. They had to walk through two miles of rice fields, cross a small stream, and climb through fences to reach the house. There Chubbie remained, while Bill was accommodated with members of the Burma Aerial Survey Company across the river at Monkey Point.

Apprehensively, they returned the next morning to assess the damage. After a full day working in the sweltering heat, they concluded that everything except a piston was intact. But that offending piston was so badly damaged it needed replacing. So they sent another frantic cable to Bernard Leete in Calcutta, who had previously offered to provide his own spare parts if the *Red Rose* needed them. He replied that he would send his reserve cylinder and piston to Rangoon and they would soon be on their way again.

By now they had only a few rupees remaining and it was time for desperate measures. Chubbie prepared a carefully worded cable to Keith in Australia: 'Miller, Herald, Melbourne. Cashless.' They didn't want anyone in Rangoon knowing the miserable state of their finances.

In the day since the forced landing, Chubbie had had time to ponder their misfortunes. On almost every travelling day they had suffered weather problems or other difficulties. Why such bad luck? Her first thought was the loss of the St Christopher medallion, until she remembered that their problems had begun long before they reached Calcutta. Perhaps a woman on a plane brought the same ill luck as a parson on a ship. Whatever the reason, she noticed with surprise that she still felt optimistic about their journey. Indeed, despite everything, she was still having the time of her life. She sent another cable to Australia saying, 'Our tail is still up.'

At least their cables were now free because they had befriended the sympathetic postmaster. They had also met an automobile-owner who allowed them to use his vehicle whenever they wanted. This saved them taxi fares, which was fortunate because they hadn't heard back from Keith—no cable, no money, nothing.

The Christmas holiday period was a difficult time to be broke. Everything was closed, including the telegraph office, so they couldn't send Keith a second cable. For two days they went without lunch. On other occasions, they dashed down to Monkey Point and fed themselves bananas from the mess. British expatriates kept asking them out, but they preferred not to accept such offers when they couldn't reciprocate, unaware that no reciprocation was required. For their would-be hosts, that vicarious link with excitement and adventure—with fame—was well worth the price of a meal.

Meanwhile, at least sightseeing was free. Burma was still loosely under the control of the British Raj. When they stood in some parts of Rangoon looking at its neat colonial buildings and churches and ornamental gardens, it was easy to imagine they were standing in Britain—until they glimpsed the longyi-dressed locals and the Shwedagon Pagoda, with its gigantic golden stupa rising towards the heavens.

After the holidays, Chubbie asked Mr Tait to phone the bank and enquire about their money. It turned out that their £30 had been sitting in the bank for the entire holiday period. They weren't destitute after all.

On New Year's Eve, the Government Advocate, Professor Egger, hosted a fancy dress dinner for them. Somebody lent Chubbie a gorgeous black and gold outfit but, as always, it was too big. She decided that 'tramp' would have to do. She bought some white trousers and cut off the legs and picked at the lower edges to produce a ragged fringe. She tugged on a torn tennis shirt, cinching it at the waist with a length of rope. Stuffing a well-worn Panama hat on her head, she circled her neck with a red handkerchief and pushed her feet into dirty old tennis shoes. To complete the ensemble, she attached a full bottle of whisky to her waist-rope. She proved extremely popular at the party, due, she was sure, to the soon-empty whisky bottle.

She would never forget Professor Egger's party decorations, which featured a miniature model of the *Red Rose* he had made himself. He attached it to a lightbulb and used its electricity source to power the tiny propeller. The plane buzzed around and around all evening to everyone's amusement and delight.

When their piston and cylinder finally arrived from Bernard Leete and the engine was repaired, they faced a new problem. The mushy paddy field had been ideal for a forced landing but was less than ideal as a runway. So they stripped everything from the plane to reduce its weight to a bare minimum. Bill even siphoned off petrol until the plane had only enough to reach the racecourse.

Chubbie's job was to stand on the mud embankment that served as the end of the makeshift runway to help Bill calculate how much run-up he had. Watching the plane hurtling towards her, she thought it terrifyingly short. However, Bill, skilful and fearless as ever, lifted off just before he reached her.

At the racecourse, they refuelled and repacked the plane. They would continue their journey the following day, 2 January 1928.

Meanwhile, all around the world, people were eager to learn of their latest adventures. Had the engine problems been repaired? Had the *Red Rose* lifted successfully off the paddy field?

No longer was the *Red Rose*'s flight just a few words slipped into a newspaper's telegraphic section. Many newspapers were publishing detailed reports, with each instalment communicating yet another drama in its seemingly unending journey. '*Red Rose* still blooming' was the headline in one newspaper when it advised its readers that the plane had indeed escaped the paddy field's muddy clutches.

That revelation led to a new question: 'What on earth will happen next?'

Chapter Ten

Rangoon's New Year's Eve party had been a last supper of sorts for Chubbie and Bill. They were about to commence the most dangerous part of their flight, the stretch that would take them south-east to Australia. Even Britain's supportive aviation experts had expressed concern about the Burma-to-Darwin run. With no RAF presence in any of the South-East Asian countries, they would be reliant on whatever the locals could muster up as landing fields. And the news from those who had flown into the region was that the haphazard results could barely be considered adequate.

Early Monday morning, they set off from Rangoon to head across the Gulf of Martaban before continuing south down Burma's narrow coastal territory. About twenty minutes into their journey, the plane started to lurch up and down like a bucking bronco. It dived suddenly, but pulled up again a moment later. Then it bounded around as if Bill had lost all control of the joystick.

Chubbie turned in her seat and shrieked, 'What's the matter?'

Bill shouted back a single, unexpected, terrifying word: 'Snake!'

The plane had been moving swiftly when he spotted the brown snake uncurling itself underneath Chubbie's seat. About three feet in length, it had a flat head, a dark cylindrical body and a blunt tail. He had no idea what type of snake it was or whether it was dangerous or not. And he wasn't keen to find out.

Unable to leave the controls to deal with the emergency, his only choice was to take his feet off the rudder pedals and try to stamp on it—hence the strange lurches and bounds as he attempted to maintain control of the plane. The last thing he needed was to be fighting a stalled engine, a diving plane and a potentially deadly snake at the same time.

When he failed to crush the snake, the wily creature slithered through the open hatchway under Chubbie's seat. 'Look out!' he screamed to Chubbie, and pointed towards the floor.

Just before they left Rangoon, Chubbie's hostess had said to her, 'Do not forget! Before you leave, have a good look in the machine for snakes. Your machine has been out in the field for some time, and all those swamps are infested with snakes. You might find that you are carrying an extra passenger if you do not make a search.'

Chubbie had thought the woman was pulling her leg. She had been so relieved that the engine was repaired and the plane was out of the paddy field and they had cash warming their pockets, that the warning had slipped her mind. Until now.

Seeing Bill pointing down, she looked at her cockpit floor. She saw an inquisitive head peeping up at her from the hatchway.

Never before had she removed her joystick from its clip so quickly. She whipped it into the air and whacked the snake over and over again. Blood splashed everywhere. She opened her eyes—half-closed in horror during her killing frenzy—and looked more closely. It didn't move. It looked dead. She waited for a moment longer. When it still didn't move, she reached down and picked up its bloodied body and tossed it over the side of the plane.

Later they learnt that the snake was called a krait and was one of the deadliest in the region. While usually found in or near water, it also liked brick piles and rat holes and the occasional house—and now planes. Sluggish or docile unless threatened, its venom was a powerful neuro-toxin that caused muscle paralysis. Once bitten, a person soon lost the ability to see or talk and died of suffocation within four to eight hours.

If Bill had been bitten, it would have proved a double fatality. The next landing was going to be difficult, even for a skilled pilot, and Chubbie had never landed a plane.

Back in Karachi, when Bill and Chubbie had talked with their RAF friends about their flight plans, a pilot who knew the Burma–Thailand region told them they'd have to fly all the way from Rangoon to Victoria Point (Kawthaung) in south Burma because there were no airfields in-between. Bill did the calculations and worked out that the distance was 650 miles, too far for comfort given the possibility of flying into petrol-guzzling headwinds.

'Then go to Tavoy,' the RAF man advised. 'You can get gasoline there but there is no place to land. However, if you come down at low tide, you will have plenty of room on the beach.'

Needing details about the moon and tides so they could set off at the appropriate time for a low-tide landing, Bill and Chubbie had visited the 'experts' in Rangoon. They were advised to land at 3 pm at Maungmagan Beach, about eight miles west of Tavoy (Dawei).

The experts were wrong. When they flew over the beach at the sug-gested time, the tide wasn't out, it was running full. And no wonder the calculations were incorrect. Chubbie would later learn that the experts' chart was dated 1882.

The *Red Rose* didn't have enough fuel to remain airborne until low tide. Bill flew up the coast looking for a suitable landing place and found a beach about nine miles north of Maungmagan. The high tide had left only a narrow strip between the jungle and water's edge, so it was a tricky landing. When the plane stopped, its wheels were in the water. Aside from their nearly catastrophic Rangoon landing, it was the most difficult of their touchdowns so far.

Hundreds of Burmese people thronged to the plane and sat in a half-circle around it, talking animatedly to each other and pointing upwards, as if the *Red Rose* was a strange bird that had materialised from the sky. No Europeans were among them and there seemed to be none living in the vicinity, so Chubbie and Bill used simple sign language to communicate that they were hungry and thirsty. A man brought over a large green coconut, which he cut using a filthy knife he had wiped on his dirty leg. Others passed them raw turtle eggs and bananas. Chubbie and Bill secretly buried the turtle eggs in the sand but ate the bananas with relief and relish.

With the worst of their hunger and thirst sated, they assessed their situation. They couldn't leave the plane unguarded, because the curious locals had already torn its fabric covering in several places. Bill didn't want Chubbie to attempt the long walk to Maungmagan because it was impossible to know what dangers she might face. And he didn't want to leave her alone with the plane because the Burmese were again trying to clamber all over it. Their only choice was to remain on the beach until the tide turned.

Even the tide seemed against them: it turned during the night, when it was too dark for them to take off. They were stranded there until the next low tide.

Bitten by sandflies and chased by crabs, they had a dreadful night. With no blankets, they had nothing between themselves and the bitter cold. They couldn't even snuggle up together for warmth and go to sleep, because the plane needed guarding. And they couldn't take turns on guard while the other slept, because the locals sat around all night talking. By daylight they were exhausted, hungry and livid.

At 10 am, the tide was low enough for the small beach to act as a runway. After Bill lifted the plane off the sand, he swooped down on the crowd who scattered in terror. It was payback for the chatter that had kept them awake all night.

The Europeans at Maungmagan had been concerned about their non-appearance and were relieved to see them land on the beach. The fuel didn't arrive from Tavoy until 3 pm, so they were forced to delay their departure until morning. At least they had a policeman to guard the plane overnight.

The expatriates put them up for the night. When Chubbie sank into her comfortable bed, she thought that even a single night of hardship showed that the simple things in life—the ones normally taken for granted—were fundamental to everyday happiness. Perhaps, for people to fully appreciate what they had, everyone needed the occasional dose of hardship.

Their second beach take-off in a row went smoothly and they headed south towards Victoria Point on the southernmost tip of Burma. There the landing strip was just a forest clearing, so primitive that Bill was worried he couldn't land on it. Forced to do so because of his low fuel supply, he stopped just short of the trees. With no room to taxi in a circle, Chubbie jumped to the ground to swing the plane around. When she stepped in front of the propeller, she was horrified to see a nasty drop only a few feet ahead.

Monkeys chattered in the lush rainforest trees as the local rubber planter welcomed them. He loved entertaining the occasional aviator who came through and he took them to his comfortable log bungalow for the night.

The next morning, as Bill looked at the clearing, he was even more troubled about his take-off. In these hot tropical climes, his fuel-laden plane needed 350 to 400 yards to lift off the ground, plus more flat terrain for him to commence his climb. But the Victoria Point runway was not only short, it faced a hill covered by trees.

Grim-faced, he stood looking at the hill. Then he shrugged and said fatalistically, 'I suppose we can get off all right.'

They did . . . just. And then another problem arose when they were airborne. They realised that their maps were packed in the fuselage and the only way to access them was to land and unpack them. Bill shouted at Chubbie; Chubbie shouted back. It turned out that he had asked her to pack the maps and she had assumed he'd already taken out those he needed.

They managed to land safely and locate the necessary maps and take off once more. But it left them with a feeling of foreboding, a feeling that every time they evaded disaster by only a whisker they were one step closer to the occasion when they wouldn't.

Again they flew into filthy weather: dense clouds and heavy rain. They had been told they could land at Penang's racecourse but it proved to be surrounded by trees and houses, making a take-off difficult. Penang's beach was too small and cluttered with fishermen's boats, so they flew another fifty miles to Taiping's polo field. It wasn't ideal either—small, surrounded by hills and covered in water. Short of fuel, they had no choice but to land there.

The next morning, when they gave their plane a final once-over, they noticed that the top fuel tank was leaking. All their efforts of the night before—checking, cleaning, filling the tanks—had been wasted. They would have to drain all the petrol into tins, lift out the tank, seal the hole and fill it again.

By the time they replaced the tank, their sweat had glued petrol, oil and dirt to their skin and clothes. As they had lost so much travelling time and as they had been told there were no Europeans at the next stop, they decided not to worry about cleaning themselves but just to get going. If they did happen to encounter a solitary countryman when they arrived in Kuala Lumpur, he would surely understand their situation and forgive their filth.

Chapter Eleven

No Europeans in Kuala Lumpur? What a cruel joke. Kuala Lumpur proved to be the seat of government in British Malaya and every official and his elegantly coiffed wife was crossing the landing field to welcome them.

Chubbie looked down at herself. Grimy khaki shirt and shorts. Dirty tennis shoes with no socks. Oil-covered legs. She also knew without checking her cracked mirror that her face was streaked with grease and oil. She looked at Bill. He hadn't shaved. His dirty shirt was fastened with a large safety pin at the neck and he too was sock-less and clad in filthy shoes. She had never felt so mortified in all her life.

They spent the night at Government House. Thanks to the loan of clothes from a fifteen-year-old girl, Chubbie was able to lunch and dine in style and to swim and play tennis. In the evening they partnered at bridge. It seemed so civilised after their many recent hardships.

Drenching rain left them looking like drowned cats by the time they reached Singapore the next day. They flew over the racecourse, which seemed the most suitable place to land, however they had been told to land on the Balestier Plain so they dutifully followed their instructions.

When they climbed from the plane, they found themselves in a couple of feet of water.

A cinematographer and a reporter splashed over to meet them, along with a swarm of locals. Within minutes, the ground was a quagmire.

'What a dreadful landing place,' was Bill's first comment to the press. He added that, in view of Singapore's size, it was one of the worst landing grounds he had encountered.

His remark wasn't tactful but was hardly inaccurate. Indeed, the *Malayan Saturday Post* would later use his remark to chide the authorities for their shortsightedness. 'This airman, quite justifiably, will take away a bad impression of Malaya's utter lack of preparedness for flying machines, except for seaplanes, because our mentality remains that of a generation ago.'

They remained in Singapore for two days, relaxing and socialising in addition to thoroughly overhauling the plane. Bill had been thinking about precautions for their flight over the Torres Strait to Darwin, the most dangerous leg of their entire journey. He decided that at their final stopover before they set off for Darwin, he would obtain thirty automobile inner tubes, a quick-action pump, and some coils of rope, which he would pack in their spares locker. If they suffered engine trouble over the sea, he would endeavour to make a pancake landing on the water. Unless they were unlucky enough to come down in rough seas, the plane should stay afloat long enough for him to pump up the inner tubes and lash them around the plane. Prior to their departure he would provide the authorities with their course and cruising speed. He would also request the authorities to advise the shipping in the area that the *Red Rose* was making the dangerous crossing and that, if they were four hours overdue, a search should be activated. If they hadn't been found by nightfall, he could use his powerful electric torch to signal to any passing planes or boats.

Over the weekend, their new friends in Singapore asked them about their future plans—after they had reached Australia, of course. With the end so close, Chubbie and Bill had also been discussing the future. Chubbie couldn't bear to go back to the prison of her married life, not after her adventures and not now she was in love with Bill. They'd had no private time together since they left Persia—the dangers of discovery and scandal were too great. But their feelings for each other hadn't changed; in fact, they had strengthened. When they were alone, they had discussed ways in which they could remain together, ways that would seem acceptable to the censorious public. The solution, they had decided, was to keep adventuring.

They told their Singapore friends that they would need to fit a new engine in Australia and relax for a while. Afterwards, they would probably make a return journey to England in the *Red Rose*. If all went according to their tentative plans, they would be back in Singapore in March. So they wouldn't be saying 'Goodbye' to their Singapore friends when they left the following day but 'Until we meet again'.

As they flew down the coast of Sumatra on Monday, 9 January, they crossed the equator and set another record. Chubbie was the first airborne woman to ever cross that invisible line.

Bill had hoped to stop only for a quick refuel at Muntok (Mentok) on the Island of Banca (Bangka); however, heavy monsoonal rain slowed their passage. When he saw Muntok's landing strip from the air, he wished they hadn't needed to land there at all. It sat on a slope and was covered in knee-high grass. At least the warm welcome from the Dutch crowds made up for the shocking landing field.

The Dutch held a reception for them that night and read out a long speech in perfect English that itemised every step of the *Red Rose*'s journey. As Chubbie listened to the speech, she felt both astonished and humbled to realise that over the past few months, as they had suffered trial after trial and had felt so alone in their suffering, people all over the world had been following their journey and taking a passionate interest in their wellbeing.

When she climbed into her bed, she thought that tonight she was resting her head in Muntok and tomorrow Batavia (Java). Within days she would be doing the same in Australia.

'The *Red Rose* draws nearer,' advised an Australian newspaper excitedly.

Muntok's Dutch residents had no intention of sleeping in, despite celebrating the *Red Rose*'s adventures a little too freely the night before. Flocking to the aerodrome soon after dawn, they watched the aviators completing their final preparations. Around 7 am, they cheered the handsome pilot and his diminutive sidekick as the pair headed towards the plane. They watched Chubbie climb into her cockpit while Bill walked around to the front of the plane and with a mighty heave spun the propeller. The engine roared. They cheered again as Bill climbed on board and began to taxi. They continued cheering as the *Red Rose* sped down the short runway and lifted into the air.

But as the plane reached 150 feet, their cheers petered out. Hands covered mouths with a collective gasp of horror. The *Red Rose* had faltered and was dropping like a stone.

Chapter Twelve

Chubbie was sitting calmly in her front cockpit when it happened. For a moment, it had seemed like any other take-off, with Bill's skills as an airman triumphing over the vicissitudes of yet another inadequate airfield. Ahead was a hillside densely covered in trees and houses, but she knew that the power of the *Red Rose*'s engine would carry them over the hilltop and on towards Batavia.

Suddenly everything went silent.

What was happening? Was Bill planning to land again? Why would he do that?

The plane gave a sickening lurch.

That was when she realised something was seriously wrong. And at only 150 feet, Bill had little room to manoeuvre.

She looked at the hillside in front of them. If he maintained their forward trajectory, the Avian would plunge into it and they would probably be killed. Yet there wasn't enough time for him to turn the plane around in an effort to save them. Even powerless, the plane's momentum was carrying them towards an almost certain death.

Then the right wing dropped and the plane began to fall sideways out of the sky.

For an interminable moment she sat there, feeling the odd weightlessness of free fall. People were regularly killed or maimed when they fell from thirty-foot buildings, yet here they were plummeting towards Earth from five times that height. She felt strangely fatalistic in that drawn-out moment. What will be, will be.

With a sickening crunch, the right wing slammed into the ground. Then the propeller struck the ground and the plane somersaulted. A moment later, it settled on the landing field, upside down and facing the opposite direction.

After the first momentary shock, when she realised that the plane was no longer moving and that she was still alive, she found herself hanging upside down, kept in place by her seatbelt. Her face ached as if someone had punched it. As she looked around, she realised that she was trapped in a mesh of wires and wreckage and was drenched in petrol. If a fire broke out, she would have little chance of survival.

She called out to Bill. He didn't respond.

There was no time to wait for help. She had to get out of the plane as quickly as possible. She tried to push aside the wreckage that trapped her, without success. As she tugged at it, she spotted a possible exit— tiny, yet so was she. She twisted around like a screw being rotated from its socket, feeling as if she were removing skin-layers in the process. Eventually, she twisted herself right out of the wreckage.

She stood beside the plane for a moment, looking at it. An overwhelming feeling of relief swept over her, relief at being free from what remained of the *Red Rose* and from the horrific image of their precious plane as her funeral pyre.

She slipped under the plane and looked inside Bill's cockpit. He wasn't there. Glancing around, she saw him lying face down in front of the plane. He wasn't moving. For a moment she thought, 'If he has gone and got killed, what am I to do?'

Racing to his side, she turned him over. Blood was pouring from his mouth. She lifted him into a sitting position, leaning his body against her own so the blood wouldn't choke him. His eyes flickered. Relief swept over her: he wasn't dead.

As his eyes closed again, she saw that his teeth had gone through the fleshy area just below his bottom lip. She lifted the flesh off his teeth and tried to stop the bleeding, to no avail.

By this time, she was surrounded by people who had rushed to their assistance. They looked aghast at the sight of her. It turned out that she too was covered in blood. Bleakly returning their gaze, she said, 'Only 1800 miles from Australia and we have now smashed our bus.'

When Bill regained consciousness, their Dutch well-wishers told them that they would take them both to hospital. She and Bill both protested, saying that they needed to see how badly their plane was damaged. But their supporters convinced them of their need for medical attention. They were also kind enough not to put the obvious into words: the plane wasn't going anywhere—with or without them.

At the hospital, the doctors cleaned off the blood and painted Chubbie's scratches with iodine. They worked on her broken nose but could do nothing about her bruises or her two rapidly blackening eyes. She would look a sorry sight for some time to come.

They told Bill he needed stitches, but he wouldn't listen. He kept talking about cameras and photographs and insurance—thankfully, an insurance company had finally relented and covered them. He tried to leave the hospital, saying he would return later to have the stitches put in, but the medical staff wouldn't let him. To pacify him, Chubbie organised to be taken back to the landing field so she could take the necessary pictures. When she returned, Bill was receiving the last of his stitches. Apart from a concussion, there was nothing seriously wrong with him, so the doctors let him leave the hospital to assess the plane's damage.

'I am broken-nosed and broken-hearted,' Chubbie told the press after they had inspected the plane. It was a daunting sight. As she totted up the damage, all her energy and optimism, her spirit and heart—indeed every ounce of courage that had kept her going for three long months—seemed to drain out of her.

Yet it could have been worse. Bill had again saved their lives. In the split second he'd had to make a decision, he had picked the one action that offered them a chance of surviving the inevitable crash. By side-slipping the plane, by forcing it to plummet towards the ground via the shortest route possible, he had avoided the deadly trees on the hillside in front of them.

Chubbie decided that, since they had lived to tell the tale with only minor injuries, and since the old bus might be reparable, some luck might still be hanging around them after all. Never one to stay broken-hearted for long, she told the press, 'Our spirit is undaunted.' She also admitted that the distance was probably too great for their small engine. They should have changed engines at the halfway point, but they had lacked the funds to do so.

They sent cables to the Avro company and others begging for assistance. Meanwhile, they decided that their wisest course would be to return to Singapore. They organised to have the *Red Rose*'s remains packed up and shipped to Singapore while their Dutch supporters booked them a passage on a small Chinese boat.

Arriving in Singapore two days after their crash, they were taken to the Colonial Secretary's bungalow to stay. A restful place with polished floors, soft comfortable lounges and silent-footed servants who attended to their every need, it provided the peace and tranquillity they needed to work out what they should do next.

Of course, everyone wanted to know what had happened. The initial reports had said that the plane suffered a broken plunger axle. When questioned by the Singapore press, Bill claimed that there had been an air-lock or choke in the fuel pipe, the type of accident that could happen to any machine.

Could the plane be fixed? Bill said that they hadn't had time to conduct a thorough examination and would do so when the plane reached Singapore. From what he had seen, the wings were smashed, but the fuselage and tail didn't seem to be in a bad condition. Whether it was reparable or not, he and Chubbie still hoped to succeed in their venture.

They received many telegrams of sympathy, including words of relief and comfort from Chubbie's husband and Bill's parents and wife. His mother didn't want him to continue the journey and seemed to think that, having provided some of the funding, her opinion carried weight. When faced with Bill's eagerness to continue—and a few pithy words about the pointlessness of quitting when they were so close to setting a world record—she backed down. They also received many telegrams congratulating them on their achievements and praising them for their determination to continue. Ironically, one of Britain's aviation authorities now praised the *Red Rose*'s flight as being among the greatest of British air achievements.

By the weekend, Bill was able to advise the press that they would remain in Singapore until the *Red Rose* was repaired and then continue their flight to Australia. The Avro company had told him that the flight would lack any advertising value unless they finished it in the same plane and the company promised to help them do so by expediting the repairs.

There was little they could do until the new parts arrived in mid February. In between stripping and preparing the *Red Rose*, they lived the life of wealthy expatriates, enjoying luncheons and dinners, bridge games and other social get-togethers. And as January turned into February, as the hot humid days crawled past, they tried not to chafe at the interminable delay.

Meanwhile, on the other side of the globe, another Avro Avian was racing down Croydon's runway. With the *Red Rose* possibly down for the count, Bert Hinkler had set his own sights on the light plane record to Australia. He would also try to smash the Smith brothers' twenty-eight-day record in the process.

Travelling with extra fuel tanks and without the weight of a passenger, he flew 1200 miles to Rome on his first day, 7 February 1928. He reached Malta on the second day, then on the third made a much longer Mediterranean crossing to Benghazi and on to Tobruk. By the end of day six, he was at Basra, a destination Chubbie and Bill hadn't reached until day twenty-seven of their more leisurely journey.

Onwards he came. Calcutta on day ten. Rangoon on day eleven. Victoria Point on day twelve. Unless something went wrong, he would arrive in Singapore by nightfall on day thirteen: 19 February.

Their spare parts would not reach them until the 20th.

Chapter Thirteen

Chubbie and Bill had heard he was coming. Indeed, who could have missed the press reports with their increasingly excited tones at his outrageously fast flight? They wondered bitterly whether the ill-luck that had dogged their own flight would turn on him for even a moment.

They were there to greet him when he landed in Singapore that evening. They helped him service his plane by torchlight. They took him out to dinner. Bill even slept in the plane overnight to protect it from their own friends, who were not only muttering comments about Bert 'taking advantage of the misfortunes of others' and 'stealing records' but had whispered the nasty word 'sabotage'.

Chubbie and Bill farewelled him the following morning and telegraphed their congratulations when he reached Darwin in an astonishing sixteen days.

And tried to hide their devastation.

What should they do next? There was no point in not continuing their flight. There were few accolades for those who came in second, and none for those who bowed out altogether. Should they race to follow him, snapping at his heels as a reminder to the world that they would have reached Australia first if not for their unbelievable run of misfortune? Or should they wait until 'Hustling Hinkler' fever had abated and the world had the energy to get excited about another record-setting endeavour?

On Saturday, 25 February, three days after Bert reached Darwin, the Singapore press advised that the *Red Rose*'s repairs were completed and that the aviators would likely recommence their journey on the Monday or Tuesday. The report was premature. The repairs were proving more difficult than anyone had expected. It was harder to fix a broken plane than to assemble a new one. Nothing fitted. Everything had to be re-welded. With the assistance of Chinese mechanics, they worked on, day after day, in the merciless humidity.

At last it was ready. On 10 March, the press reported that the *Red Rose* would be transported to the racecourse the following day. There it would take to the air once more, to complete the five-hour flight test required for an airworthiness certificate.

Excitement gripped Singapore. While the world's press had poured out its sympathy for the downed aviators, Singapore had felt personally devastated. Expatriates and islanders had turned out in force to cheer the aviators when they set off for Muntok on 9 January, and they had comforted the battered and dispirited pair on their ignominious return a few days later. In the weeks that followed, Singapore had tried to lift the duo's spirits as well as helping with the plane's repairs. It was as if Bill and Chubbie and the *Red Rose* were now part of the island's fabric—honorary citizens in all but name.

Carefully the plane was lifted onto a trailer attached to the back of a lorry. An advance guard was sent out to clear the road of other vehicles to help ensure a safe passage. Slowly the lorry moved out from the warehouse and began the fifteen-mile journey to the racecourse. No one would breathe comfortably until the lorry reached its destination.

More locals—thousands more—waited at the racecourse and mobbed the plane, making it difficult for Bill to take to the air. At last a space was cleared and he took off, to fly around and around the racecourse for five hours. After he landed, he announced to the waiting press that they would leave for Muntok the following Tuesday.

In truth, they would have preferred to bypass Banca Island. It seemed like tempting fate to go back to the site of their record-ruining crash. However, they had promised the kindly Dutch to visit them again when—or if—they were able to continue their flight.

Bill continued, 'Admiration has been expressed in all quarters at the determination of Mrs Miller to continue the flight, which has met with so much ill-luck.'

The flight was all about Chubbie now. For many, her participation had been the most interesting feature of the *Red Rose*'s flight from the start. Now, she was all they had left. Bert Hinkler had beaten every record that Bill or the *Red Rose* had previously set by travelling farther, faster and solo. Chubbie alone would be their pathway to glory—the first woman to make the perilous flight from England to Australia—if nothing else went wrong on their journey to Darwin.

At 7 am on Tuesday, 13 March, they took off from the Singapore racecourse, eagerly watched by all their Singaporean well-wishers. The local press expressed everyone's thoughts when it remarked: 'Great interest is felt in the effort of the two aviators, who are continuing their flight after suffering set-backs which were enough to discourage even the stoutest heart.'

It was impossible for Chubbie not to feel a sense of trepidation as the *Red Rose* lifted into the sky. She wondered if it would rise to the occasion or if something else was waiting in the wings—or in the fuselage or engine—that would announce its presence at the worst possible moment.

But the flight to Muntok proved uneventful. Both the plane and engine worked perfectly. The landing site was also in better condition. The Singapore consul had written to the Muntok authorities, asking that the grass be cut before the *Red Rose* returned. The ground was still uneven, but they could at least see its undulations. They landed safely and were greeted affectionately by their many Dutch friends.

In the early hours of the following morning, Chubbie was awoken by a loud noise. A Chinese funeral band was playing a mournful refrain accompanied by the monotonous beating of drums. She found it impossible to get back to sleep, not only because of the noise. A feeling of ill omen crept through her. Why a funeral dirge of all things, in Muntok of all places, on this morning of all mornings?

They left for the landing field in the dark, wanting a dawn take-off so the journey would be completed before the worst of the day's heat. Flying in humid tropical conditions was not only uncomfortable for them, it added further stress to their well-worn engine.

The *Red Rose* faced the landing strip. A sense of déjà vu settled over everyone. The Muntok crash had been horrifying, not just for Chubbie and Bill but for all of the spectators.

Bill pushed the throttle forward and the plane sped down the landing strip towards the tree-covered hillside. It lifted off the ground at exactly the same point as previously.

Everyone held their breaths. The plane kept rising and soared over the hillside.

Bill didn't tempt fate by circling to dip his wing in farewell.

As they left the island and began flying over the sea, Bill shrieked a single word that Chubbie could hear over the engine drone. 'Alright!' She turned around and saw that he was smiling.

Rain pummelled them again as they flew towards Batavia, but they were long past caring about a simple drenching. Rain and dense clouds enveloped them for much of the next day's journey to Surabaya in West Java. They flew past a smoking volcano and were glad it didn't pick that moment to erupt.

Surabaya was their last 'civilised' landing place, although they had another two overnight stops before they attacked the Torres Strait. Bill sent a cable to the Shell Company requesting that fuel supplies be laid down for them at Darwin. He added optimistically that they anticipated the successful completion of their journey.

Each day though, the weather conditions deteriorated as if the elements were conspiring against them. An hour out of Surabaya, they ran into another curtain of grey clouds and heavy tropical rain, the ugliest storm they had endured in their five-month journey.

They stopped overnight at Bima on the island of Sumbawa. The next day they faced more torrential rain, more thick clouds in mountainous country, more hours when they couldn't see the ground below them.

When they reached Atambua in Dutch Timor (West Timor), their final overnight stop, they were dismayed. Not only was the landing field covered in long grass—except for a small mown strip in the middle—it was also covered in water. Bill managed to land safely, but he was uncertain whether he would be able to take off again.

He asked the Dutch commander if more grass could be cut. Before long, the local gaol had disgorged a gang of convicts who, with hands and feet chained together, cleared a long wide landing strip.

The commander and lieutenant offered to help service the plane. They jury-rigged a sun shelter—bamboo poles covered with a tarpaulin—to protect them all from the burning sun. Nothing protected them from the malarial mosquitoes, which feasted on their exposed flesh.

At 5 pm, the heavens opened. Everyone crawled under the plane for protection. The water rose and continued rising. When it was a foot deep, Bill said it would be impossible to take off the next morning. They covered the plane with the tarpaulin and left it there until the rain eased.

The rain that drowned Atambua had also drenched Darwin. Bill received a cable from the Shell Company saying that continuous heavy rain had fallen on Darwin since Friday without any sign of it abating. Since visibility was poor and the landing ground boggy, it would be best if they postponed their arrival.

At least the news distracted them from the frustration of their enforced delay.

The rain in Atambua cleared the next day and the ground dried quickly, although Bill still wasn't sure if it would be firm enough for a safe departure. He had already discarded the idea of taking with them the inner tubes, quick-action pump and coils of rope. The take-off would be difficult enough as it was without this extra weight. They both accepted that, if they were forced to ditch into the sea, the *Red Rose* would float for a mere half hour. Only a miracle would save them.

When Bill examined the ground the following morning, Monday, 19 March, his concerns didn't abate. It was still too boggy. Soon the locals brought hundreds of feet of matting which they laid down on the landing strip.

When Chubbie saw the quantity of matting, she wondered if the walls and roofs of every house in the district had been stripped. She hoped not. The matting wouldn't be of much use to anyone afterwards.

With fervent wishes of 'God speed' following them, the *Red Rose* picked up speed. The matting separated the plane's wheels from the worst of the bogginess although the water-logged ground still seemed reluctant to release them. Chubbie's stomach was in a knot by the time the plane lifted off the ground, missing the trees by a mere six feet.

She hoped it would be the last drama they faced before they reached Australia.

With such a long distance to travel, they didn't circle the landing strip and waggle a goodbye. Instead, they climbed 5000 feet to cross the mountains and then headed towards the sea.

The weather refused to favour them even on this final leg of their journey. The air was hot and humid, and mist shrouded the island. After they crossed the shoreline, rain soaked them again, barely easing throughout their journey.

For hours, all they saw beneath them was the sea. No passing ships. Nothing else to occupy their attention. Chubbie found it strangely eerie and was glad Bill sat just a couple of feet behind her. She hated to think what it would be like to undertake such a journey on her own.

They were halfway to Darwin and flying at about 1000 feet when the engine made a strange noise. A popping, spluttering sound. The plane lost height. She turned to Bill and yelled, 'What's happening?' He shrugged to indicate that he didn't know.

Soon the alarming noise died away and they began to climb again, as if their gutsy little plane had wrested control from the recalcitrant engine and was determined to get them to Darwin. She took a few deep breaths to calm her racing heart while the plane flew steadily on.

Then it happened again. The engine coughed and spluttered. The plane sank. As they hadn't yet regained their previous altitude, they lost even more height. A moment later the spluttering ceased and the engine ran smoothly. The plane gained altitude again. She waited tensely to see if the problem had fixed itself . . . and waited.

The engine spluttered its indignation again.

Darwin was still three hours away. Each time the engine misfired, the plane lost more altitude. If the problem continued, they would soon run out of sky.

When she again asked what was happening, Bill sent her a note saying, 'I don't know.' His next message made her stomach sink into her dirty tennis shoes. 'I'm afraid she won't stay the course. But, anyway, we've done our best.'

His words lacked any maudlin sentimentality. There was no evidence of fear, only a calm acceptance of the fate that awaited them.

The engine spluttered and gravity pulled the plane down again. This time it kept sinking. As the ocean loomed closer, she thought, 'This is it.' That strange balance of bad luck and good luck that had kept them going for 158 days was ending with only a couple of hours left to fly. She turned to Bill and saw him kiss his hand to the sea and sky, both a farewell and an acknowledgement that mankind was kidding itself when it thought it had any dominion over nature.

In that drawn-out fall, she wondered if they could tie the air-cushions and life jackets together and float until they sighted land. The rain was torrential and the heavy clouds made the sea look especially grey and ominous beneath them. Then the spluttering ceased and the engine roared, and they began to regain altitude.

The gut-wrenching cycle of spluttering and sinking, followed by smooth running, continued. Somehow they maintained enough altitude to stay airborne while the plane ate up more miles to Australia. When they were an hour out of Darwin, Bill sent her a note saying, 'Seventy miles to go and we're losing altitude again. But we might just do it.'

Visibility remained poor, so he was navigating by compass alone. According to his calculations, they should soon reach Darwin, although he still couldn't see any evidence of land. Was the compass working properly? To be lost over this vast expanse of water with a troublesome engine would be their death knell.

As if a curtain had been pulled back, the clouds suddenly dissipated and they could see Bathurst Island, off the coast of Darwin. Soon they saw Darwin about ten miles ahead. Chubbie swivelled in her seat and grinned at him as she pointed towards the town. She turned up her thumb in the universal signal of success and he did the same. Then they reached out and shook hands over the top of his cockpit windscreen.

As they flew over Darwin's airfield, they saw that the landing conditions were appalling. They saw something else as well. Despite the fog and rain and sandstorms they had endured—despite the dramas caused by the persistent engine trouble, the joyriding snake, the forced landing in Rangoon and the crash in Muntok; despite their scrimping and saving, their constant hunger and thirst, and the many other hardships and heartaches they had suffered in their effort to complete this most extraordinary of record-setting journeys—there was no one at Darwin's airfield to greet them.

Chapter Fourteen

When they arrived at Darwin, they had completed all but the last stages of a flight that is perhaps unique in its story of adventure and disappointment.

The Sydney Morning Herald, 20 March 1928

D arwin hadn't intended to snub them.

The previous day, when its officials received no response to their warning about the horrendous weather conditions, they had assumed that the *Red Rose* was on its way. Despite threatening clouds and the occasional light shower, hundreds of people had motored out to the landing paddock near the prison at Fannie Bay to greet them. They kept waiting as the dark clouds turned into heavy monsoonal rain. They continued waiting until a message arrived saying that the aviators had received the warning telegram and hadn't left Timor.

Deciding that the aviators would wait there until they received word of improved weather conditions, the town's powers-that-be cancelled all plans for a welcoming party and an official reception. Not only was the rain torrential and the visibility poor, the middle of the airfield was a swamp and the grass was five feet high and impossible to mow because of the monsoonal weather. In fact, it was too long to provide a safe landing according to the sergeant who had attended Bert Hinkler's plane.

The officials asked if anyone had any ideas for making the landing field safer. Should they direct the plane to the nearby racecourse at Fannie Bay? No, the racecourse was little better. What about painting a white cross on the landing strip? No, the rain would wash it away. As one bad idea followed another, they decided to delay the *Red Rose*'s flight until Wednesday to allow time for the rain to clear and the grass to be mown.

But Darwin's message to the aviators didn't get through. And the *Red Rose* beat Bill's telegram to Darwin saying they were on their way.

Only one person saw the *Red Rose* land: Mrs Dempsey, the wife of the local gaol superintendent. She heard a plane overhead and went outside to see what was happening. Providentially, her husband had taken it upon himself to assist the aviators by laying down a white calico guide and attaching red bunting to the telephone poles, for which Bill would later thank him profusely. Mrs Dempsey saw the plane roll to a stop in one of the boggiest parts of the runway and the aviators step out into knee-high mud.

When word reached Darwin that the *Red Rose* had been sighted, fleets of cars raced to the airfield carrying the mayor and other prominent citizens and officials. Far from being ignored, Chubbie and Bill were to be feted.

Telegrams flooded in, 450 in total, including congratulations from Bert Hinkler and from Prime Minister Stanley Bruce. The Prime Minister wrote, 'On behalf of the government of the Commonwealth and the people of Australia, I desire to congratulate you and Mrs Miller on the completion of your flight to Australia. We are grateful that despite the difficulties and delays which beset you on the journey your task has at length been safely accomplished.'

Unfortunately, Chubbie and Bill also received word that no steps would be taken to officially recognise Chubbie's achievement, even though she was the first woman to travel by air from England to Australia and her flight was the longest ever undertaken by a woman. If she had piloted the plane, the government's response would have been different.

Others, however, recognised her contribution. The Shell Company's telegram said: 'Please convey our heartiest congratulations to Mrs Miller on her safe arrival in Darwin. Her success in being the first woman to fly to Australia is a fitting culmination to the splendid achievements of her countrymen: the Smith brothers, Paver, McIntosh, and Hinkler.'

Back in England, the editor of *The Aeroplane*—one of the few aviation experts who had supported the venture—praised the *Red Rose*'s trip as one of the pluckiest flights in aviation history and declared that Bill had proved himself a first-class aviator. He added, 'Perhaps the greatest credit is due to Mrs Miller, for it was her undefeatable enthusiasm and optimism which made the attempt possible.' He explained that she had raised the necessary capital by hard work and persistence, and had never lost her sense of humour.

The press in general were more interested in Chubbie's achievement than Bill's and knew the public would be as well. Of Bill, the reporters provided only a bare description: he was five feet eight inches tall and weighed ten stone seven pounds. Chubbie, by comparison, was tiny, only five feet and a half-inch in height and weighing a mere seven stone. Dressed in shorts and a white open-necked shirt, she had dark smartly shingled hair and a smiling sunburnt face—a 'chubby' face indeed, observed one of the journalists, deciding that this was the reason for her nickname. And her cheery nature and charm enchanted everyone she met.

After a few days to rest and to recondition their plane, they farewelled Darwin with a low flyover of the mayor's house, terrifying the local citizens who thought the plane was about to crash. Onwards they flew to Newcastle Waters, Brunette Downs and Camooweal (just inside the Queensland border).

Chubbie would later tell the press that, when they were about twenty-five miles out of Newcastle Waters, they couldn't find the windmill shown on the poorly marked Civil Aviation map. Not wanting to get lost, as Hinkler had done, they decided to land and question two men on packhorses. The horsemen were so casual—in that outback Australian kind of way—that they showed no surprise at the sight of a plane dropping from the sky onto the ground beside them. One of the pair, an elderly man, remarked that he had travelled 500 miles in five months as if it were quite an achievement. When he asked Chubbie where she had come from and she replied London, he showed no more interest than if she had said Darwin.

They hopped across the countryside until they reached Brisbane. There they were given a civic reception and both were asked to address the gathering. Bill spoke first, offering his thanks for the welcome and saying how much aviation could do for those living in Australia's back-country. Chubbie stood up to loud cheers and applause and a hearty rendition of 'For She's a Jolly Good Fellow'. Speaking in a soft voice, she told the audience that she had never felt so nervous in all her life, that she was no speaker and felt rather silly. All she could say was that she was grateful for all the kindness shown them throughout the trip and that she was proud to be Australian. She thanked them all from the bottom of her heart and sat down again.

While the audience heard only a terrified but nonetheless gracious speaker—a housewife who had privately said that she wanted to turn tail and flee back to England when she realised she would have to speak in front of an audience—the press encountered a feisty record-setting aviator, who was peeved at being pipped. When asked about her greatest disappointment or frustration, she replied, 'That Hinkler butted in before us—which of course he could not have done but for the crash.'

A short time later she retracted the comment, saying that she hadn't used the expression attributed to her and that she had never seriously implied anything of the kind. She had learnt the first of many lessons of fame—that those in the public eye have to think carefully before they speak.

Around 5 pm on Saturday, 31 March, a welcoming party of silver-winged aircraft set out from the Australian Aerial Derby at Sydney's Mascot aerodrome to meet the *Red Rose* on its journey south from Newcastle. The late afternoon sun was hiding behind golden banks of clouds when, around 5.30 pm, the returning squadron could be seen against the darkening sky. 'Here they are!' cried the 100,000-strong crowd. Looming larger and larger, the planes flew in a perfect formation towards the airfield and then circled for ten minutes as the crowd cheered. The crowd cheered even louder when one silver bird detached itself from the flock and descended towards the aerodrome, landing gracefully in the middle of the water-logged fields. Taxiing to the foot of the official stand, it stopped in a sea of muddy water and sodden grass.

An Aero Club captain waded to the plane and held his arms out to Chubbie. She climbed from the cockpit and looked askance at the surrounding water. Another man could be seen splashing his way to the plane, dressed in his best suit; it was Chubbie's husband. But Keith had time only for a perfunctory kiss before Chubbie, with a wry smile, let the Aero Club captain pick her up and start carrying her to the waiting car.

Behind them came Bill, riding piggyback on another muscular frame. Once in the car, they were driven around the inside fence of the aerodrome so the crowds could get a close-up look at them. Then they were officially welcomed and taken to a reception at the Town Hall.

Over the next two months, Chubbie saw more Australian cities and towns than she could later remember. They travelled to Canberra, where they were the guests of honour at an official luncheon held at Parliament House; then on to Melbourne and to Hobart. When they landed in Tasmania, Australia's southern-most state, their flight became the longest ever made in a light plane. But few cared by then. Hinkler's triumph meant that those extra miles were no longer of any importance.

After touring the island, they returned to Sydney to begin a paid speaking tour of New South Wales. Bill flew them around the country-side and was always the first to speak. He would then introduce Chubbie, who was the main attraction. With practice, she transformed from being nervous and softly spoken to a professional speaker: confident, amusing and always charming. 'I was just the baggage,' she would declare with a twinkle, her self-deprecating humour delighting her audiences.

As Chubbie and Bill spoke in theatres and halls and clubs across New South Wales, the *Southern Cross* roared across the Pacific, arguably the greatest flight ever made until Neil Armstrong landed on the moon. Twenty-five years after the first heavier-than-air flight, the Earth had at last been circumnavigated. And Australian aviators had been responsible for covering much of that distance through multiple flights from England to Australia and the *Southern Cross*'s flight from North America.

Chubbie first met the *Southern Cross*'s four-man crew in Sydney on Sunday, 11 June, the day they arrived at Mascot aerodrome. She and Bill joined them at a number of functions in the aftermath, including a celebratory luncheon hosted by the New South Wales government. There she sat among the state's cabinet ministers and other political and aviation elite. She was the only woman present.

She met them again in Canberra on 15 June at a federal government function. She and Bill stood on the welcoming platform with the Australian Prime Minister and the federal political elite as Stanley Bruce praised Kingsford Smith and his crew and handed them a £5000 cheque.

The six adventurers felt an instant affinity, which developed into a strong friendship. Who else knew what it was really like: the ecstasy of flight, the tedious yet exhausting hours in the air, the moments of terror, the compulsion, despite everything, to go back up and do it all over again. The *Southern Cross*'s navigator, Captain Harry Lyon, who was about to return to America, told them that he and his colleagues had been approached about participating in a Hollywood motion picture for a hefty payment. Make-believe flying, seemingly, was more lucrative than real exploits. But the *Southern Cross*'s two Australian pilots, Charles Kingsford Smith and Charles Ulm, were not planning on returning to America, so he wondered if Chubbie and Bill would be interested in becoming his Hollywood pilots.

A few days later, Harry telegraphed them to ask for a speedy decision as he needed to book their passages. They met up in Sydney for further discussions. It turned out that Harry was thinking about more than just a Hollywood film. An Atlantic flight, in fact. A successful crossing would mean that, between them, they had circumnavigated the world. He had also seen the attention bestowed on Chubbie for her part in the *Red Rose*'s flight. And everyone had just heard about Amelia Earhart's flight across the Atlantic—as a passenger, like Chubbie—and the attention it was generating. What if Chubbie was to *co-pilot* an Atlantic flight?

Chubbie and Bill had known that interest in the *Red Rose*'s flight was waning and would die away altogether after they finished their tour. The *Southern Cross*'s arrival had seen to that. The question 'What next?' had already been on their lips. Their options were limited. Few people or sponsors would be interested in a return flight to England after Bert Hinkler's achievement. And Chubbie couldn't bear to return to her unhappy married life, to become the woman who had once done something important but now lived in ignominious obscurity. With these new enticements on offer, they couldn't help themselves—they said, 'Yes!'

A flurry of activity followed as they made the necessary preparations. Chubbie wrote to her husband and mother, saying that she had been offered a flying opportunity that was too good to turn down so she was sailing to America. She deliberately sent them letters rather than cables as this gave them no time to send forbidding responses. She had shed the cocoon and was making her own way in life.

The most heart-wrenching decision was their need to dispose of the *Red Rose*. It had carried them through so much—more successfully in fact than most people realised. They hadn't broadcast to the world that both the Muntok crash and the near-disaster over the Torres Strait had not been the engine's fault. The engine had died over Muntok because Bill had forgotten to turn the petrol on. And the engine had struggled over the Torres Strait because he had left the reserve tap on, so oil kept clogging up the plugs. They had survived because the plugs cleared themselves every so often.

They didn't have an opportunity to say goodbye to their trusty plane. It was in Cooma being repaired. They sold it to R.A. Charlton of Sydney, who kept it for only seven months before selling it to J.R. Palmer, a Sydney stockbroker and aviation enthusiast. In January 1929, Palmer flew a doctor to Scone aboard the *Red Rose* to operate on a critically ill patient, and the publicity for this flight demonstrated to the New South Wales public the value of Queensland's recently established Flying Doctor Service. Over the next few years, the

Red Rose passed from hand to hand until it was destroyed by fire after a crash-landing at Singleton, New South Wales, in 1936.

The spectators began gathering at Sydney's Circular Quay early on 23 June to say thank-you and goodbye to the two Americans of the *Southern Cross* crew, Harry Lyon and Jim Warner, the radio operator. Few knew that Chubbie and Bill were sailing out with them; their plans were too sudden.

Sydney had turned on a splendid aviators' farewell: a crisp winter's day with a cloudless sky of cornflower-blue. A police band played as rainbow-coloured streamers thrown from deck and dock trailed down the ship's side like a mermaid's tresses.

The six members of the *Southern Cross* and *Red Rose* crews were whisked past the crowd and bundled on board. For a moment, few recognised the pilots, Charles Kingsford Smith and Charles Ulm, who were dressed in their new Royal Australian Air Force uniforms with the golden stripes of their recently acquired ranks glinting on their royal-blue sleeves.

The band started playing patriotic tunes, including 'The Stars and Stripes Forever' and 'The Star-Spangled Banner'. An RAAF plane circled overhead, the drone of its engine heard only when the band paused between songs. The crowd waited hungrily, keen to see the faces of their heroes, to feel as if they were part of this event, a part of history in the making.

At last, only minutes before the scheduled departure time, the four members of the *Southern Cross* crew appeared on deck with Bill and Chubbie beside them. The crowd went berserk, cheering and waving hands and handkerchiefs. After Kingswood Smith and Ulm slipped ashore again, the *Sonoma* pulled away from the dock and headed into the harbour. Every ferryboat captain in the vicinity tugged on his horn as a final raucous farewell.

It was the first time Chubbie had sailed along Sydney's beautiful harbour and out through the heads into the open ocean. It was also the last. The Australian aviatrix—as the Americans would soon call her—would never return.

Part Two
DREAMS

Chapter Fifteen

America loves a hero. The celebrations began as soon as the *Malolo*—their ship from Honolulu—appeared out of San Francisco's fog and passed through the Golden Gate heads. Planes roared overhead scattering a vast flock of squawking seagulls. The coastguard cutter *Golden Gate* ploughed through the water beside them as it escorted their ship to the dock, an honour bestowed only on vessels carrying the most famous of the famous.

Everyone wanted to personally congratulate the *Southern Cross*'s two American crewmen, as if the well-wishers could draw the mantle of glory over their own shoulders by shaking the men's hands or, better yet, kissing them. The plane's navigator, bluff and hearty Harry Lyon, was the type to count the kisses: 284 from Australian lasses, he had previously told the Australian press. Since Harry and Jim were accompanied by the *Red Rose*'s crew—known internationally because of the snake-in-the-plane incident, if nothing else—America also embraced them in its celebrations.

Chubbie and Bill disembarked with the *Southern Cross* crewmen, and trooped aboard the *Golden Gate* for a ceremonial trip across

117

the bay to Oakland. The *Southern Cross* had departed from Oakland's airfield six weeks earlier without—the city was embarrassed to admit—any fanfare whatsoever. At Oakland, the crews climbed into two open-topped cars for the ticker-tape parade to the Town Hall. As Chubbie waved to the cheering crowds lining Oakland's streets, she tried not to feel like a gatecrasher.

At the Town Hall, the mayor shepherded them upstairs to a private room where he was holding a small function before the main festivities. Turning to Chubbie, he asked, 'What would you like to drink?'

She looked at him in bewilderment and replied, 'Well . . . I thought there was a prohibition in America.'

Amid howls of laughter, he swept open some sliding doors. She saw row upon row of distinctively labelled bottles with glasses scattered among them. As she gasped in surprise, a few of the women around her joked that they were drinking more under Prohibition than ever before. When she saw the amount of alcohol they consumed, she had no reason to disbelieve them.

The absurdity of Prohibition and its Kafkaesque bureaucracy would strike them again a few months later when US customs officials attempted to drain the alcohol from one of Bill's compasses. Its presence, they claimed, breached Prohibition laws.

In the following weeks, the two crews were honoured at breakfasts, buffets and banquets, meeting California's rich and powerful as well as the stage and screen stars the world fawned over. They even enjoyed a yachting party until Chubbie fell overboard and nearly drowned. Semi-conscious and with two cracked ribs, she was going under for the second time when Bill and Harry threw themselves into the water and rescued her.

Los Angeles—Hollywood—drew them south; however, little was happening with the film contract. In the end, the project fell through.

Their hopes of obtaining backing for an Atlantic flight were soon realised, though. Los Angeles was becoming more interested in air travel every day, according to the *Los Angeles Times*, and some of its financiers were keen to transform it into the world's aeronautical centre. On 20 July, Harry announced to the press that he, Bill and Chubbie would fly from London to Los Angeles the following spring in a tri-motored plane built especially for them in Los Angeles. The plane would cost $80,000 to $100,000, according to the financiers. It was to be an all-metal, closed-cabin monoplane with a 78-foot wingspan and a 1700-gallon fuel capacity—a condor compared to Chubbie and Bill's recently sold wren.

Early in August, Harry had to rush to Washington to see his gravely ill father. Thinking it would be a valuable opportunity to discuss their Atlantic plans with navy and government officials, he took Chubbie and Bill on the flights with him. Soon after their arrival, Chubbie's loose lips landed her in trouble again. 'You can't get any decent cigarettes or soap in this bloody country,' the tired traveller complained, not expecting her comment to be picked up by the nation's press.

While the flappers of Australia and England saw 'bloody' as a deliciously naughty word that reflected their modernity, America interpreted it as an insult to their homeland. Chubbie denied the report, saying that she had never made such a statement and that she was grateful for America's kindness and hospitality. It was another reminder of the importance of minding her tongue.

Then another scandal broke. Reportedly, Harry Lyon was a bigamist, with wives in Boston and San Francisco. Harry ducked his head for a time and stopped talking to the press. Thus, the public had heard nothing about his plan for an interim record-setting flight, also with Bill as his pilot, until two days before its commencement.

Their destination was the fishhook-shaped Bermuda archipelago, some 800 miles south-east of New York. Such a flight had never previously been undertaken because of the difficulty of finding the twenty-square-mile pinhead in the vast Atlantic Ocean. Cocky Harry had no doubts about his navigational abilities. 'If Captain Lancaster keeps the old bus up in the air,' he told the press, 'I don't expect to have any trouble finding Bermuda. Out in the Pacific, which is a real ocean, they have islands that are really small.'

If Harry failed to find that pinhead though, Bill's fuel tanks would be dry long before he could double-back to the American coastline. And, while his amphibian—which had a seaplane's floats as well as a land plane's wheels—could set down on the ocean surface, a violent sea was just as deadly for amphibians and seaplanes as for any other small vessel.

Chubbie and her new friend Amelia Earhart stood chatting on Long Island's shore on Sunday morning, 28 October 1928, as they watched the green-and-yellow *Flying Fish* hurtle across the surface of Manhasset Bay. The two women had felt an immediate affinity when they recently met, having both risen to fame as passengers on record-setting international flights. Chubbie had hoped to be on board the *Flying Fish* for its historic flight to Bermuda until the flight's backer, the publisher and publicist George Palmer Putnam, chose to accompany Bill and Harry. Putnam had also backed Amelia's Atlantic flight and would later become her husband.

Manhasset Bay had little tidal current and a low tidal displacement, creating an ideal runway for amphibians and seaplanes. On this idyllic autumn day, the bay was as flat as a plate-glass window—too flat, as it happened, because it caused a suction that kept Bill's heavily fuel-laden plane glued to the water. After four frustrating hours, with more and more gear offloaded in unsuccessful attempts to lighten its weight, the men decided to siphon off all but 80 gallons of fuel and head towards Hampton Roads near Norfolk, Virginia. The shorter distance from there to Bermuda would reduce the amphibian's fuel requirements.

Chubbie was invited on board a second amphibian, which was carrying mechanics and would follow the *Flying Fish*. Eighty miles from Long Island, Bill's engine cut out, forcing him to glide down onto Barnegat Bay. Chubbie's pilot landed as well, allowing the mechanics to investigate. They discovered water in the fuel tank. Bill would have come down in the unforgiving Atlantic Ocean if his initial take-off had been successful.

After his fuel supply was replaced, the two machines set off again; but they encountered bad weather near Atlantic City, forcing them to stop there for the night. By the time the mechanics finished over-hauling the engine the following day, the extremely low tide made it difficult to move the amphibian from the shore onto the water. It was 5 pm by the time the *Flying Fish* reached Hampton Roads.

Chubbie's amphibian didn't make it there at all. A stiff northwest wind forced it down off the Virginia Capes. Without a radio, they drifted for hours until a tugboat stumbled across them and attached a tow line to prevent them drifting out to sea. The tug radioed the coast-guard; however, it was 9 pm before a patrol boat reached them and towed them to shore.

On Tuesday, Putnam told the press that the *Flying Fish* needed further adjustments, which would take a day. On Wednesday, he announced that the plane would fly to a fishing village, some twenty-seven miles closer to Bermuda. On Thursday, he advised that weather forecasts indicated poor conditions along the route to Bermuda. The following Tuesday, he cancelled the flight.

Bill's first chance at American glory had failed.

Back in Los Angeles, the manufacturer of the proposed plane needed advice about equipment and other essentials for the transatlantic flight Harry was planning, and required one of the trio on hand to provide assistance. Bill was negotiating a work contract with Cirrus Aero Engines Limited and Harry was more puff than pragmatism, so this task fell to Chubbie.

She travelled across America again, this time by train, having already seen more of the vast country than most Americans would see in a lifetime. When she discussed the flight plan with their backers, they mentioned that the flight needed a radio operator and asked if she would be willing to take on the role.

'Certainly,' was her response. She was always keen to learn something new and anything to do with planes excited her. Besides, the more aviation skills she possessed, the greater her chance of being employed in America's aviation industry.

'Do you know anything about wireless?'

'No, but I'll find out,' she said decisively.

She rented an apartment in Los Angeles and attended classes at the YMCA School, the only woman in a room full of men. She learnt how to use and repair a wireless radio. Learning Morse Code was especially difficult. There were only so many dots and dashes the brain could comfortably process or the hand jot down. Most people found it overwhelming and many students failed or dropped out. However, she was determined to master the skill. She was lent a little Morse-tapping machine and practised in her apartment at night and on the weekends. After four months, she was delighted to see the respect in the backers' eyes when she proved her proficiency in all the skills required by a radio operator.

Afterwards, she returned to New York, where Bill was residing. Bill had had a visitor while she was in Los Angeles: his wife Kiki. Since he had been away for more than a year and showed no sign of returning home, Kiki had left the children in England and travelled to America to find out what was happening with their marriage. Bill later told Chubbie that he had asked Kiki for a divorce and that her response had been a demand for $10,000 for her upkeep and that of the children. Without it, she wouldn't release him.

Chubbie was thankful she didn't have to face the woman. How could she look her in the eye after taking her husband? Kiki's obstinacy, though, dimmed her hopes that she and Bill could ever have anything but an illicit relationship, that they could ever live without the fear that their adultery would one day be exposed to the world.

Meanwhile, Bill's negotiations with Cirrus Aero Engines had proved successful. He was employed as a test pilot and demonstrator at a monthly salary of $500. The company also sponsored him to fly the 9000-mile Caribbean Circle, a flight that had ended in mishap for all previous flyers. The route would take him from New York down the eastern seaboard to Miami and across to Havana. Then he would island-hop via Puerto Rico to South America. From there he would travel west to Panama and Mexico City, around the Gulf of Mexico to Miami and back to New York. While there was no financial reward, the Central Union Trust had offered a gold medal to any pilot who could successfully fly the circle.

The American press showed little interest in his Caribbean challenge, although Britain's *Flight* magazine devoted a full page to the subject, more column inches than it had allocated to the *Red Rose's* entire flight. Bill sent the press detailed accounts of his journey, which began early in March 1929, but few newspapers published them. However, the press showed more interest on 7 April when his plane crashed at Trinidad. His engine had stalled on take-off, smashing the aircraft and sending him to hospital. His internal injuries required surgery aboard the ship on his way back to New York and then months of rehabilitation.

Bill's second chance at American glory had failed.

Under the circumstances, it was probably fortunate that the Atlantic plane wasn't ready in time for their mid-1929 attempt at crossing the Atlantic. However, the flight's cancellation meant that Bill's third chance at glory had failed. Publicity-wise, he was unsellable.

While American newspapers had spent the summer of 1928 talking about Chubbie's involvement in the proposed Atlantic flight, few people knew that she wasn't a licensed pilot. Although she was skilled at flying a dual-control aircraft—as she had proved in Los Angeles when she had taken control of a twelve-seat passenger plane—she hadn't actually performed any take-offs or landings. So, when she returned to New York, she rented a room near New Jersey's Red Bank airport and quietly commenced lessons with the Airview Flying Service.

Having total control of a plane thrilled her more than anything she had ever experienced. She flew for as many hours as possible, and the rest of her time was spent learning about engines and pottering around the planes themselves. As she practised soaring and swooping and rolling and diving, she dreamed of a time when she would be paid to take a plane up into the air, when she would be respected for her abilities as a pilot rather than being patronised simply because she was a woman.

Most women at this time had no real comprehension of how patronising the world's attitudes were because they had never experienced anything different. Since she had set off on the *Red Rose* flight though, Chubbie's eyes had been opened. In her world travels, she had received looks of respect from many men for her achievements in a male domain and for possessing character attributes like courage, which were normally credited only to men. She had no desire to ever go back to the world of domesticity.

In her morning flights above Red Bank, she noticed that the *Blue Comet* passenger train passed beneath her each morning. One day, partly for the practice and partly for the thrill, she dropped down towards the railway tracks and raced the train. Her old training plane had a maximum speed of about seventy miles per hour and was able to keep pace with the *Comet* as it chugged towards the seashore. Gradually, though, the train outpaced her. As it pulled further and further ahead, the fireman stuck his hand out the window and waved at her while the engineer blew a victorious toot.

She was circling the tracks the next morning when the *Comet* came into sight. Swooping down, she kept pace with it for a while, but once more it pulled ahead. Again, the fireman and engineer announced their triumph with a taunting wave and toot.

After her third day of defeat, it was war. She was determined to beat the annoying *Comet*. Each day she waited until the train came into sight. Down she pounced and the race was on.

Her vented frustration became the source of much amusement among her fellow pilots. They made bets on her likely success. The look on her face when she landed each day was answer enough. Those who bet in her favour inevitably lost.

Early in April 1929, she passed all her tests and was granted a United States private pilot's licence. With her return to New York, the daily battle ended, but she didn't forget her foes. She wrote to the railway company complimenting them on the train's operation and the crew's friendliness. In reply, she received an invitation to ride in the locomotive with the horn-blowing engineer, a charming gentleman who told her how much he had relished their daily skirmishes.

While Chubbie was gaining her pilot's licence and Bill was attempting to complete the Caribbean Circle, the *Southern Cross* disappeared in outback Western Australia. Kingsford Smith and his crew were eventually discovered alive, but decidedly unwell; however, his friends Keith Anderson and Robert Hitchcock died after the *Kookaburra* crash-landed while searching for them. A newspaper circulation war raged in Australia's capital cities at this time and a desk-bound editor decided to boost his newspaper's sales by printing the claim that the *Southern Cross*'s disappearance had been a publicity stunt. Thus began the Coffee Royal Affair, so named because one of Kingsford Smith's crew had attempted to make light of their dire situation by joking that at least they had Coffee Royal (coffee and brandy) to drink while they waited to be rescued.

Chubbie and Bill found themselves caught up in this drama when the press revealed that the *Kookaburra* had had a faulty compass, and that the compass had originally come from the *Red Rose*. Reportedly, Bill had asked its purchaser if he could keep the compass because it had saved his life; but Robert Hitchcock, who had been the *Red Rose*'s Sydney-based mechanic, had instead passed the compass to his solicitor, saying that Bill and Chubbie owed him wages. When he needed a compass for the rescue mission, he had collected it from his solicitor and had taken it on board the *Kookaburra*.

When the news reached Chubbie and Bill that Australia thought their compass was largely responsible for the aviators' deaths, they were devastated. They wrote a letter to the Australian press saying that they had paid Mr Hitchcock a liberal salary and had asked repeatedly for the compass to be sent to them. The compass had worked perfectly for their own travels, so they wondered if the aviators had failed to properly compensate it when they fitted it into the *Kookaburra*. A newly installed compass required its magnets to be readjusted because of the different amounts of magnetism in each plane. 'We greatly regret the tragic manner in which the two brave men met their end, but feel strongly on the subject of being held responsible in any way.'

At the subsequent inquiry, a mechanic testified that the *Red Rose*'s compass had been working perfectly when the *Kookaburra* flew from Richmond to Broken Hill. He suspected that the problem began at Broken Hill when a thief stole the steel toolkit and spare parts from the plane, which would have affected the compass's magnets. The inquiry exonerated the *Southern Cross*'s crew of instigating a publicity stunt; however, the mud that had already stuck to Kingsford Smith wouldn't wash away until after his death.

The baseless attack and its consequences were a warning to Chubbie and Bill of the dangers celebrities faced from a press more interested in sensationalism and sales than fairness, justice and simple honesty. In a strange parallel, Chubbie would face a similar backlash as her own star rose in America.

Chapter Sixteen

An air race solely for women? Elizabeth McQueen was intrigued by the idea. Although not a pilot herself, she was founder and president of the Women's International Association of Aeronautics and had long supported and promoted women in aviation. She knew that male pilots had been racing against each other ever since the Wrights' ugly duckling had hopped off the ground a quarter century previously. Since women had been piloting planes for nearly as long as men, wasn't it time that the world's female aviators had an air race of their own?

The person to approach was Clifford Henderson, the man charged with reviving the fortunes of the flagging National Air Races. Henderson was both a shrewd automobile salesman and a pilot. When he had a customer on the hook, he would reel them in by taking them up to the heavens and bringing them back down again. Afterwards, he had no need to point out how mundane their earthbound existence was. Instead he would mention that in their new automobile they would also experience the thrum of the engine, the wind caressing their hair, the thrill of speed . . .

He was a very successful automobile salesman.

The previous year he had run the National Air Races at Los Angeles and had shown the world that he was also an artistic director of extraordinary talent. Now he was turning those talents towards the 1929 National Air Races at Cleveland.

Henderson envisioned an aerial circus that would outdo the great P.T. Barnum himself. What were dancing horses and spinning acrobats compared to his own vision of 'The Greatest Show on Earth'? When he closed his eyes he could hear the growl of aero engines and smell the gasoline fumes. He could see the kaleidoscope of colours as airborne chariots sprinted for the finish line. He could feel the heart-stopping tension as airborne gladiators darted around pylons while locked in mortal combat with their foes. He could even sense the silent, almost menacing, presence of the huge German dirigible, *Graf Zeppelin*, looming overhead as it paused on its round-the-world trip. He wouldn't create a show that spectators merely enjoyed; he planned to intoxicate their senses with an aerial extravaganza.

If he could entice the world's famous aviators by offering a large enough purse, their names would attract the crowds who paid the entrance fees that financed the show. The elite aviators were the show-stoppers whose antics would keep the audience spellbound. Some flew because it was their only source of income. Others were circus artists or show-offs or cowboys. But the best had an intrinsic understanding of the principles of flight and were so attuned to their planes that the relationship almost transcended the physical. And their presence was so magnetic that just being near them both awed and inspired.

When these aviators registered to participate, the top aviation companies would sponsor them and would be inspired to improve their aircraft designs in the hope of achieving a winning result and a marketing edge. The aviation companies would then purchase display stands in Cleveland's newly built exhibition hall to market their wares.

Hopefully, the crowds drawn to watch the air show would make their way into the 200,000 square-foot hall with its spangle-covered chandeliers and sateen-draped walls. They would gape at the jewel-studded model airplane worth $400,000 and the full-size aircraft suspended from the ceiling. Some would be tempted to exchange the vicarious thrill of watching for the buzz of actually flying and would purchase lessons from the flying schools manning their own stalls in the exhibition hall. Pilots—visitors as well as racers—would head over to the stands of the race-winning aviation companies with a view to upgrading their planes.

The previous National Air Races had shown that air shows were not merely avenues for financing aviators and thrilling spectators. Rather, the flow-on effect was to provide a bridge between the old days of barnstorming and the serious future of commercial aviation. Critical to any air show's success, though, were the drawcards that would attract the public. So what better event to add to his aerial extravaganza than the world's first air race flown solely by women?

The female air derby was announced in May 1929, a month after Chubbie obtained her licence. It would be held in conjunction with the Cleveland races the following August. The pilots were to fly from Santa Monica, California, to Cleveland, Ohio, a distance of nearly 3000 miles in nine days. The female derby's major sponsor was the National Exchange Club, a chain of 800 branches that aimed to promote the 'exchange of ideas'—among its strictly male membership. The prize pool for the derby winners was an appealing $8000, while cash prizes for different stages of the journey brought the pot of gold at the end of this aviation rainbow to a highly motivating $25,000.

Fourteen of the country's top female aviators immediately registered their interest, Amelia Earhart and Ruth Elder among them. Tall willowy Amelia, nicknamed 'Lady Lindy' because of her physical resemblance to America's most famous aviator, was the country's pre-eminent

The 1929 Powder Puff Derby

= Flightpath

250 miles

aviatrix; the 'first woman to fly the Atlantic', albeit as a passenger. Ruth Elder—the beauty of the bunch, according to the press—had also attempted to cross the Atlantic as a passenger. Her jaunt had ended in an ignominious ocean ditching that simultaneously launched her Hollywood career.

The derby wasn't only open to American aviators. Irish-born Lady Mary Heath, the first British woman to hold a commercial flying licence, and Germany's Thea Rasche also put up their hands. Lady Mary later cancelled her registration, however Thea, known as Germany's 'Flying Fraulein', would be among the women to line up at Santa Monica on 18 August.

Chubbie was determined to join the derby. She had arrived in America filled with plans and dreams but none had yet reached fruition. To most in the aviation world, she was just a glory-seeker, one of the many hangers-on who used the industry to gain fame and fortune. She realised that if she wanted to be taken seriously, she needed to prove she was a serious pilot. Winning a place in the air derby would show the aviation world that she was up there with the best.

She registered for the derby and then put out feelers for a plane. She was introduced to Lawrence Bell, vice president and general sales manager of Reuben Fleet's Consolidated Aircraft Company. Bell was one of the industry's best salesmen. He saw the airways as highways and recognised that, if the public could be convinced that 'even a woman' could fly, the potential market for aircraft sales would double. He listened with interest to her sales pitch about the marketing value of having a Fleet plane in an air derby that would generate a huge amount of publicity (more than all the male derbies held in 1929 combined, as it happened). He offered her a new open cockpit, two-seat Fleet biplane equipped with a Kinner five-cylinder radial engine. Before she could take possession though, the plane had to be adapted for racing and practically rebuilt around her small frame. Among other things, the factory had to add special extensions to the rudder pedals to enable her to reach them.

To get to the starting post, she would need to fly from the company's Buffalo base in New York State all the way to California—alone. She had never flown such a long distance before, not while piloting a plane at least. During the *Red Rose* flight, Bill had planned the route, Bill had undertaken all the take-offs and landings, Bill had managed the controls during rough weather. He had also been there as a comforting presence during the long, lonely and sometimes terrifying hours in the air. Having to leave him in New York and cross the country by herself was an intimidating thought. She had seen firsthand from the *Red Rose* flight how much could go wrong. Although she had learnt a lot from Bill and from her flight training about the mechanical side of aviation, she didn't have enough skills to solve all the problems she might encounter during such an arduous flight.

Additionally, attempting to navigate unknown territory with only a map on her lap and a compass on the instrument panel was never easy. It was hard for many non-aviators to comprehend the difficulties. Cross-winds would nudge her plane this way and that so she would have to make regular course corrections. Her compass sat in alcohol, so turbulence would make it jump around and it always lagged in registering her plane's change of direction. Moreover, instead of pointing north towards the plane's nose when the plane itself was travelling north, it pointed downwards towards the earth's magnetic pole. Thus, she would rarely be able to navigate by compass alone. Over and over again she would need to glance at the compass to see if she was heading in the right direction then lean over the cockpit—first one side, then the other—to examine the terrain. When she spotted a noteworthy feature, she would have to find it on her map and mark it with her finger then hold her finger there until she found the next feature.

This finger-plotting technique would help ensure she was travelling the right way—if there were features to be found and she identified the correct one, of course.

On Saturday, 10 August, she pushed aside her fears and climbed into her little blue plane with its bright yellow wings to begin the 3000-plus mile journey across continental America. She aimed to fly as much of the derby route as possible—backwards, of course. Airfields were not always easy to spot so she would have an advantage if she had located and circled the landing sites before she had to find them during the pressure of the race. Of course, she could always follow the tongue-in-cheek advice of humourist Will Rogers, an aviation aficionado. He suggested that a pilot in search of an airfield should simply look for a place where two or three deadly high-tension lines intersected.

She had informed the race authorities that she would arrive at Santa Monica in the middle of the week. The race was due to start the following Sunday so this would allow her a few spare days in case anything went wrong.

It did. She got lost.

There was no point cursing herself for her stupidity. Where possible she, like all pilots, endeavoured to use the 'iron compass' as a navigational instrument—the railroad tracks that ran as directly as possible from one town to another. However, where two or more tracks left a town, it was surprisingly easy, because of the compass issues, to follow the wrong tracks. That's how she had become 'momentarily disoriented', in the pilot's vernacular. She had followed the railroad tracks that ended up heading north towards Santa Fe, rather than west to California. Forced to land to get her bearings, she damaged her engine. She managed to take off, though, and nurse it as far as Lordsburg, New Mexico, where she wired Los Angeles for repairs and advised the race authorities that she hoped to resume her flight on Friday. It would be a tight schedule. From Lordsburg, she still had 600 miles to fly to reach the starting line.

Amelia Earhart, Ruth Elder and some of the other derbyists had parked their planes at Santa Monica's Clover Field aerodrome long before Chubbie had even set off from Buffalo, giving them plenty of preparation and relaxation time before the big race. By early Saturday, 17 August, sixteen of the twenty registered planes were at the aerodrome. Chubbie's wasn't among them. She didn't arrive until Saturday afternoon. After her arduous transcontinental flight, she had less than twenty-four hours to overhaul her plane and to rest. It wasn't the best way to commence a gruelling nine-day air race.

At the aerodrome, her plane was inscribed with the number 43—her own choice—and registered with five other planes in the light division. These were the smaller, sportier planes with engines under a 510 cubic-inch displacement. The other fourteen planes formed the heavy division. Larger, faster planes, they were often used commercially and were generating the most press attention.

Chubbie's was the only Fleet aircraft in the derby. In fact, most of the participants' planes were one-off models because manufacturers recognised the value of sponsoring a single pilot to showcase their company's wares. The Travel Air Manufacturing Company, however, had seven planes in the race. Most were owned by the derbyists themselves because its light fast planes were popular among racers. Worryingly, though, trouble had already brewed in one of the Travel Air planes, that of twenty-three-year-old, tousle-haired Louise Thaden, who was being sponsored by the company itself.

Travel Air had been forced to work swiftly to complete five new planes before the big race. Louise's plane was last off the factory line. By the time it taxied from its Wichita hangar, there was no time for anything but a single test flight. As she started her journey to California, Travel Air co-founder Walter Beech and his pilot followed her in a second plane to make sure everything went smoothly.

Halfway between Tulsa and Fort Worth, Louise slipped into a groggy daze. When she finally spotted the airport ahead, she abandoned the usual landing etiquette of entering the circuit as she waited her turn, and instead barrelled straight in, much too fast, as if she were a nervous pilot making her first solo landing. After alighting from the plane, she collapsed to the ground, unconscious.

It turned out that she was suffering from carbon monoxide poisoning. For some reason, her new plane's exhaust was being channelled back into the open cockpit. If she had remained airborne for much longer, she would have fallen unconscious and dived to her death.

With four other brand-new Travel Air planes in the derby, Beech worried that it might be a design or manufacturing flaw rather than an idiosyncrasy in Louise's plane. He had no time, though, to pull the plane apart and locate the problem before the race. Instead, he jury-rigged a breathing tube by running a four-inch pipe into the cockpit.

Louise refused to be deterred by her close encounter with death. When she took off again for Santa Monica, she kept her mouth glued to the air tube, hoping that her decision to continue with such a serious defect wouldn't be one her family would later regret.

Neither Louise nor Chubbie nor any of the other derbyists had flown in an air race before, so they had no real comprehension of the challenges they would face. Yet at some level they were aware that this derby was more than just a race across the country to see who reached Cleveland first. When they reached the finishing line—whatever their position in the race ladder—the person who arrived there would be intrinsically different to the person who had departed from Santa Monica.

Each woman was flying a flimsy machine driven by an erratic engine and would inevitably encounter trouble. Each stage would test her proficiency as a pilot, her mathematical skill as she calculated routes, her spatial aptitude as she read maps, and her ability to sense trouble and calmly deal with it. Each stage would also test her emotional resilience and determination, not only because of the stress associated with racing and dangling prize money, but because of the inevitable lack of sleep and the difficult flying conditions. As the race start drew closer, each woman was asking herself how she would be judged—indeed how she would judge herself—when she arrived at Cleveland. If, of course, she made it.

Chapter Seventeen

As 2 pm neared on Sunday, 18 August 1929, more than 20,000 people crowded the edges of the Clover Field aerodrome and swarmed over a neighbouring hill, eager to watch the start of this world-first air race. Most of the derbyists' planes had been hangared elsewhere overnight so the spectators saw the planes flying in from different directions. One by one they glided down and took their places in two horizontal rows. The spectators saw Chubbie and the other women climb out and inspect their planes one last time: fuel valves, stabiliser adjustments, flying wires, ailerons. Some gave their machines an affectionate pat—almost a 'touch wood' caress—before heading over to register their arrival.

Microphones installed on the landing field allowed the derbyists to speak to the crowds before the race began. The pilot everyone wanted to hear was Amelia Earhart. Similarly to Charles 'Lucky Lindy' Lindbergh, she was worshipped by the public—although she hated the adulation. Humble and self-effacing, she believed she hadn't earned it. 'I was just baggage, a sack of potatoes,' she had told the press after spending the entire Atlantic flight in the passenger seat. She also knew that the Earhart mystique that entranced the world was merely the product of a clever publicity campaign. She was determined to achieve success through her own aviation skills, so she would know—in her heart at least—that she was worthy of the public's adoration. Her success, or otherwise, in the derby would answer many questions that had long troubled her.

An ardent feminist, Amelia regularly used her pre-eminent position to advocate for the equality of women and for the welfare of her sister aviators. As the Santa Monica spectators hung on her every word, she told the world, 'I believe it will mean more for all of us to get through to Cleveland safely than to break records.'

Although the female derbyists were competing against each other for the prizes and accolades, there were significant differences between them and male air race competitors. Not only did the women have a deep concern for each other's wellbeing, each of them was determined to prove that she was as skilled and capable as any male pilot and deserved equal consideration in employment opportunities.

Marvel Crosson, with the optimistic number 1 painted on her new Travel Air (she was the first to register for the derby), had long talked about the problems facing female aviators. The raven-haired twenty-five-year-old ran an aviation business in San Diego, acting as a purchasing agent for her brother, a commercial aviator in Alaska. Not only had she piloted planes across the hazardous expanses of the frozen north, she had recently set the women's altitude record at 23,996 feet. Yet, despite the considerable acclaim for her business sense and aviation abilities, she still encountered prejudice from male pilots. 'These good fellows never forgot I was a girl!' she said of the other San Diego pilots. 'There was a shade of condescension in their pal-ship. They acted as though it was a pleasant thing for a girl to be interested in flying, but "just among us men" it was of no importance. I could feel the sex line drawn against me, in spite of the fact that they were splendid fellows and pals of my brother Joe.'

She and the other derbyists wanted to be paid to fly, not to be a token distraction. Not only would the derby be a personal quest for success, the women hoped that they as a group—as a gender—would show the aviation world how capable female aviators truly were.

The women standing behind the microphones at Clover Field were dressed in a range of styles and colours: coveralls, knickerbockers and puttees, moleskin coats, the occasional skirt. Chubbie wore white coveralls with a pair of black-strapped, high-heeled shoes peeping out from underneath them. She wasn't trying to be feminine: the heels helped increase her reach, both on the ground and in the cockpit, where they provided leverage.

After the ceremonies were completed, they headed back to their motley collection of aircraft, which ranged in size from Amelia's big five-passenger Lockheed Vega monoplane to Chubbie's tiny Fleet biplane.

Edith Foltz's Eaglerock Bullet monoplane, one of the light planes in Chubbie's division, was attracting considerable attention from the spectators and other derbyists. A revolutionary design, it was the first aircraft to be built with retractable landing gear. It hadn't yet gained its nickname, the 'Killer Bullet'.

Edith, Amelia, Chubbie and the other female pilots climbed into their cockpits. Some carried so many bouquets and good luck charms that they joked that their planes would be too heavy to take off.

Chubbie sat there scanning her instrument panel and glancing at her map, wondering if she had missed anything. As the hot Californian sun beat down on her, she licked parched lips and wiped sweaty hands on her coveralls. She wriggled to get a comfortable perch on the compulsory parachute under her bottom—it felt as hard as a rock—and wished that the derby officials would hurry up and start the race.

The light planes were in the front row, with Phoebe Omlie scheduled to take off first and Chubbie second, the order in which their registration papers had been received. The other planes would follow at one-minute intervals. Only nineteen of the twenty registered planes were lined up. Mary Haizlip's plane hadn't yet arrived in Santa Monica, although she hoped to join the race the following day.

Humourist Will Rogers was at the airfield to farewell the derbyists. As he looked at the planes squatting on the landing field and thought about their female pilots, he mused out loud, 'It looks like a Powder Puff Derby to me.' The remark wasn't intentionally sexist, just one of his witty word images, but the name stuck. Thereafter, the women's air derby would be known colloquially as the Powder Puff Derby.

As the engines throbbed, a hush settled over the crowd. At 2 pm the crack of the starting pistol—fired in Cleveland and relayed by radio across the country—echoed across the aerodrome, the signal the race authorities were waiting for. The starter official began his countdown by dropping, or swiping downwards, the red flag nine times. Phoebe's engine throttled to a crescendo. When the red and white flags dropped together—the go signal—her plane zoomed down the runway and soared into the air, accompanied by a bellow of elation from the watching crowds.

Chubbie's eyes focused on the starter official. One red flag, two . . . When both flags dropped together, she too hurtled down the runway.

Over the following seventeen minutes, the remaining planes took to the air. Like a swarm of dragonflies, they darted across the narrow coastal plain and headed towards the ranges, their tiny forms soon lost in the distant haze.

Except for one plane. Amelia's orange Vega had taken off and then banked back so she could return to the landing field. Her starter mechanism had shortcircuited and fumes from burning rubber filled her cabin.

Mechanics dashed to her plane and made hasty repairs. When she took off again, her supporters could only hope that the lost thirteen minutes would not prove critical in determining her final race result.

San Bernardino, a mere seventy miles away, was their first stop. The California sun baked them every mile of their journey. But visibility was good, so it was easy flying.

Phoebe Omlie, in her red-and-yellow closed-cockpit Monocoupe, was first over the finishing line, making it clear she was a strong contender for line honours in Chubbie's division. Although some of the press had snidely dismissed all the female pilots as 'Atlantic fliers or housewives', Phoebe was one of the derbyists who made their living from the aviation industry.

The twenty-six-year-old had been the first woman to obtain both an American transport licence and an airplane mechanic's licence. She was a daredevil at heart. While still in her teens, she had danced the Charleston on the wings of airborne planes and hung from a trapeze secured only by her teeth. She had earned a Hollywood stunt movie deal after taking out the record for the highest female parachute jump. She had also set the world's female altitude record in 1928, although fellow derbyist Marvel Crosson had afterwards beaten it. Recent crashes had left her body badly broken, forcing her to walk with a cane, however she refused to give up flying. She had almost been eliminated from the race in the days before its commencement when nightfall and an empty fuel tank forced her down in a Santa Monica hayfield. An officious sheriff dismissed her explanation and arrested her for suspected drug smuggling. It took Amelia Earhart's intervention—and a threat to call President Hoover—before Phoebe was released.

The fastest time in the heavy division was flown by Florence Barnes, nicknamed 'Pancho' after a life-altering trip to Mexico. Pancho was flying a new Travel Air, rated by the company as the third fastest behind Marvel Crosson's and Louise Thaden's. The twenty-eight-year-old was the most outrageous of the group, a cigar-chomping, cussing barnstormer and stunt pilot whose wealthy family had married her off to a clergyman in a desperate attempt to curb her wild ways. An affair introduced her to the joys of sex. Later in life, she would run a private club for air force men, naming it with saucy directness as the Happy Bottom Riding Club.

Landing at San Bernardino was easiest for Phoebe and Pancho and the other early arrivals. While the authorities there had assured the race committee that the landing field would be sprinkled with water just before the derbyists arrived to prevent a dust cloud arising, they hadn't realised that cars and trucks would converge on the landing field and park around its perimeters, generating their own dust cloud.

Opal Kunz was the first to experience trouble. Blinded by the dust, she was ten feet out in her altitude calculations and landed heavily, damaging her undercarriage. Neva Paris, following Opal in, saw the blue-and-orange plane stranded in the middle of the landing strip. Swerving her own plane, she came in diagonally at a high speed, yet managed to execute a perfect landing. Amelia, coming in behind them, overshot the strip and looked like she might plunge into the crowd. As the spectators scattered, a path opened for her plane. She brought it to a halt just before reaching the perimeter.

One of the nineteen pilots failed to reach San Bernardino. Mary von Mach, a less experienced pilot than most of the others, had the ill luck to be targeted by a bunch of male redneck aviators who wanted to 'escort' her to her destination. When one buzzed her plane as if to start a dogfight, she turned tail and fled. The other derbyists signed a petition allowing her to start again from Santa Monica the next day.

Chubbie, the second to take off, was the second last to arrive. Despite the best efforts of San Bernardino's Exchange Club, she had lost her way. The men had climbed onto the flat top of a theatre and painted 'San Bernardino' in twelve-foot-high aluminium letters. Nearby they had painted two arrows, one pointing towards the airport and the other to magnetic north. In the words of one proud painter, 'Even an aviator with the blind staggers couldn't miss it.'

Tired, nervous, stressed, Chubbie wandered in the afternoon heat as far as Redland, five miles beyond San Bernardino, before realising her error. By the time she found her way back, she had been flying for well over an hour and was the last in the time-elapsed rankings by twenty minutes. One pressman sniggered, 'She could have made it as quickly in an automobile.'

That night they were treated to a banquet. Marvel, Amelia and some of the other pilots gave short speeches. Later, they watched the film *The Flying Fool* starring their own Pancho Barnes. Although delighted to see their friend on the silver screen, they would have appreciated a quieter night as they had a 4 am wake-up call. So they were especially annoyed when they returned to their hotel and discovered that they would have oversee their planes' servicing before they could get any sleep.

Then came more bad news. They were locked in a battle with the race organisers.

The derbyists had only received their final race itinerary the day before the race began. When they saw that Calexico, California, was one of their landing places, they complained to the Santa Monica race authorities that its runway was too short for the heavier planes. Recognising the merit of their complaint, the Santa Monica officials agreed that they could bypass Calexico and stop instead at Yuma, Arizona. Accordingly, some of the derbyists organised to have deliveries of oil, fuel and spare parts sent to the Yuma airfield.

However, when the Cleveland authorities were informed of the itinerary change, the race committee chairman, Floyd J. Logan, wired the San Bernardino race authorities to say that the derbyists must stick to the original route. If they didn't, they would be disqualified.

The women couldn't understand Logan's obduracy. Surely anyone with even a smidgeon of flying experience would understand their concern. Heavy planes. Short runway. Dangerous combination.

Hot-blooded Pancho would have none of it. At midnight, she roused the women from their beds so they could sign a petition. It began: 'We, the undersigned pilots in the women's air derby, hereby declare we will go no farther than this point unless routed by or through Yuma instead of Calexico.' Chubbie was the sixth to add her signature.

This battle could easily have fractured the rapport developing between the women. Instead, it unified them under a powerful leader. To an outsider, Amelia might have seemed the group's obvious leader because of her international reputation, her calm measured authority, and her extremely heavy Vega. However, an explosive implacable force is sometimes required to make authority figures take notice of dissatisfaction in the ranks. Rich and spirited Pancho, who had nothing to lose either financially or socially, was a natural for the role. Her passion and righteous anger united the women against their common foe.

A mass walk-out wasn't what the race committee wanted. Dr Fred Ayers, chairman of the San Bernardino race committee, telephoned Logan to inform him of the petition and strike ultimatum. Logan refused to budge. He claimed that the route had been chosen three weeks earlier and that, while he was vitally concerned for the pilots' welfare, he would accept no itinerary changes. Then he snapped a goodbye and left his telephone off the hook.

It was 2 am by this time and Ayers was desperate. He phoned Clifford Henderson and explained the seriousness of the situation. Henderson agreed to go at once to Logan's house and negotiate a compromise. At 2.30 am, word came through that the derbyists would be permitted to bypass Calexico so long as they flew low enough over the checkpoint to allow the race authorities to read their numbers.

Some of the derbyists had already had an hour or two of sleep, others none at all. They would get little more because of their early wake-up call. Logan's intransigence meant that these female pilots, who hadn't benefitted from the intense military training given to most of the world's elite male pilots, would have to fly over rugged mountain ranges and hot desert floors while suffering from sleep deprivation. It was a recipe for trouble if ever there was one.

Chapter Eighteen

Grumbling about their lack of sleep and muttering imprecations at the slumbering race committee chairman, the derbyists headed to the airport early the following morning. As they concentrated on their critical pre-flight checks, Ruth Elder noticed she had a serious problem. A mechanic had poured fuel into her oil tank. She wasn't looking as glamorous as usual when she vented her anger and frustration. She didn't know if there would be enough time to clean and refill the tank before she was scheduled to take off.

The departure schedule was in the reverse order to their arrival, an advantage for Chubbie because of her late landing. She felt sorry for the pilots who were scheduled to take off last. As the ground was still ankle-deep in dust, the first few planes would churn it up so badly that the swirling particles would reduce visibility for those at the tail end. Even more dangerously, dust could be sucked into the filters and intakes, clogging and damaging an engine's internals to the point that it could fail.

The women's machines soon squatted one behind the other in an orderly row with their propellers ticking over. White-coated officials scuttled around the field carrying flags and stopwatches and official paperwork. At 6.45 am, the starter stood near the first plane and lifted his flag. One by one the women zoomed down the runway and took off. Ruth Elder was so eager to get going she made a false start. Blanche Noyes' attendant forgot to remove her plane's wheel chocks until a boy said, 'Say, mister, you better pull those big blocks out or she'll never get to Cleveland.'

Fuelled by adrenaline, Chubbie and the other pilots flew off into the haze of the eastern sunrise. For the light-plane pilots, it was better to head towards the Banning Pass, a wide windswept cutting between the San Gorgonio and San Jacinto mountain ranges that served as the gateway to the Imperial Valley on the eastern slopes. From there they would travel south-east to Calexico, which lay on the Mexican border.

Others like Louise and Marvel and Amelia, who were flying aircraft with more powerful engines, decided to save time by climbing above the Santa Rosa Mountains on a more direct route. Amelia was leading the derbyists as she buzzed the checkpoint at Calexico airport at 7.28 am and then headed east across the desert towards Yuma, Arizona.

Claire Fahy was coming third of the six light planes in Chubbie's division when she set off from San Bernardino in her Travel Air biplane. She was just about to fly over the Calexico landing field when she heard an alarming noise: the twang of a bracing wire snapping in two. Her biplane's upper and lower wings were joined together by struts and multi-strand metal bracing wires. If one strand frayed, the others would hold the wings together and maintain the plane's structural integrity until it could be landed and repaired. But when Claire heard the bracing wire snapping, she knew that her plane had just been transformed from an airborne wonder into a potentially deadly coffin. She had no time to wonder how a stranded-metal wire could snap in two before she heard that distinctive twang for a second time. She pushed her plane's nose towards the ground for an emergency landing.

'I must have had a horseshoe about me somewhere,' she would later tell reporters, 'for the fact that I was over the field surely saved my life.'

When she inspected the bracing wires, she could find no sign of fraying in either breakage. Both had separated as if they had been cut by pliers yet there were no cut marks on either end of the fractured wires. What else could have caused such a destructive breakage? When her test-pilot husband arrived, he agreed that a single fracture of that nature would be extraordinarily unlucky, but two was preposterous. After inspecting the damage, he could think of only one agent that would cut through two stranded metal wires in such a way: acid. He wondered if someone had deliberately tampered with the plane. He urged Claire to pull out of the race. She didn't take much convincing to agree.

Chubbie's light-plane division had just been reduced to five.

The Flying Fraulein was experiencing problems as well. Thea had been asked by the Moth Aircraft Corporation to fly a de Havilland Gipsy Moth, which also put her in Chubbie's light-plane division. Her plane wasn't ready in time for the race so she was given a substitute at the last minute, another grey and silver Gipsy Moth. She'd had little time to test-fly it before the race began. To add to her concerns, she had received a disturbing telegram, which was tucked away in her pocket.

Her engine had started cutting out soon after she left San Bernardino. As she neared Calexico, it began to cough. Then it cut out altogether, forcing her to make an emergency landing in an alfalfa field ten miles north of Calexico. She overshot the field and ran into the road, buckling the landing gear. Cut and bruised, she climbed from the Moth and assessed the damage.

Locals gathered, intrigued to discover that the trouser-clad pilot was a woman—and a German at that. One of the locals, a mechanic, watched her remove the fuel clarifier. When he saw that it contained scraps of rubber, fibre and other impurities, he and other witnesses signed a statement to that effect for the race authorities. Thea telegraphed the race committee to say that her plane was down and damaged. She hoped to continue in the race if the repairs were successful.

Although Yuma lay due east of Calexico, the direct route between the two towns ran through the northernmost tip of Mexico. When the derbyists balanced the risk of having their planes confiscated—or stolen—if they were forced down on the Mexican side of the border, most decided that the time gained and the potential money earned from a fast leg to Yuma made the risk worthwhile.

Evelyn Trout—nicknamed 'Bobbi' because of her bobbed haircut—was one of the women who took the shortcut. She had established an altitude record two months previously in the light plane she was now flying in Chubbie's division; however, her newly installed engine was proving troublesome. Like Thea's engine, it kept cutting out. Then it stopped altogether when she was about ten miles west of Yuma.

She was too far from Yuma to glide there. Spotting a smooth field near Los Algodones, Mexico, she steered towards it. Just before she came in to land, she saw that the field had been ploughed into deep furrows. She had no altitude or power to change direction. By the time her plane came to a halt, it was on its back and badly damaged. She too was out of the derby.

With Bobbi and Claire eliminated, only four pilots remained in Chubbie's light plane division. Whether Thea could continue was also uncertain. With three cash prizes provided for each division, Chubbie knew that all she had to do was to keep her plane in the air until she reached Cleveland and her chances of winning a cash prize—and the consequent honours—were high.

Even at 9 am, Yuma was so hot that Chubbie felt as though she had stuck her face in the open door of a blazing furnace. Sand was everywhere, even on the 160-acre landing field. Amelia was the first over the finishing line. For the next half hour, the sight of her plane—nose down in a sand dune—was a warning to her fellow derbyists to be careful of soft sand lest their aircraft end up in the same humiliating position as that of the famous aviator.

Amelia called Los Angeles and ordered a new propeller. In an act of team-spirit—one that many would later regret—the other derbyists decided to wait with her at Yuma until the new propeller was delivered and attached.

The temperature rose until it was well over 100 degrees Fahrenheit. Chubbie and the others lay under the wings of their planes and snoozed while the local residents raced home to collect food and cold beverages for them. By the time Amelia's plane was repaired, the sun was at its apex, a particularly bad time to be flying in desert regions.

In the sweltering heat, their planes were sluggish and needed every inch of the sandy Yuma runway to take off. As they headed towards Phoenix, the barren desert floor beneath them was soon replaced by rugged treeless mountains, and yet more barren desert—a drab monotony broken only by the terror of flying over it. Vicious downdraughts followed by equally vicious updraughts threw their planes around like yo-yos on a giant's string. Wondering if their machines could withstand such gyrations, Chubbie and the other pilots kept a grim watch for suitable landing areas.

At last, in the clear desert air, the fertile green of Phoenix could be seen ahead. Louise crossed the finishing line first; however, Pancho nosed her from first place in the heavy division on elapsed time. Chubbie landed fifth, relieved to know that her flight time was only a few minutes slower than those of the leaders in her division. After the embarrassment of the first day's flight, she was holding her own.

Another banquet had been organised for their evening entertainment, much to their annoyance—they were desperate for sleep. They also needed time to prepare their planes and map out their routes. Instead, they felt like circus exhibits.

As they sat around making small talk with their hosts, and listening to interminable speeches praising people they didn't know and activities they didn't care about, news began to spread. Marvel was missing.

Chapter Nineteen

At first Marvel's friends weren't worried when she failed to reach Phoenix. Half a dozen of the derbyists had already been forced down without any major mishaps. Indeed, forced landings were so common that some of the women carried 'protection' in case they came down in territory where dangerous animals roamed—or dangerous men. Feisty Marvel carried a revolver. She had told the race authorities she would fire off a bullet if she needed to make contact with searchers.

A search party was out looking for her. Earlier that afternoon, a cowboy had ridden into Wellton, a small town thirty miles east of Yuma, to tell the authorities that he'd seen a plane plunging to the ground in the distance. Soon, a well-driller, some ranch-hands and a child reported that they too had seen a plane similar to Marvel's falling in a spin from about 1000 feet. They saw it slam into a thick growth of cottonwood trees in inaccessible country near the Gila River north of Wellton.

As the searchers combed the countryside, they didn't hear any cries for help or the distinctive crack of a bullet. They didn't hear or see anything at all, which was worrying. The terrain was rough: rocky desert country partly covered in ten-foot brush. If Marvel had managed to parachute successfully, there were few clear stretches for her to land safely.

Scout planes failed to spot anything. Further search parties headed out into the darkness. They lit beacon fires in the hope she might see them and answer with a signal of her own. Another group would head out just before dawn to beat through the brush. They would find her, surely, sooner or later.

When the news broke that Marvel's plane had been seen spinning into the earth, Claire Fahy was the first to mention the ugly word 'sabotage'. She was adamant that someone had tampered with her plane. She would later tell the authorities that when she took the broken wires back home and showed them to the factory employees, all agreed that they had never known natural circumstances to cause such a break. So, if her own plane had been sabotaged, could someone have tampered with Marvel's plane as well?

Thea Rasche reported that her plane had been forced down because impurities had entered the fuel system in 'some strange manner'. She declined to say openly that she suspected tampering. Instead, she pulled a telegram from her pocket and handed it to the race authorities. Its message was short and simple: 'Beware of sabotage.'

Ruth Elder told the race authorities that she had found fuel in her oil tank that morning. While she thought the cause was more likely a mechanic's idiocy than a deliberate act, she felt it best to report her own experience.

The organisers asked themselves why anyone would try to sabotage the women's planes. If such a thing had happened, was it intended to lessen the chances of some of the competitors so as to improve the chances of others? A small fortune was at stake for the winners and crimes had been committed for much less. Of course, if sabotage had indeed taken place, it didn't mean that a derbyist was necessarily to blame. Other planes were accompanying the derbyists, carrying timers and race officials, family and friends. And locals were involved at each of the landing places. If one of them had made a large bet on the outcome, the person might have wanted to control the results.

Who else could it be? A disgruntled man determined to keep women out of the air? A religious reactionary appalled at the behaviour of these cigarette-smoking, alcohol-drinking, trouser-wearing she-devils?

Santa Monica publisher-cum-derby-sponsor Robert Holliday wondered if the race authorities themselves were partly responsible. He sent a telegram to the race committee saying that the women's planes had not been properly guarded overnight at San Bernardino, allowing curiosity seekers to swarm over them. An official who had inspected the planes there had told him that a quarter of the planes had suffered various degrees of damage. He strongly advised the committee to launch an investigation and recommended that the race be delayed until the committee could ensure that the planes were properly guarded and inspected at all future landing sites.

As the list of mishaps grew, the San Bernardino district attorney's office ordered a formal investigation. All of the race officials there, including the field guards and service mechanics, were called in and questioned about what they had seen and heard and otherwise experienced during the hours the planes had been in town.

The chairman of the San Bernardino race committee, Dr Ayers, supported the investigation although he told journalists that he couldn't believe that tampering had taken place. He added ruefully, 'I do believe, however, that there was a woeful lack of preparation for the cross-country race.'

Dr Ayers also revealed that Marvel had told him that her engine had been overheating and had shown signs of reduced oil pressure on the leg to San Bernardino. However, officials of the company that was maintaining Marvel's plane said she hadn't mentioned any such problem to their mechanic.

When Walter Beech was questioned about Marvel's new Travel Air, he reported that she had experienced engine trouble on her trip to Santa Monica. A new engine had arrived in time to be installed; however, the changeover had not been made for reasons unknown to him.

The press asked the engine's manufacturers why the new engine hadn't been installed. Wright Aeronautical advised that they had instead taken parts from the new engine to replace worn parts in the old engine. The company assured the press that the rebuilt motor had passed all the necessary tests before the derby began.

During his own interview with the press, Beech had also made a disturbing admission. He said that, before Marvel took her plane from the factory, he had warned her to guard against sabotage. When the press demanded to know what had prompted such a warning, he declined to say.

A sombre group of women awoke on the third morning of the derby. There was still no news of Marvel. The race officials had delayed the start from 6 am to 8 am to allow them time to catch up on sleep. When they arrived at the airport, they were pleased to find that the morning's forecast was good: a clear sky with light variable winds. They should reach their next stop by midday, before the worst of the desert heat.

One by one the derbyists took off in reverse order of their arrival and followed their compass settings towards Douglas, Arizona. Chubbie had passed the bluffs and rock-strewn valleys and was flying over flat empty terrain when she heard her engine splutter. She immediately wondered if she was a victim of the jinx—if not the saboteur—afflicting the air derby. According to a signed note from her mechanic, her fuels tanks were full. So what was causing the engine to falter? She was near Elfrida, twenty-five miles north of Douglas, when she was forced down. She landed on the bumpy ground without damaging her plane and turned her attention to the engine to work out what had incapacitated it.

As she and the other derbyists knew, pilots without mechanical skills didn't last long as soloists, particularly if they made cross-country flights. Female pilots who had to land in the wilds couldn't flutter their lashes and beg a big strong man to help them. They had to solve the problem themselves. Mechanical trouble-shooting was a systematic exercise. The most likely explanation for her spluttering engine was that the fuel wasn't getting through. The problem could be a blockage in the fuel line—like Thea had suffered—or an empty fuel tank. The second was the easiest to test. She cleaned the dipstick then dipped it into her fuel tank and pulled it out again. It was dry. The tank was empty. Yet the mechanic had assured her—in a signed letter, no less—that he had filled it. Uncertain whether her plight was the result of a mechanic's stupidity or a saboteur's machinations, she set off to walk towards a ranch house she had spotted from the air.

The derby report written by esteemed aviation journalist Cy Caldwell had disparaged the derbyists for their 'unfeminine' attire, in particular the coveralls and sturdy shoes most of the female pilots wore. The fact that they never knew when they might need to walk cross-country—or stumble, if the terrain was particularly rough—was one of the many reasons why female pilots wore practical male-style clothes rather than the silk dresses and delicate pumps he suggested. In this instance, the countryside she was passing through was home to rattlesnakes, scorpions and black widow spiders.

The ranchers were astonished to see a female pilot appear as if from nowhere. They collected enough fuel to get her to Douglas and headed back to the plane with her.

She took to the air again, hoping she hadn't lost too much time. When she spotted the Douglas airfield in the distance, she headed directly towards it. Then her engine went quiet.

It was an eerie silence. Worse, it was an infuriating silence. She didn't have enough altitude to glide to the airfield. She would have to land on the sage and cacti-covered desert floor within sight of it.

This time she wasn't so lucky. Vicious cactus spikes ripped into her fuselage. Even before she slipped down from her cockpit she could tell that it would take hours to fix, hours that would be added to her elapsed-time clock and push her even further to the back of the light-plane division.

The race authorities had spotted her plane and sent mechanics to undertake the repairs. She refused to leave, remaining to help the men fix the extensive damage. As the hours passed and the elapsed-time clock ticked on, the stresses of the previous week overwhelmed her. Questions whirled around in her mind, demanding answers that no one seemed able to provide. How had her plane run out of petrol when the tank was supposed to be full? What had happened to Marvel? What was going on?

The mechanics working on her plane were aware of her escalating distress. And given that they now knew Marvel's fate, they couldn't blame her.

The race officials had refrained from informing the derbyists of Marvel's death until they reached Douglas for fear that the news would distract them. While most of the derbyists had expected the worst by that time, the reality was both heartbreaking and confronting.

The search party looking for Marvel had spent Monday night exploring the dense vegetation on the Gila River's banks. Dawn was breaking on Tuesday morning when they found her body on boulder-strewn ground near the river bed in an isolated ravine. She was nestled in the silken folds of her partly opened parachute. They could see why she hadn't been able to alert them via a gunshot or bonfire or cry for help. It looked like every bone in her body was broken.

Her wrecked plane lay 300 feet away. Both her smashed cockpit clock and watch had stopped at 12.16. They wondered what had happened in that quarter-hour after her departure from Yuma. Her body was some distance from the plane, suggesting that she had attempted to bail out as it had spun to the ground. Had her plane's altitude been too low for her parachute to fully open?

Another investigation began, this time a coronial inquest into Marvel's death. The Los Angeles Department of Commerce also opened a crash investigation, recognising the importance of determining if the sabotage charges had any substance. Once the news of Marvel's death had been released, more of the derbyists mentioned their own problems. Bobbi Trout, who'd had engine difficulties, Opal Kunz, who'd been blown off course on the Douglas leg, and Chubbie, when she at last arrived at the Douglas airfield, all expressed concerns about the possibility of tampering.

Race officials had stopped Chubbie's elapsed-time clock when it fell dark, knowing that she couldn't continue her flight until the light of day. She and the mechanics worked through the night until the damage was repaired. At daybreak on Wednesday morning, she flew on to Douglas, landing at the airfield well before the scheduled departure time. She ordered a thorough cleaning and inspection of her fuel tank to try to work out what might have happened.

For the most part, these additional suggestions of tampering were treated lightly by the race officials, although they made a point of communicating them to the investigators. Nonetheless, the race officials took special precautions. They posted guards around the airfield and ordered that all the derbyists' planes be carefully inspected.

Most of the derbyists also dismissed the sabotage claims. Some went so far as to suggest that the claims were merely the products of minds overwrought by the hard grind of flying such a long race. Yet tensions remained high. That evening, instead of slipping across the border to enjoy Mexico's nightlife, the women remained in their hotel rooms studying maps and calculating courses. The next morning, they gave their planes an extra inspection and allowed experts to repack their parachutes.

Unease hovered like a ghostly presence as they prepared for the day's flight. Once Chubbie and the other pilots settled into their cockpits, though, they forced themselves to push aside their thoughts and feelings about Marvel's death. For their own survival, it was critical that they focused on the next leg of their flight. A distracted pilot could easily become a dead pilot. Another dead pilot.

Chapter Twenty

'Grim Reaper Stalks Women Flyers' was the comforting headline in one of the nation's newspapers that morning. Another published a photo of Marvel with the caption that she was the 'first fatality' in the women's derby—as if, naturally, there would be more.

On hearing of Marvel's death, many men jumped at the opportunity to air their views about female aviators. El Paso's mayor, who was to greet the women when they landed at his town later that morning, told his council, 'Such races are all right for grown, active, able-bodied men, but they are too much for women.' One columnist was even blunter: 'Women pilots are too emotional, vain and frivolous to fly, and are hazards to themselves and others.'

Chubbie and Amelia had predicted this would happen. While sharing a hotel room in Phoenix on the night Marvel disappeared, they had discussed the public's perception of deaths in the aviation world. While a male pilot's death was simply a sad part of the job, a female pilot's death horrified the public. Why? They decided that the community's horror was just another sign of the public's unwillingness to accept women's autonomy, that society still felt that women needed to be protected from themselves. How long would it take society to accept that women were perfectly capable of making their own decisions and living with the consequences? Didn't they realise that female pilots took to the air knowing the risks? Since deaths would inevitably occur, surely it was about time the public got used to it.

Louise Thaden agreed. Indeed, like many other aviators, a part of her almost revelled in the idea of a flaming death. 'If your time has come,' she would later write, 'it is a glorious way in which to cross over. Smell of burning oil, the feel of strength and power beneath your hands. So quick has been the transition from life to death there must still linger in your mind's eye the everlasting beauty and joy of flight.'

Of course, her view was idealised, romantic, naïve. It offered a perception of death that ignored the greater possibility of excruciating suffering, along with likely pangs of regret. Importantly though, she and the other derbyists recognised that they were blazing a new trail and that, at some point in any such journey, trailblazers inevitably faced the reality of death. 'There has never been nor will there ever be progress without sacrifice of human life,' Louise concluded, with calm acceptance.

The welcome at El Paso was almost overwhelming. There is nothing like a tragic death to spawn huge publicity and draw out the ghouls. Crowds began gathering from 7 am. By the time the mosquito-like drones could be heard, there were so many people jamming the airfield's perimeter that squads of soldiers and motorcycle policemen were screaming 'Stay back! Stay back!' They feared the crowd would break though and mob the aircraft and pilots.

The press asked the derbyists how they felt about Marvel's death and whether the race should proceed. Amelia was the first to land at El Paso and to communicate the group's view that the race must continue. She made her usual remarks about women being the same as men in the air, that gender was never an issue. As for Marvel's death, she advised, 'There is no question as to her ability and there has never been a thought among us that foul play might have caused the accident.'

The press asked her opinion about the cause of Marvel's death.

'Marvel had motor trouble,' Amelia stated flatly. 'She was flying so low when the motor quit that she had no chance to use her parachute. She took a sporting chance and jumped. She lost. That is one of the tough breaks of the game.'

As it turned out, the Department of Commerce's inspector had reached a different conclusion. He could find no evidence that Marvel's engine or plane had failed before the crash. He had, however, seen vomited matter on the side of her fuselage and suspected that a sudden illness triggered by the extreme heat had caused her to lose control.

Louise Thaden had her own suspicions about what might have happened. Although it seemed most likely that Marvel had developed sunstroke at Yuma while they waited for Amelia's propeller, another possibility kept intruding into her thoughts. Vomiting was a sign of nausea, which was one of the symptoms of carbon monoxide poisoning. In high doses, carbon monoxide could kill in minutes. Dizziness and disorientation were symptoms as well. The pilots' seats in the Travel Air cockpits were low. Had Marvel, feeling nauseous, undone her seatbelt so she could vomit over the side? Had she remained there, dizzy and disoriented, with no control of her machine?

Aviators knew what happened to pilots who were not wearing seatbelts when their open-cockpit planes went into a spin. They were tossed out. If carbon monoxide poisoning was indeed the cause, could there be an intermittent exhaust problem in any of the other new Travel Airs, as there had been in hers?

The company wondered the same. A factory team was sent to meet the derbyists at their Midland stop the next day. The mechanics were ordered to examine all the Travel Airs and to follow the derbyists for the rest of the race—just in case.

By this time the other investigations were winding up. The Moth Aircraft Corporation's expert had found no evidence of tampering in the Flying Fraulein's plane, while other investigators determined that the telegram warning of sabotage was a malicious prank. Mechanics from the sponsoring oil companies, along with other witnesses, had testified that Marvel supervised her own servicing and that a mechanic had worked all night on Claire's plane. An inexperienced and now publicly humiliated mechanic had pumped the fuel into Ruth Elder's oil tank. And interviews with the relevant personnel at the San Bernardino airfield had elicited nothing troubling.

The only remaining charge was the claim by the Fahys of acid on the bracing wires. When Claire's husband refused to travel to San Bernardino to be questioned, the authorities decided that the Fahy accusation had no merit either. Seemingly, there was no basis whatsoever for the sinister charge of sabotage.

Meanwhile, cavalry from Fort Bliss patrolled El Paso's airport, just in case.

Swirling clouds of black sand descended on El Paso while the derbyists sat through their luncheon. When pilots from the east reported thunderclouds in that direction, the race officials decided to cancel the day's remaining flight.

With day four now completed, Louise Thaden was the fastest of the heavies with an elapsed time of six hours and forty-eight minutes while Phoebe Omlie, at eight hours and thirty-five minutes, continued to lead the light-plane division. Edith Foltz, flying the Eaglerock Bullet, was only an hour behind Phoebe. Chubbie was in third place—a distant third, though, as her elapsed time of eighteen hours and thirty-one minutes was twice as long as that of the other pilots in her division. However, Thea was hot on her trail. The weather-induced delay allowed her to catch up with the other derbyists at El Paso. Thea's elapsed time was then re-calculated at nine hours and fifty-nine minutes. Chubbie was back in fourth place again.

The women used the unexpected free afternoon to make a concerted attack on El Paso's beauty shops. In the evening, some headed across the Rio Grande into Ciudad Juárez, Mexico, to party. The incorrigible Pancho Barnes was among the revellers. Later, pious prohibitionists would blame her weakness for the evil nectar—she accepted a dare to down a jug of beer—for the problems she would suffer on the next day of the derby.

When an El Paso journalist asked Chubbie about her chances in the race, she admitted, 'While I do not think I have much chance of winning, I am going to keep on trying.'

'Keep flying' had become the derbyists' unspoken rallying cry. They felt they had no choice but to keep flying the derby. If they abandoned it because of Marvel's tragic death, the world would instantly diminish them and their achievements. They would be considered too emotional, too capricious, too *female* to be able to handle the serious life-and-death challenges faced by aviators. Not only would such a judgement affect their own hopes and dreams, it would be detrimental to those of future female aviators. They were going to finish this race whatever came their way.

Like Chubbie, some of the other derbyists were also refusing to let their individual odds deter them from completing the race. The two Marys—Mary von Mach and Mary Haizlip—kept flying even though their delayed starts meant they had little chance of any honours. And Bobbi Trout, although officially out of the race, had decided to rejoin the derbyists in her repaired plane as an untimed follower.

The delayed and downed pilots were keen to remain a part of this trailblazing event because a powerful spirit of camaraderie had developed between the women. In the past, they had all coped on their own with the emotional and social burdens that came with their desire to fly, and with the scorn and dismissal emanating from the male-dominated aviation world. But now they were no longer alone. Those trousered, bobbed pilots lounging against the nearby planes were kindred spirits who had experienced a similar journey. They could share stories and offer advice about dealing with difficult family members, pursed-lipped neighbours and disgruntled males.

Something else was developing as well. The San Bernardino strike had proved that a unified female voice was a powerful force. Out of the Powder Puff Derby camaraderie came an international organisation for women pilots—The Ninety-Nines—that the derbyists would establish in the latter months of 1929. It would outlive them all.

Chapter Twenty-One

'Hunt the ceiling' was the advice given to Chubbie and the other pilots when they arrived at the El Paso airfield on Thursday morning. With the 6000-foot Davis and Guadalupe mountains ahead of them, the authorities wanted to make sure there were no other fatalities. Thankfully, the forecast was for clear weather ahead.

Through no fault of the organisers, it would be the most arduous day in the entire derby. In addition to the pre-planned route, the derbyists had to start the day by flying to Pecos, their intended stopover the previous night. From there they would fly to Midland and Abilene, and then rest for the night at Fort Worth.

The leg to Pecos wasn't difficult. They flew across the mountains and reached the flat country before the sun could heat the thermal stew. Chubbie was fourth across the finish line at Pecos, beaten only by Phoebe in her division. Although the investigators had dismissed the sabotage claims, Chubbie's jinx hadn't lifted. Her fuel gauge had smashed during her landing, which would delay her departure until repairs were completed.

Stuck at the airfield, she had a firsthand view of the other planes coming in to land on what would prove the most drama-filled stopping point in the nine-day derby.

Petite Blanche Noyes, a budding actress with large limpid eyes, had only received her pilot's licence two months previously and had been accepted into the derby by virtue of a fiddled flight history. Like many other female pilots, she had been taught by her flyboy husband. Piloting the Travel Air they both owned, she was placed in the first half of the heavy division when she took off from El Paso.

Ten miles short of Pecos, while flying at 2000 feet, she caught a whiff of the one smell that made every pilot's heart race. She whipped her head backwards and forwards looking for its source and saw a wisp of smoke coming from the baggage compartment. She reached over to wrench the fire extinguisher from its brackets. It wouldn't budge. She tugged at it with increasing panic, but still it wouldn't budge.

For a moment she thought about bailing out. Then she abandoned the idea. Marvel's death had left them wary about relying on parachutes. And she didn't relish telling her husband that she had smashed their primary source of income.

Smoke was now billowing from the baggage compartment. She would have to land as fast as possible. She looked down and was relieved to see she had left the mountain territory and was flying over Texan prairie land. She sideslipped to keep the smoke away from her face and lungs, grateful she had remembered this simple manoeuvre from her recent lessons. As she neared the ground, she changed direction just enough to miss the worst of the vegetation, but not enough to miss it all. Her plane slammed into the ground and skidded through mesquite and sagebrush nearly three feet high.

She leapt from her seat and tugged again at the fire extinguisher. It still wouldn't shift. Terrified, she mustered every ounce of her strength and yanked it once more. The casing that held the extinguisher lifted up, along with some of the plane's wooden flooring. She turned the extinguisher towards the fire. The wretched thing wouldn't work.

Tossing it aside in disgust, she grabbed her burning valise and pitched it overboard, before jumping down to join it. She scooped up handfuls of desert sand and hurled them at the flames that were now licking the air. When the fire had been smothered, she poked through the burnt clothing and flying equipment in the baggage compartment to try to discover what might have sparked the fire.

A flaming cigarette butt, seemingly.

She didn't smoke.

She paused for a moment to assess the situation. Her plane still seemed airworthy, but she was in the backcountry and would be out of race contention unless she could get herself into the air again. She had never cranked a propeller before. Ignoring the pain in her burnt hands, she pulled the propeller over and over again with the brute force of the desperate. It was four exhausting minutes before the engine caught and she heard a blessed thrum.

Climbing back on board, she gunned the engine in an attempt to pry the plane loose from the undergrowth. As it wrenched itself free, she could feel the sagebrush clawing and tearing the fuselage. A downward list in the final stages of her take-off indicated that her landing gear was seriously damaged as well. She had no idea if she would be able to land safely at Pecos or if she had just used up the last of her luck.

As the derbyists completed their 180-mile leg to Pecos, they were determined to refuel and fly off again without too much delay. Only a few minutes separated the elapsed times of some of the prize contenders, a minuscule difference when the prize for the winner of this stage was $1000. The women were landing so quickly after each other that it was obvious to the race officials there would be little room to manoeuvre if any plane landed badly.

The landing strip itself was only small. The town's people had come out in force to clear as much sagebrush and mesquite as possible from the designated area, yet they seemed to be unaware that the planes would need to be stationed somewhere while the service trucks refuelled them. When the derbyists were scheduled to fly in, the locals parked their cars and trucks around the landing strip to obtain the best vantage point.

The spectators and waiting racers saw Amelia's orange Vega follow Chubbie's Fleet down. Hearing another drone, they glanced up and saw Blanche's Travel Air circling the landing field as if hesitant to land. When they peered more closely, they realised that its lower yellow wing was shredded and its landing gear mangled. Blanche wasn't just being hesitant; she was warning them that she was in serious trouble.

Voices yelled, 'It's going to be a crack-up! Get fire extinguishers! Call an ambulance!' Others shooed back the spectators, fearing that an out-of-control plane might plough into the crowds.

Chubbie and the other pilots watched anxiously as their friend came in to land, aware that she was one of the less-experienced pilots in the derby. Showing a skill that belied her lack of flying hours, Blanche set her plane down on its right wheel with all the precision and delicacy of a ballerina. As its momentum slowed, it dropped gently onto its smashed left wheel and began to ground-loop.

She was down and safe. As the spectators cheered, they saw her burst into tears of relief.

A reporter from the *Pecos Enterprise* expressed his admiration for Blanche's 'death-defying feat' in landing safely. What also astonished him was that after her plane had been patched up she took off again to continue the race, 'as game as they can make them'.

Meanwhile, Pancho had been speeding to catch up with the other derbyists. Forced to return to El Paso because of engine trouble, she had stomped around for two hours until the repairs were completed. Weather issues and engine trouble had already allowed Louise Thaden to take the elapsed-time lead, so she knew she'd have to scrounge every second out of the race if she was to win back the lead.

Coming in to land, she couldn't see the ground in front of her. She— and all other pilots—had to raise her plane's nose to reduce airspeed, which meant that her only view of the landing field came from sticking her head over the cockpit side. In her haste to set down, she only looked over the left side to line up the runway. If she had looked out the right side, she would have noticed the Chevrolet touring car parked at the corner of the landing field directly in front of her. To her shock—and that of the car's owner—she slammed into it.

As the horrified owner raced over to his car and drove it off to the city, she assessed her plane's damage. Both right wings smashed. The struts on the left side broken. Extensive damage to other parts of the plane. She too was out of the race.

Chapter Twenty-Two

Another grand luncheon. More fried chicken.

Chubbie and the other women silently fumed at the delay, aware that the sun would continue heating the earth and would spawn more thermals—or worse—while they made small talk with the Midland locals.

The next stretch, to the refuelling stop at Abilene, was well marked by roads and railway tracks, which usually allowed pilots to fly at a comfortably low altitude. However, the derbyists had to maintain a higher altitude on this stretch because of cross-winds and thermal-induced turbulence. In fact, the flying was so hard through much of the stretch from Douglas to Fort Worth that some of the women ended up with blisters on their hands.

Chubbie was flying at 1500 feet, concentrating on fighting the thermals, when it happened. A roar engulfed her as if a train was running over her. Her plane started rotating like a spinning top. Her senses swam. She had no idea what was happening.

Then her plane stopped spinning as unexpectedly as it had started. She was upright, although still enveloped by the mind-shattering roar.

Her head cleared enough to identify the problem. She had been swept up in a twister, one of those mini-tornadoes of rotating heated air that danced along the hot ground, making its presence known only when the dust sucked into its vortex outlined its shape like a ghostly apparition. It was a freak of nature that pilots feared even more than an airborne fire because there was little they could do to counter nature at its most ferocious and deadly.

She looked around her. The rotating winds were pushing her plane towards the ground. She had to get out of its clutches. She considered bailing out, but had no idea what effect the twister would have on her flimsy parachute. It might shred the canopy as if it were tissue paper. It might twist the lines around each other and prevent the canopy from opening.

She looked at the altimeter. It was gyrating wildly. She couldn't work out if she was high enough to survive a jump. With a fatalistic shrug, she decided to remain with her plane and ride it out.

The twister shot her from its grasp as quickly as it had seized her. Looking down, she was thankful she hadn't tried to parachute to safety. She had dropped more than 1200 feet and was only a few hundred feet from the ground.

She climbed so she could see a broader expanse of the terrain. She had no idea where she was and needed to regain her bearings. When she looked at her map and compared the navigational features, she discovered that the twister had thrown her backwards by a half-hour's flying time.

'Hangar tales' were what aviators called them, the stories that pilots told their companions at the end of a day's flying. By now, most of the derbyists had a good one to tell. Some were dramas like Blanche's and Chubbie's, which left their listeners shaking their heads in wonder that they had lived to tell the tale. Others were humorous, like the tale Ruth Elder would tell the following night after they flew from Fort Worth to Wichita.

The fertile plains of Oklahoma and Kansas were a welcome sight after the desert country of Arizona and Texas. Navigation was easier because the farmer's fields were one-mile squares creating a landscape that looked like a chequerboard. However, the wind was gusty and Ruth, like Chubbie, was flying an open-cockpit plane. As she pinched one end of her map between her thumb and forefinger so she could get a good look at its markings, a gust of wind buffeted the aircraft. The map was torn from her hand, leaving only a piece the size of a postage stamp clutched between her fingers.

After travelling a bit further, she was worried she might have gone off course. She landed on a flat area of pasture near a homestead, intending to ask directions. Cattle lounged in the distance, but she wasn't concerned because she had more than enough room to take off again without trouble. However, the noise of the plane landing had disturbed them. They looked up and started lumbering towards her.

That's when she remembered that her plane had a bright red fuselage. She prayed, 'Please God, let them all be cows.'

Fortunately, they were.

Wichita called itself the aviation capital of the world, despite sitting in tornado alley. The reception it offered the racers was the most exciting of them all. An army plane equipped with a short-wave transmitter joined the planes before they reached Wichita and followed them in, transmitting an account of the final leg of their journey that was re-broadcast from a local radio station. As each pilot stepped from the cockpit, she was handed a microphone and asked to comment on the race. Afterwards a personal hostess chauffeured her to the evening's events in a car with the pilot's name on the side.

At the evening's banquet, each of the aviators was asked to speak. The reporter for *The Wichita Eagle* praised Chubbie's as one of the best tributes the city had ever received. 'I think Wichita is the very nicest city we have landed in since the derby started in Santa Monica,' she told the 300 attendees, 'and you have truly given us a reception that we always will remember.'

The Wichita press noticed that there was little talk about sabotage, although it was clear from Thea Rasche's answers that she wasn't convinced by the investigators' reports. 'I never saw gasoline that dirty,' she said in reference to the muck in her fuel system. 'All that dirt couldn't have been in the tank unless someone had put it there.'

Chubbie too was still wondering why she had run out of fuel. She told the reporter, 'They said it was a mistake that I had not enough gasoline for the hop, but it seems like a rather peculiar mistake. It has cost me a good deal.' She added that she had had stinking luck and that, to top it all off, she was losing her voice from all the talking. But, otherwise, she was having a wonderful time.

As exhaustion sapped their energy, and as the parachutes beneath them felt increasingly like concrete, they flew onwards to Kansas City and East St Louis on Saturday then to Terre Haute and Cincinnati and Columbus on Sunday. Engine trouble forced Chubbie down in a meadow near Xenia, Ohio, halfway between Cincinnati and Columbus. When she alighted from her plane, she was shocked to discover she had stopped a mere six inches from a pit that hadn't been visible from the air.

Forced to wait for a new cylinder to be flown from Cleveland, she decided to spend the night at a nearby farmhouse and complete her journey to Columbus in the morning. She missed the last of the race dinners that had been organised in their honour, as well as her fellow derbyists' delight that fried chicken was at last off the menu. They'd had to resort to drastic measures, though, sending word to the Columbus race authorities that they would eat anything at the banquet dinner—anything but fried chicken!

Monday, 26 August, dawned clear and dry. The starting flag wouldn't drop until 1 pm so the women were able to sleep in for the first time. Most chose not to do so—for long at least. They wanted their planes in prime condition for the race to the finishing line. Dressed in their once-white coveralls, they slid under the bellies of their planes and scrubbed off dirt and oil and bugs before giving them a final polish. Like Chubbie, most had no interest in domestic chores, but they would do anything to maintain their precious machines. They knew that a slick ship was a fast ship and also a good-looking one.

The 'Flying Debutante', Ruth Nichols, had been having a beneficially uneventful race and was sitting in third place in the heavy division when she took her Rearwin up for a post-maintenance test flight. Columbus airport was being upgraded and a concrete runway laid. As it wasn't yet completed, Ruth and the other pilots had to fly over the new section and land on the old runway.

The sound of a plane coming in to land inevitably drew the derbyists' attention. Looking skywards, they recognised it as Ruth's red-and-white Rearwin. They saw it drift slightly in a cross-wind as it passed over the new section. They glanced down to see where it would touch down if it continued on the same course. A steamroller smoothed the concrete at the junction of the new and old runways.

They looked back at Ruth's plane. It hadn't changed course. She mustn't have seen the steamroller.

Onwards the steamroller ran. Onwards the plane flew. With a horrifying inevitability, the two converged. Ruth's plane struck the steamroller and somersaulted across the soft dirt of the old runway. Over and over the plane tumbled until it came to rest on its back.

The siren's warning wail chilled the blood of every pilot at the aerodrome. Before the plane had even stopped moving, people were running towards it. Astonishingly, they saw a body wriggle out of the wreckage. Ruth was alive, but the Rearwin was a wreck. With only 120 miles to go, she was out of the race.

For the first time, the pilots were to take off in the order of their derby positions. This meant that the first to cross the finish line would be the winner.

One by one the fourteen surviving planes raced down the runway and soared into the haze. As bright as a flock of toucans, they flew across Ohio in a final bid for derby honours. Louise Thaden was the first to rocket across the finish line in Cleveland, to an ear-blasting roar from the crowds. And for the first time, the spectators besieged her rather than Amelia, who took Ruth Nichols' third-place position.

When Louise took the microphone to address the crowds, she began, 'Hello folks. The sunburn derby is now over.' She walked away with over $4000 in winnings from the air race organisers and another $6000 in stage prizes and other payments.

Over the next hour, most of the other derbyists crossed the finishing line then parked in front of the main grandstand. As they stepped from their planes and looked around them, the gaps were obvious. Marvel was gone and her ship, with its bold number 1, was probably now in a garbage dump somewhere. Margaret Perry had been diagnosed with typhoid a few days earlier and, crying with frustration, had been admitted to hospital where she would remain for some weeks. Claire Fahy was at her home in California. The other three downed pilots, though, were making their way to Cleveland, where they would all be reunited. There they would celebrate their achievements and retell the funniest and scariest and most outrageous of their hangar tales: Phoebe's drug-smuggling charge, Louise's carbon monoxide poisoning, Chubbie's twister, Blanche's fire, Ruth Elder's cows, Ruth Nichols' steamroller, Pancho's invisible Chevy. Each tale of triumph or ruefully acknowledged failure was a badge of belonging that no one could ever take from them. The race had ended, but the spirit of friendship would live on.

When the race organisers stepped up to the microphones to announce the winners, Chubbie was astonished to receive third place in the light-plane division and a prize of $325. Phoebe had maintained first place, Edith Foltz had come second, and the Flying Fraulein fourth.

Many years later, when Louise Thaden wrote her memoir, she could still remember the sight of Chubbie's face as she received her derby prize, a grin stretched from ear to ear.

The Cleveland air races had commenced two days prior in front of 100,000 spectators. Before the end of the races on 2 September, many more were expected to walk through the gate, eager to see the feats of the nation's best aviators. Charles Lindbergh was among the attendees.

A reporter managed to corner him for an interview and questioned him about the aviation industry. He talked at length about the development of large passenger and transport planes for transcontinental trips and the need to speed up these journeys by developing night-flying instruments. When asked about parachutes in passenger planes, he said that he thought them unnecessary. He expressed his opinions about lighter-than-air dirigibles like the *Graf Zeppelin*, about gliders as training tools, about autogyros and other experimental planes, and about the industry in general.

The journalist asked him about the women's derby. He said that he had followed it with interest.

So, what effect did he think it would have on aviation? Did women have a real place in aviation?

After offering his lengthy opinions on so many other topics, Lindbergh's response was that he didn't care to say.

The 2800-mile National Women's Air Race had been a long, gruelling marathon across difficult—indeed dangerous—territory. It had required outstanding navigational and piloting skills. Above all, it had required pluck, courage and an emotional resilience that women were constantly told they didn't have. Yet despite the extraordinary achievements of these female aviators—these 'Powder Puff' derby-ists, 'ladybirds', 'petticoat pilots', 'flying flappers', 'sweethearts of the air' ('Can't we just be called "pilots"?' Amelia Earhart begged)—even the King of Aviation wasn't willing to accept these magnificent young women as men's aerial equals.

Chapter Twenty-Three

Clifford Henderson's dream had come to fruition. Some 450,000 spectators paid to see the greatest assemblage of planes and pilots in the history of aviation. So much food was sold that the hot dogs, if laid end to end, would have stretched from Cleveland to Boston. And the energy from the opened soda pop bottles could have dispatched the derbyists' nemesis, Floyd J. Logan, all the way from Cleveland to Atlanta, whether he wanted to go there or not.

The spectators were not only interested in watching the parachute-jumping, high-speed racing, war manoeuvring, aerobatics and other hair-raising stunts by male aviators. For the first time ever, women were participating.

Those with a keen interest in human nature asked the experts why so many people were so eager to watch others—male or female—risk their lives. Mehran K. Thomson PhD, author of the recently published *The Springs of Human Action*, provided the answer. Thrills! 'We live for the thrilling moments in life,' he told the press, 'and endure the rest.'

For some spectators, the idea of watching women risking their lives was even more thrilling than watching men. And, according to the program, they would have the opportunity to do so for the first time. Three of the closed-circuit events—the air races flown around a course visible to spectators—were open only to women.

Chubbie hadn't known what a closed-circuit event was until the Fleet company told her she was entered in a few of them. The first was a pylon race scheduled for the day after they reached Cleveland. She hadn't known what a pylon race was either.

The company sent a test pilot to instruct her. He explained that the race was flown over a five-mile course marked by three tower-like, red-and-white-checked pylons that created a racetrack in the sky. The judges and pressmen stood atop the pylons so they had a bird's eye view of the planes' movements. Chubbie would have to fly ten laps of the five-mile course to complete the fifty-mile race. She must count the laps to make sure she had completed the course because if she landed too soon she would be disqualified. She must also fly outside and not inside the pylons or she would be disqualified. The winner was the pilot who completed the course in the shortest possible time. It was tricky and dangerous flying, definitely not for the fainthearted.

Indeed, in past pylon races, planes had sometimes collided or slammed into the ground, killing their male pilots. So what would happen when these less experienced female pilots competed in such a deadly event?

When Chubbie arrived at the starting line, she discovered that the test pilot had nosed her plane into a rut and broken the propeller. It seemed that she was out of the race before she had even climbed into her cockpit. Furious to the point of tears at the lost opportunity, she stood there for a moment looking strangely elegant in her dirty white coveralls and high-heeled black lizard shoes. Then she snapped at the test pilot, 'Well, you'll have to let me have your machine!'

'No!' he retorted. He needed it for his own race. As they glared at each other, the company president came along and told him to lend Chubbie his plane.

The race was about to start. The test pilot taxied his plane to the starting line. Chubbie climbed into the cockpit and sat at the controls—and realised she had a problem. She couldn't reach the rudder. Her own cockpit had been modified to fit her diminutive frame whereas the test pilot's cockpit was the usual design, built for a man.

She refused to pull out. The challenge of the race had an appeal of its own. Someone stuffed cushions behind her back so she could sit further forward in the seat. Then they left her alone to fly.

She looked across at the flagman, waiting for his signal. She was to be first to take off, followed by Phoebe Omlie, then Amelia. Fourth was the famous British flyer, Lady Mary Heath, the only registrant who had previously flown a pylon race. Blanche Noyes would set off last. Two other derbyists, Edith Foltz and Thea Rasche, had also registered for the race but had been forced to pull out because of problems with their planes.

All of the contestants had been derbyists, except Lady Heath who had registered but withdrawn before the derby. A rumour had spread that she had withdrawn because she thought her presence would not be fair to the other pilots. The comment from a member of England's peerage, whether true or not, was a reminder of Britain's historic snootiness towards the colonies and generated resentment among the American pilots. An atmosphere of international rivalry developed as the women declared they were 'out to get' their famous British rival in this pylon race. America versus the Home Country. Chubbie, on paper the weakest pilot in the race, was largely forgotten.

The flag dropped and she opened her throttle. Her plane shot across the field. Gently she pulled back on the stick and lifted into the air. She was off and racing.

Down the straight stretch towards the first pylon. The circuit was five miles long so each straight was around 3000 yards. Chubbie leaned forward to try to reach the rudder, bracing herself with one hand. The cushions, no longer wedged between her back and the seat, popped out from behind her and were gone. She would now have to fly this unfamiliar plane across an unfamiliar course in an unfamiliar race while teetering on the edge of her seat.

When she looked back to see where the other planes were, she realised that she had headed towards the pylon for the ten-mile laps, rather than the five-mile laps. She had just lost time on the critical first leg.

By the time she was back on track, Amelia had caught up with her and was jockeying for position. The rules said that Amelia must keep at least 150 feet to the right and at least fifty feet above and mustn't attempt to pass between Chubbie and the pylon. Chubbie kept glancing around, checking Amelia's whereabouts as she came into the turn, worried that she might be caught in the deadly turbulence of her friend's plane.

The first turn was a critical learning experience. 'Turns win the race' was the advice from the experts. She tried not to bank for the turn too soon because she risked crashing into the pylon. Banking too late was almost inevitable because of her inexperience, which shot her too far beyond the pylon and wasted precious time.

Along the straight towards the second pylon. She tried not to take the second turn too sharply, because she would lose too much speed. And she tried not to take it too widely because any extra distance wasted time in this time-elapsed race. All the while she had to keep an eye on the nearby planes as they jostled for the best turning position, and for the slipstream of those who had already sped around the pylon.

Another straight stretch; another turn. While she and the other inexperienced pilots headed horizontally around the pylons, the more experienced Lady Heath climbed in the straight stretches and then dived towards the pylons. The English aviator reached her lowest altitude when she was halfway around the pylon, with her plane nearly vertical and a wingtip almost skimming the ground; then she would climb again for the second half of the turn. This meant that Chubbie also had to look out for planes that might be above her and beginning to dive for the turn.

It was clear from the start that Phoebe was racing around the circuit at an astonishing pace. And Lady Heath, with her outstanding piloting skills, was definitely in the money for one of the other prizes.

More straight stretches. More turns. Every so often Chubbie would spot the grandstand—a kaleidoscope of colours—then it would be gone. One moment she was counting the laps. The next she had lost track of the number. She decided to do one more lap for good measure . . . and another. When she saw officials trying to flag her down, she realised she must have completed the course. She would later discover that she'd flown fourteen laps instead of the required ten. She would also learn that the seasoned campaigners attached pieces of tape to their instrument panel, one for each required lap, and peeled them off as they went past the checkpoint.

Phoebe was clearly the winner. The timekeepers reported that she had sped around the course at an extraordinary 112.4 miles per hour. The crowd was cheering her when the judges announced she had been disqualified for cutting a corner when she rounded the second pylon. And Amelia was also disqualified for fouling Chubbie on the fourth lap, much to Chubbie's distress because of their friendship.

Chubbie's look of astonishment at having come second at 98.7 miles per hour—a faster speed than both Lady Mary and Amelia—turned into a delighted smile when she was called to take Phoebe's place on the podium. The punters were equally astonished. Most had been backing Phoebe, Lady Mary or Amelia. Chubbie had won what the press regarded as the most colourful event of the day along with a prize of $500 and a huge trophy. As the first race of its kind ever held for women, pictures of the trophy and her glowing face were published in many of the world's newspapers.

Phoebe protested her disqualification, saying that she had re-circled the missed pylon. Chubbie supported her claim, despite the impact this would have on her own prize and winnings. Mary Heath did so as well. The race committee reversed the disqualification; however, instead of sliding Chubbie back to second place, it allowed the two pilots to tie for first place position and allocated Phoebe $500 as well.

After the Cleveland races, Chubbie returned the Fleet to its owners. Ultimately, it passed into the hands of Frank Goldsborough, the son of the late Brice Goldsborough who had died in an attempted Atlantic crossing in 1927. In May 1930, Frank used Chubbie's plane to set junior transcontinental flight records. Two months later, he crashed the plane and died from his injuries. It was his twentieth birthday.

Chapter Twenty-Four

S he had done it. Her derby success—in particular, her pylon race win—had proved to the aviation world that she was among the elite of the elite. She had finally shed the 'Melbourne housewife' persona, not only from the world's perspective but, as importantly, from her own.

Consolidated Aircraft's managers were so pleased that they gave her a handsome bonus. And other manufacturers came knocking.

Fairchild Airplane Manufacturing Company approached her about taking part in the National Air Tour for the Edsel B. Ford Reliability Trophy—or the Ford Reliability Tour, as it was commonly known. Ford was president of his father's Ford Motor Company, which manufactured aircraft as well as automobiles. The tour's aim was to promote the aviation industry and display the speed and reliability of the planes entered in the tour. An invitation to participate was an honour indeed.

Two other female pilots would join the aerial cavalcade, derbyist Mary Haizlip and barnstormer Frances Harrell, who would later die in a pylon-race crash. As the first extensive aerial competition to pit men and women against each other, it had piqued the media's attention and Fairchild was going to make the most of it.

When Chubbie, with her down-to-earth Australian pragmatism, saw the pretentious flying attire they wanted her to wear, she couldn't help being amused. White kid jodhpurs—how was she going to keep them clean? White silk shirt and black tie. White V-neck jumper with a black line as a trim. White kid Norfolk jacket lined with lamb's wool. White helmet and black boots. She would look like a little white pixie.

Fairchild didn't stop there. Her plane—an open-cockpit Kreider-Reisner biplane—was also all-white with a black trim. She was to be accompanied by two other white Fairchild planes, one piloted by a male derby first-prize winner.

The White Fleet, as it was soon called, flew from Buffalo to Detroit in an arrow-shaped formation with Chubbie in the lead, as if she were the Queen of Sheba and the other planes were filled with her minions. The formation brought a smile of satisfaction to her face and that of every other female aviator who had suffered disparagement from the world's men.

Among the twenty-nine registered tour planes was a Great Lakes trainer Bill was piloting. Not only did the tour pit men against women, it pitted teacher against student. Many a man's sense of self-worth would struggle to cope with the prospect of being beaten by a student, let alone a female student, let alone an illicit lover. But Bill was different. He was proud of her achievements. He was determined to do everything possible to assist her escalating career and had become her unofficial manager.

On 5 October 1929, the thirty-two-city tour began. The tour planes, along with another dozen aircraft carrying officials and journalists, crossed the border to Windsor, Ontario, to begin their seventeen-day trip. It would take them to Montreal, then down the Atlantic seaboard states to Florida, from whence they would dog-leg through the Midwest and return to the Ford airfield on 21 October.

The flying was hard: 5100 miles in seventeen days with two flights per day and a formal dinner every evening. Chubbie soon learnt what some of the men thought of the women's involvement. She had never previously flown the route so she was grateful when a male pilot offered to lead the way. It wasn't long before she realised he was leading her astray. She broke off and returned to navigating for herself, accepting it as one of life's useful lessons. It probably wasn't personal, just further evidence of many men's unwillingness to welcome female aviators into their industry.

Onwards flew the cavalcade of planes. As they roared over towns and cities like an aerial motorcade, eyes lifted to watch them. At each stopping place, the town's citizens couldn't help gazing for a moment longer at the tiny virginal-looking female pilot. Extraordinarily, by the end of the second day, she was coming eighth in the competition, beating all but seven of the male pilots. Many of the beaten men were celebrities in the industry like humourist Will Rogers' personal pilot, Wiley Post, with his rakish eye-patch.

The tour wasn't an air race as such, although points were awarded for speed. Points were also awarded for other flying skills, including stick-ability: the pilots had to take off with a full load in as short a distance as possible ('unstick') and land in the shortest distance possible ('stick') in their brakeless machines. The race authorities had a formula for calculating each of the variables and moved the pilots up and down the tour ladder based on the points gained or lost. Chubbie's success in this test had helped move her up a few places.

She could have been out of the tour on day five. 'Woman saves boy's life' was the headline in some of the country's newspapers. It wasn't quite true. When she landed at Richmond, Virginia, on 9 October, she was horrified to realise that her still speeding plane was about to collide with a boy who had foolishly dashed onto the landing strip. She threw her plane into a ground-loop. In doing so, she risked a rollover, a particularly dangerous mishap in an open-cockpit aircraft, which lacked overhead protection. Her wheel caved under the strain of the sudden turn, but the damage proved to be only minor and she was able to continue with the tour, albeit with a drop in placing.

She was back in eighth place by the end of the tour, much to her own and Fairchild's satisfaction. Whipping the majority of the male pilots proved as pleasing as being handed a purse containing $500.

She had not only outshone most of the other male pilots, she had outshone her own lover.

On 3 September 1929, the day after the Cleveland races ended, frenzied buying had seen the Dow Jones Industrial Average peak. By the time the Ford Reliability Tour finished on 21 October, the stock market had dropped sixteen per cent from its high. Few were worried, though. The market was still considered 'fundamentally sound'.

Then on 24 October 1929, the Wall Street Crash began. When the market later rallied, the seers thought the correction was over, unaware that the raging bull had turned into a hibernating bear. A world that had only recently survived the Great War and the Spanish Flu epidemic was about to face another hardship of devastating proportions.

Chapter Twenty-Five

Chubbie didn't hesitate when she was offered one of the most dangerous jobs in the world. New Jersey's recently established Victor Aircraft Company was building a new plane and wanted her to become its chief test pilot at an income of nearly $4000 per year. It was one for the record books. When she accepted, she became the first female test pilot in the history of international aviation.

The role of a test pilot wasn't simply to climb into the cockpit of a newly built plane, speed down the runway and see if it would fly. That was part of the job, naturally, and had been since planes had first taken to the sky—and fallen out of it.

The first deadly test flight of a heavier-than-air plane had killed Frenchman Eugène Lefebvre in 1909. Thereafter, aircraft on test flights had regularly crashed. Wings fell off. Engines fell out of their mounts. At least parachutes had improved a test pilot's survival odds, although early versions had alarmingly high failure rates.

Like all aviators, Chubbie knew the risks. Indeed, what pilot hadn't heard the stories about the Alexander Aircraft Company's problems with its revolutionary Eaglerock Bullet, the model Edith Foltz had flown in the derby on an 'experimental' licence. For commercial sales, the plane needed to pass stringent government accreditation tests, including those that changed its centre of gravity by moving crates of sand that had been loaded on board. The Bullet's first accreditation test pilot—who flew the plane a few weeks after the derby—successfully parachuted out when he encountered a deadly problem and was paid $100 for his endeavours. A week later, the widow of the second was paid $250. The third demanded $500 to put the plane through the rigorous certification process. He too had a successful bail out. The fourth demanded $1000 in advance before he flew the plane, and the money passed to his estate.

Part of the problem was that test pilots couldn't bail out the instant a plane encountered difficulties. In fact, they had to deliberately generate problem situations in order to truly test the aircraft.

Of course, only a small amount of a chief test pilot's time was actually spent in the air. More time was devoted to the planning and analysis stages. First, Chubbie and the designers had to prepare a flight plan so she would know what they wanted her to assess. When she took to the air, she had to stick as rigidly as possible to this flight plan. Afterwards, she had to communicate her observations to the ground teams so they could implement any necessary changes.

Not any pilot could be a test pilot. What the Victor Aircraft Company saw in Chubbie was, firstly, the life-saving asset required by all test pilots: quick reflexes. Almost as importantly, she had the intuitive feel for aircraft that allowed her to sense, both physically and mentally, when one was behaving oddly, and the mental calmness and clarity needed to cope with multiple problems at the same time. She also had the practical intelligence of an aviation mechanic and, to top it all off, she was a good communicator.

Chubbie told the press she was to test-fly a new type of plane—one that could take off in a hundred feet and land at about twenty miles an hour, one with a surprisingly thick wing and terrific lift. If all went well, the company planned to build her a racing version, which she would take on a demonstration tour through Florida and the west coast during the winter months.

When she took up Victor Aircraft's first plane for its maiden flight early in December 1929, the press announced 'First woman test pilot'. She told them that the experience was thrilling but not scary. She was too busy following her flight plan and assessing the results to have any time to be frightened.

Victor's plane flew, but unfortunately the company didn't. When the receivers turned up a short time later, she was out of a job.

Charles T. Stork saw a different side of Chubbie—her bright-eyed bubbliness—when he chatted to her and Bill at a cocktail party early in 1930. His company, the C.T. Stork Corporation, was looking for staff. Liking the looks and skills of the engaging pair, he organised to meet with them to discuss his proposal.

At his office, he explained that his company had recently obtained the metropolitan distribution rights for Cirrus engines, Irvin parachutes, Savoia-Marchetti amphibians, Stinson Juniors and Great Lakes trainers. He wondered if the role of demonstration pilot would appeal to them. When they said that it would, he offered each of them a retainer along with a large percentage of any sales they made.

Just as they were about to shake hands on the deal, he asked, 'Have you both got commercial licences?'

With her usual frankness, Chubbie was about to blurt out that they only had private licences when Bill butted in. 'Oh yes, yes, we have got those,' he lied.

'That's alright then,' said Stork, 'because you must have a commercial licence to fly prospective customers to give them a demonstration.' They agreed on a starting date the following week.

In the privacy of the building's lift, Chubbie protested, 'Bill, we don't have commercial licences. What are we going to do?'

'We're going to get them,' he reassured her. He too had been horrified at the thought of losing such an ideal job until he remembered that their friend J.R. Booth had a flying club in Ottawa, Canada, and had offered to help them if they ever needed anything. He told her he would telegraph Booth straight away and ask him to approach the Canadian Air Force about conducting the commercial licence tests. If they caught the overnight train, they would be in Ottawa by morning and could have the licences in their pockets by nightfall.

Chubbie had grown up in outback Australia, where the vibrant yellows and oranges and reds warned of its extreme heat. Canada, by contrast, was like a black-and-white photo, its lack of colour attesting to a different extreme: an environment so wickedly cold that she found it difficult to breathe.

Booth was waiting for them at Ottawa when their train pulled in around 8.30 am. He handed fur coats to the shivering pair. As they snuggled into them, Chubbie wondered with horror what it would be like high in the freezing sky in an open cockpit.

Booth told them he had arranged everything, including accommodation, and that they were booked in for their medical tests that afternoon. When they explained that they hadn't time to stay overnight, he took them out to lunch and plied them with warm food and alcohol—legally purchased alcohol. It helped them to thaw out. It also created a new problem: when they left the restaurant, Chubbie was drunk.

Her medical test was first. The doctor began his examination by saying that he would check her eyesight. When he saw her eyes roll, he asked what was wrong. She admitted that she had just come from America and had over-indulged at the Silver Slipper. The sympathetic doctor said he would put off the eye tests until the end of his examination.

She passed both the medical and flight tests, as did Bill. Still dressed in the same clothes they had worn to their meeting with Stork—with the addition each of a new toothbrush—they headed back to New York carrying the precious commercial licences that would open the door to paid employment.

The huge Stork showroom was like a playground for the wealthy. Situated in 'airplane row' at 1782 Broadway, New York, it was decorated as a hangar, with a mock airport and seaplane base visible through the open hangar doors at the rear. Chubbie and Bill, penniless celebrities in their own right, would be hobnobbing daily with the rich and powerful.

Among the demonstration planes was a Stinson Junior, a high-wing, closed-cockpit monoplane built for private users. Eddie Stinson, the company owner, insisted that they travel to Detroit and learn everything about the plane before they attempted to sell it. He later sent Chubbie a letter saying that she flew as well as any man. She was thrilled to receive the letter—and to sell one of his planes to a Jewish importer. The commission was large and for a time they felt like they were living in clover. She thought she had also sold a Savoia-Marchetti amphibian to a young man driving a handsome Duesenberg automobile; however, she was never paid a commission, probably because she and Bill found themselves out of work a short time later.

It was a bad time to be attempting to sell luxury items. In the deteriorating economic climate, the market for private planes had collapsed. Aviation companies were jettisoning staff to stay afloat, and Chubbie and Bill were among those sacrificed.

In the nine months since the Powder Puff Derby, the press had taken an increasing interest in Chubbie's extracurricular activities. No longer were the newspapers reporting only her flight plans and race wins. She had inched her way up, flight by exhausting flight, until she was seated on the nation's aviation pedestal.

Or perhaps 'teetering' was a better word. The press could fawn one moment and lash the next. She hadn't yet experienced its fury, but it would come, she knew, if the secret of her relationship with Bill was exposed. The press generally referred to him as her manager or associate. While some might suspect the truth, none had alluded to it—mercifully. She didn't have the luxury of Pancho Barnes' money, which allowed the shameless aviator to say, 'To hell with everyone! I'll do what I want!' No aviation company would sponsor a 'wanton woman' to market its product. No lecture organiser would employ an 'adulteress' to inspire its audience. She had to maintain a constant vigilance about what she said and did, all the while hoping that nothing untoward would happen that might unwittingly bring their relationship to the public's attention.

Speaking engagements were regularly added to her calendar, and she was one of the celebrities invited to participate in 'America's first radio television theatre' in Jersey City on 3 April 1930. It seemed appropriate that a pilot should be on the stage for this inaugural broadcast, a portrayal of both the visible and the invisible speeding through the ether. The production didn't quite proceed according to plan. The broadcast ended up as ghostly flickering images combined with gurgling noises. Nonetheless, the proud Jersey City mayor announced this first to be a complete success.

The theme of most of Chubbie's talks was women's advancement, both generally and in the aviation industry. Like Amelia, she used every opportunity to motivate women to strive for more than society wanted to allow them.

Social constraints still bound most of the world's women, both personally and professionally. There were only two careers in which women could evade or rise above these conventions: the Hollywood movie industry and the world of aviation. Movie stars still largely relied on their looks and feminine wiles to achieve career success so the industry itself was a long way from the forefront of feminism. Female aviators, however, were different. Their skills put them at the vanguard of feminism, whether they personally wanted to be there or not.

Meanwhile, Harry Lyon still emitted the occasional rumble, telling a Lion's Club meeting in April 1930 that his planned transatlantic flight would take place that summer with Bill and Chubbie as his pilots. It was news to Chubbie. They had pretty much given up on him and, instead, she had been making plans of her own.

The Atlantic was still alluring. No woman had yet piloted a solo flight across it. Chubbie found a promoter who was willing to back her flight from Newfoundland to London. To minimise the risk, her equipment was to include an iron mike—a gyrocompass—similar to those used on ocean liners, which would help guide the plane over a planned course.

Her promoter spent two-and-a-half months raising funds for the venture only to find that the plane couldn't be equipped and tested in time for the most favourable weather window: 30 June to 15 July. A New York pressman calculated that if she had been successful, the financial reward would have been about $3 million.

After abandoning her Atlantic flight plans, she was among the twenty-five female aviators who registered to fly in the lucrative 1930 Powder Puff Derby. However, on receiving the paperwork, they learnt that stringent restrictions had been imposed on the female pilots, among them that surgeons would follow them for the entire route.

Chubbie was disgusted. 'After being used to navigating a heavier plane,' she told the press, 'I object to flying a flivver plane, which the committee requires, and to being trailed by a plane carrying surgeons. These conditions do not apply to the men's derby.'

She, Amelia Earhart and many of the other well-known female aviators pulled out of the race. They knew that their decision would cost them financially at a time of increasing economic difficulty. Nonetheless, a critical principle was at stake. Every time they took to the air, they saw themselves as living proof that women could be men's equals. Thus, the race committee's rules were a slap in the face. They were determined to take a firm stand in the hope that their embargo would send a powerful feminist message and would force the race committee to rectify the situation the following year. Only six of the original twenty-five registrants ended up taking off from California to race to Chicago.

With no other job prospects in the offing, Chubbie knew that she and Bill would soon be struggling for money. While the economic downturn made it hard for all pilots to obtain work, female pilots, by a strange twist, found it slightly easier because their scarcity made them a curiosity.

It meant that the future for both of them rested largely on her shoulders. She would have to be the one to find a new source of income. She would have to undertake the task—life-threatening, perhaps—that earned the money. And she would have to accept that some of her hard-earned money would go to support Kiki and her children.

She was beginning to resent it. All of it.

Chapter Twenty-Six

'Japan?'

The incredulity in Guy Vaughan's voice was almost embarrassing. Still, Chubbie wouldn't let it deter her.

Naturally she would have preferred the less dangerous option of finding paid employment. To get a job though, she needed to remind the aviation world that she existed. Since publicity and race winnings from the 1930 Powder Puff Derby were no longer within reach, her only solution was to set a new aviation record.

No one had yet crossed the North Pacific.

Some 5500 miles separated the American west coast from Japan. The Aleutian Islands lay between them, a potential refuelling site. If she succeeded in making such a flight, her name would be printed in the record books alongside Lindbergh and Kingsford Smith.

She couldn't afford to buy a plane, so she decided to try to loan one. First, though, she needed a good engine. The *Red Rose* flight had proved that a sound engine was critical, not only for success but for survival.

When she approached Guy Vaughan, general manager of the Curtiss-Wright Corporation, and enquired about borrowing an engine, he asked what she wanted it for. He couldn't conceal his disbelief when she told him.

Vaughan was in fact horrified. Anyone who had read Kingsford Smith's recently published tale of his transpacific flight would know that the man had only succeeded because of his piloting brilliance and the brute strength that enabled him to control the bucking plane through hours of wild storms. Yet here was this slip of a girl proposing a similar venture. He declared that she had no idea what was involved in such a flight and would drown herself. Under no condition would he lend her an engine for such a risky venture.

She begged and begged.

He eventually weakened, unable to resist the skilled aviator's pretty face and pleading eyes. He agreed to lend her a Wright Whirlwind J-6-5 engine on one condition: that she promised to fly over land.

Thinking quickly, Chubbie suggested a transcontinental flight. No woman had yet attempted to set a record for a flight from the east to west coast of America, or vice-versa. He gave his handshake of approval.

Now all she needed was a plane.

Someone mentioned the plane Errett Williams had flown in the 1929 National Air Races, the plane that had won him $15,000 in prize money in a three-month period. Reportedly, it was dumped in the Alexander Aircraft Company's junkyard. It had developed a serious image problem.

Like Edith Foltz, Williams had flown an Eaglerock Bullet under an experimental licence in the 1929 National Air Races. The Bullet was a revolutionary design, years ahead of its time. Until its advent, most aeronautical engineers had rationalised that the best way to increase a plane's speed was to increase its engine's power. The Bullet's designer had recognised that horsepower could be used more effectively if the airframe was designed differently. Among a number of innovations, the Bullet's landing gear retracted and tucked itself into the wing, significantly reducing drag.

However, the Bullet's problems arose when the company attempted to obtain the Air Commerce Bureau's commercial accreditation. Under its testing regulations, the fully-laden four-seat plane had to be made to spin six times to the left and six times to the right and to recover from each set of spins in only one-and-a-half turns. To make a plane spin, the process is to pull back the throttle and hold the nose up. With the loss of airspeed comes a loss of lift (the aircraft stops flying) and then a stall followed by a spin. Alexander's test pilots had tried to push the Bullet into a spin but it refused to oblige, merely falling away in a wide spiral with the pilot in complete control. Obviously, they needed a crack test pilot like Williams to make an annoyingly well-behaved plane behave badly.

On 16 September 1929, Williams took a Bullet up to 7000 feet and put it through its paces, allowing it to slip into a nose-down spin. One rotation . . . two . . . three . . . five. All was looking good. Then its nose rose and its tail dropped and he realised that the Bullet was no longer recoverable. It had settled into a flat spin, a pilot's nightmare because the nose couldn't be pushed down far enough to pick up sufficient air speed to fly out of trouble. After twenty-six rotations, Williams gave up. His senses were swimming and he was barely conscious. Only his primeval survival instinct pushed him up through the escape hatch in the cockpit's roof.

After the Bullet killed two of the three accreditation test pilots who followed Williams, the company changed the design by extending the fuselage length and producing a slightly different wing shape. The new model ultimately received the necessary accreditation; but only because the Air Commerce Bureau at last recognised that it was an unspinnable aircraft, which made it a safe aircraft. None were ever sold. Once it had been dubbed the Killer Bullet, interest from prospective buyers evaporated.

Chubbie used her aviation contacts to catch a lift to Colorado Springs. There she asked the Alexander Aircraft Company's management about Williams' racing plane. They said that it had never received the necessary certificate of accreditation, which she already knew. She told them about her transcontinental flight plans and assured them that she wouldn't do anything that might trigger the spin problem. They agreed to give her the plane. They also reconditioned it, painting it fire-engine red with thin white outlines on the fuselage and windows.

The dramas of her flight back to New York in the Bullet produced a story she would later call 'my best joke on newspapermen', a story she would regularly tell at speaking engagements. The joke happened at Kansas City.

A number of pressmen were at the airport waiting for her to arrive from Wichita. They saw the Bullet swing over the field and land fast . . . without its landing gear down. It skidded along the soft cinder track for some distance then stopped with its nose poking into the ground.

They raced towards the plane accompanied by aviators and ground staff, a doctor and an ambulance. When they saw her climb up through the escape hatch in the cockpit roof, they cried, 'Are you hurt?'

'No,' she replied calmly. 'The wheels wouldn't come down and I had to land without them.'

They were amazed at her composure. She seemed blissfully ignorant of the fact that a four-inch dip on either wing could have proved fatal.

'The funny part of it,' she later told her audiences, 'was that everyone believed me.' She paused for a moment, so she had the audience's complete attention. Then she added, 'If you go inside my plane now, you will see "WHEELS!" written in big letters on the instrument panel. What really happened that day was that I forgot to put down the landing gear.'

Of course, the airport mechanics had ribbed her mercilessly after her botched landing. They were the ones who had made the 'wheels' sign. The problem was that she had momentarily forgotten that her plane had retractable landing gear. Moreover, she hadn't received adequate landing-gear training in the first place, which wasn't helped by the fact that the plane had no instruction sheet or warnings lights or alarm bells or a big lever with 'Up' and 'Down' symbols.

Still, it was a good lesson. Better to have bungled an airport landing than an emergency landing in the wilderness. She made sure she knew exactly what she had to do before she set off again for New York to complete the preparations for her transcontinental flight.

Two weeks later *The New York Times* announced, to her intense frustration, that Laura Ingalls was also planning a transcontinental flight—shades of the *Red Rose* flight all over again. Laura hadn't flown in the 1929 Powder Puff Derby; however, she was an experienced pilot. She had recently beaten the world's aviators, men as well as women, to set a new barrel-roll record.

And Laura took to the air first. When she reached Los Angeles on 8 October in a flying time of thirty hours and thirty minutes, Chubbie decided that her only option was to beat it.

For the previous few years, the fad had been for endurance flights, like the *Red Rose's*. Now, flyers were shuttling across the country or dashing between towns in search of ever more obscure speed records. Not only did these flights grip the minds and stimulate the imaginations of the public at an increasingly difficult economic time, but the leading aircraft and engine manufacturers also took interest. These flights demonstrated the practical value of more streamlined planes with more powerful engines, not only for the promotional value that lay in air racing but for commercial aviation. As every businessman knew, faster usually meant cheaper, and cheaper meant more profits.

Chubbie's Bullet had a 120-horsepower engine, a cruising speed of 110 miles per hour, a top speed of 145 miles per hour and carried 100 gallons of fuel. She wasn't planning to make a non-stop record attempt, which would have necessitated night-time flying and required blind-flying instruments she didn't have. Morever, it was actually faster to make refuelling stops. The fuel quantities required for non-stop flights turned usually sprightly planes into lumbering elephants, as Kingsford Smith had learnt firsthand. The *Southern Cross* was so overladen with fuel when it left Suva, Fiji—it carried the equivalent weight of fifty-seven men—that after twenty minutes of flying it had climbed no higher than fifteen feet. Fortunately, the ocean swell wasn't sixteen feet.

Her own flight would also be more arduous than Laura's, although the press made little mention of the fact. Laura had followed a pilot plane, which was responsible for navigation, so all she'd had to do was zoom along behind it. Chubbie had to do everything herself, a truly solo flight.

Before she left New York, she took out her maps and drew her first day's course. Then she jotted down the distances: 50 miles, 100 miles, 150 miles and so on. She calculated her compass courses and added those details to her maps. She would have to do the same each night of her flight. She knew that when she took to the air she couldn't rely on someone else to lead her to safety. Her success depended on her own thorough preparations—and, of course, good luck.

The pressmen noticed that Chubbie wasn't decked out like a pilot when she headed across New York's Curtiss Field airport on Monday, 13 October 1930. Instead, she was dressed demurely in a brown tweed skirt, a tan and red sweater, stockings, brown shoes and a cloche hat. She looked little different to the average woman walking along a New York street.

She maintained the same demure image when she climbed onto a wing and posed for a picture while cleaning her windscreen. But she didn't look quite so housewifely when she scrambled onto the top of her plane and slipped feet first into the cockpit, her only mode of entry and exit because of the extra fuel tanks sitting on the passenger seats.

She shoved several cushions behind her to allow her to reach the rudder bar and controls. Then, with a cheery wave, this twentieth-century woman gunned her plane's engine and roared down the runway.

'I'm so tired,' she told the Indianapolis press, after flying for six hours and thirty-sixty minutes. 'It's the longest non-stop flight I've made alone.' Then she begged for a cigarette.

The press asked how her trip had been.

'Filthy! You should have seen the Alleghenies. Fog, mist, rain. I discovered myself twenty miles off my course.'

The Allegheny Mountains near the Atlantic seaboard created the most problems for pilots heading west from New York. The pre-flight weather forecasts had indicated that the conditions looked good all the way to Wichita, with a high ceiling and good visibility over the range. Instead, she encountered a low ceiling and poor visibility, causing her to fly off course, and delaying her journey by nearly an hour. After completing the mountain crossing, the fog and haze were so bad over Pennsylvania that she missed seeing the city of Pittsburgh altogether.

The journalists asked her to smile for the cameras.

'I'm too disappointed with the report of the weather conditions west of here to smile,' she told them.

The picture published the next day showed her clutching her hair with one hand and reading a sheet of paper held by the other, her face wearing a look of consternation bordering on horror.

But she refused to be deterred by the news of rain at Wichita and a 400-foot cloud ceiling. After a refuelling break of only twenty-eight minutes, she was off again, planning to refuel at Wichita and stop at Albuquerque.

She didn't make it to Wichita. Torrential rain between St Louis and Kansas City affected her engine, forcing her to land among startled sheep grazing on a private landing field in the suburbs of Kansas City. The only good news was that she had clipped half-an-hour off Laura Ingalls' New York to Kansas City flight time.

Fog-bound the next morning, she told the press that she had no choice but to delay her departure. She also expressed concern that the adverse weather might destroy her chances of beating Laura's record. She kept a close eye on the weather and, when a window opened in the afternoon, she took to the sky again. Two hours later she reached Wichita, where she stopped for the night. She was forty-four minutes ahead of her rival.

Meanwhile, Laura—now attempting a west–east record—was grounded by bad weather in Amarillo, Texas, and was unable to continue her own leg to Wichita. If the weather had been better, these two rivals for transcontinental glory would have spent the night in the same town.

Visibility remained poor when Chubbie took off for Albuquerque, New Mexico. Laura slipped by on a parallel course. After a quick lunch and refuel, Chubbie flew to Winslow, Arizona, where she spent the night. The morning's forecast reported strong winds along her route and heavy fog on the west coast but again she wouldn't let it deter her. Fighting headwinds most of the way, she reached Los Angeles on 16 October in a total flight time of twenty-five hours and forty-four minutes. She had beaten Laura's record by nearly five hours.

'I've been up at 4.30 every morning for a week,' the worn-out aviator told the press. 'Now I'm going to have the luxury of sleeping in a few mornings.'

As she rested in Los Angeles, she heard that Laura had reached New York on 18 October in twenty-five hours and thirty-five minutes, nine minutes faster than Chubbie's east–west time. Laura's first transcontinental record had lasted only eight days. Now Chubbie's had been beaten in two.

A low cloud ceiling hung over much of southern California on Sunday, 19 October, delaying Chubbie's departure on her west–east flight. The sun was nearing its apex by the time the fog lifted enough for her to take off for Winslow. As the afternoon progressed, as the sun drifted towards the horizon, she checked her cockpit clock and her maps and calculations with increasing concern. Simple maths provided the answer to the question she didn't want answered. She had no chance of reaching Winslow by nightfall.

She had never made a night-time landing before. She wondered if she should try to find a closer landing field. The terrain below was dangerously rugged, with few spots to land safely in the event of trouble. If she was unable to reach a town before dusk and was forced to bail out, she might be marooned in the mountains or forests—if she survived the landing. Better to stay the course, she decided. Having landed at Winslow a few days before, she at least knew the location of the airfield.

The sun set at 5.45 pm. She kept flying as its last lingering glow disappeared and darkness wrapped itself around her. She relied solely on her compass calculations, hoping that wind-drift hadn't blown her off course. As the minutes passed, her fear grew.

It was nearing 6.30 pm by the time she saw the lights of Winslow. Her intense relief soon dissipated when she flew over the town and failed to see the distinctive stretch of parallel lights. When darkness fell, the airfield officials must have concluded that she had landed elsewhere. She would have to land without any lights at all.

During flight training, pilots were given simple instructions about night-time landings. Don't. Not without the relevant instruments, that is. Night-time's gloom made it frighteningly difficult to see objects—or abysses—and to judge distances. Many an aviator hadn't lived to tell his hangar tale about an attempted landing after nightfall.

At least her familiarity with Winslow allowed her to find the airfield, despite the darkness. A runway landing minimised her chances of smashing into unseen objects or collapsing into cavities. Nonetheless, her ability to judge the distance between her landing gear and the ground's surface was seriously impaired. She made her assessment then braced for the impact.

Her plane slammed into the runway and threw itself into a ground-loop, a sure sign of landing-gear damage. She hung on as it looped, waiting tensely to see if its momentum would hurl it over. Gradually, it slowed down and came to a halt. The plane was in one piece and so was she.

When the mechanics examined her plane the next day, they said that the damaged tailskid and bent propeller could be fixed that day; however, they would have to fly in a new wheel from Los Angeles. Two days later, when the repairs were completed, she was on her way again.

The weather refused to help her. At Albuquerque, when she mentioned her plan for a 6 am departure the next day, the officials told her to forget it. Thick fog covered Amarillo and its vicinity. It was Friday before she could continue her journey.

Her propeller, not properly aligned after the Winslow landing, slowed her down on her flight to Wichita so she employed the aviation capital's mechanics to straighten it. A tailwind at 5000 feet blew her to Columbus, nearly freezing her along the way. She decided to thaw out overnight and complete the final leg the following morning, Sunday, 26 October.

Over the next few days, the country's newspapers published photos of her standing on the wing of her plane and waving, with a delighted smile on her sunburned face. Her flight time from Los Angeles to New York was twenty-one hours and forty-seven minutes, beating Laura's record by a decisive four hours.

Chapter Twenty-Seven

At last, a job of sorts.

A Pittsburgh organisation, Aerial Enterprises Incorporated, wanted her to fly from Pittsburgh to Havana and back again, carrying an illuminated scroll from Pittsburgh's mayor to Cuba's president, General Gerardo Machado y Morales. The purpose of her trip would be to promote Pittsburgh's potential as an air centre. America was a heavy investor in Cuba's sugar industry; accordingly, an air route between these two cities could prove a worthwhile business venture.

Aerial Enterprises was to pay her $1000 for the return flight, the first half to be paid when she took off from Pittsburgh—hopefully on 10 or 11 November 1930—and the second half after she reached her destination. Additionally, she was provided with an upfront payment of $250 to cover costs associated with the flight. It wasn't enough to finance blind-flying instruments or other extras; however, she had managed without them on her transcontinental flight and hoped they wouldn't prove necessary this time.

She flew to Pittsburgh a few days beforehand, with Bill accompanying her, and on Sunday, 9 November, they thrilled 3000 spectators at the Butler airfield by performing spectacular aerobatics. But on Monday she advised the press that her next day's departure had been cancelled because of poor weather. On Tuesday, when she was told that low clouds and rain covered the eastern seaboard down to the Gulf of Mexico, she grumbled, 'I'll be here the whole winter.' On Wednesday, when there was no improvement, she groaned, 'I'll be here for the rest of my life.'

The fog wasn't the only problem. The smoke belching from the Steel City's factories, forges and steam mills was being trapped by the hunkering cloud layer, compounding the visibility issues.

Thursday was the 13th. A *Pittsburgh Press* journalist decided to find out if she would risk such a trip on the 13th. Before he could pose the question though, Chubbie laid down some interview ground-rules. 'Please, don't ask me the bunk.' At his blank look, she explained what 'the bunk' was: 'Do you like babies? Do you cook? Do you admire the American housewife? What do you think of aviation's future?'

Suspecting she would consider his own question bunk, he asked it anyway.

She responded dismissively, 'The number thirteen means absolutely nothing to me.'

He thought it a surprisingly disdainful response from a 100-pound, five-foot bit of femininity who was about to fly over the Appalachians with only a compass to guide her.

She explained that in her mind thirteen was not a bad number. She had been born on the 13th.

He slipped in a question about women's employment in the aviation industry. She replied, 'Women are seriously handicapped by the fact that transport companies refuse them jobs as pilots on the theory that scared passengers will not ride with them.'

It was even worse than that. Many American companies rejected female applicants on the grounds that *female* passengers wouldn't trust them, as if that said it all. But the derby's Edith Foltz, a one-time co-pilot for a charter air-transport company, had made a point of asking her female passengers how they felt about flying in a plane piloted by a woman. Far from being concerned, she reported, they were delighted.

Chubbie told the journalist that women pilots were also more cautious than men, which was safer for plane and passenger alike, yet work opportunities were few. 'Women's best bet in aviation is promotional work,' she summed up. 'But that's off now because of the general depression.'

The journalist asked about her Cuban flight plans. She said that she would refuel at Jacksonville, Florida, then fly to Miami to clear customs. 'If I have good tail winds, it will take me eleven to twelve hours. If not, it's in the lap of the gods.'

How would she know when it was time to head off?

She told him that when the night weather charts indicated favourable weather she would be called at 4 am and taken to the airfield. 'Will you be there?' she asked disingenuously. Her eyes twinkled at his look of horror.

As it happened, neither of them were at the airfield on Thursday or Friday or Saturday. On Sunday, the *Pittsburgh Press* began its update: 'Mrs J.M. Keith Miller, who came to Pittsburgh to fly to Cuba, stayed to learn about fog.'

Each day she waited at the airport. Each afternoon she returned to her accommodation at the Hotel Schenley—the 'Waldorf of Pittsburgh'—the type of hotel she could only have dreamed about when she was a Melbourne journalist's wife.

Her reluctance to fly through bad weather led the hovering pressmen to nickname her 'The Cautious Lady'. However, pilots understood the problem. They had a simple expression to describe it: cumulo-granite. Cloud-covered rock. It was deadly.

One morning, when the reporters arrived at the airport, they called out to her, 'Is the Cautious Lady getting off today?'

'Not if the birds are walking on the ground,' she replied with a laugh. 'You boys may think I am an old woman, but my neck is not going to be broken by any fool stunt!'

One journalist admitted that they didn't really mind the early starts and delays because she was such a good sport.

Meanwhile, the American press was reporting daily on Cuba's deteriorating political situation. Elections there were generally corrupt and the losing party often revolted. General Machado y Morales, who had won the 1924 election, took control at a time of collapsing sugar prices and financial turmoil. His solution was to establish an authoritarian dictatorship. On 11 November, the day Chubbie was originally due to fly to Havana, the press advised that student riots were spreading rapidly over Cuba. Machado declared martial law on the 13th. He sent out heavily armed soldiers to patrol Havana's streets, with orders to shoot any civilians who disobeyed them.

She couldn't have picked a worse time to be flying to Cuba.

Finally, a good weather forecast. As she headed to her plane early on Wednesday, 19 November, the pressmen asked if she had any worries about her trip. She expressed continuing concern about bad weather over the mountains.

What about the dangers of a forced water landing while crossing from Florida to Cuba?

She pointed towards her rubber boat and said with a grin, 'It's for getting away from sharks.'

At 7.42 am, her red Bullet rocketed down the runway and climbed into the Pittsburgh clouds. Just before 10 am, it landed again, forced back by a wall of fog over the Alleghenies. 'I never saw such fog in my life,' she grumbled. 'It was just too much of a gamble.' She added feelingly, 'If it were not for the nuisance I am making of myself to these newspaper boys, I would not have minded coming back.'

Naturally, the pressmen teased her. She was delighted to turn the tables on them the following morning, telling them that their own newspapers had reported that the same fog had thwarted the round-the-world flier Lieutenant Eric Nelson—a man!—along with passenger and mail planes.

The treacherous fog covered the city the next morning and the next. She waited at the airport for hours before returning to her hotel for the fourteenth night. This was not the publicity she had been hoping for—the positive publicity she needed to finance her aviation career. If she remained grounded in Pittsburgh for much longer, she risked becoming the country's laughing stock.

On Saturday, 22 November, the weather forecasters announced that conditions along her route were the best since she had reached Pittsburgh. Considering how dreadful they had been, it wasn't a decisive vote of confidence, but it propelled her from Pittsburgh's clutches at 10.17 am.

'The best' proved only to be fog's absence from the arrow heads of the Alleghenies. Instead, turbulent air over the mountains tossed her plane around as if it were as insubstantial as a cotton ball. As the ranges gentled into soft slopes, clouds the colour of cigarette ash amassed. Soon rain pounded at her cockpit, as if the Furies were demanding entry. Then a headwind tried to drive her back to Pittsburgh, back to the merciless teasing of the journalists.

As her clock's hour-hand inexorably progressed, she calculated that she had no chance of reaching Jacksonville by nightfall. Unwilling to tempt fate with a second night-time landing, she set down at the naval

airport near Savannah, Georgia. She had so many checks and preparations to undertake that she delayed telephoning Pittsburgh until she
reached her hotel at 10.30 pm.

Her surprise at the relief in her backers' voices changed to mortification when she discovered that they had feared the worst and had
activated a search. The major air operators had asked their pilots to
keep a lookout while the airports along the Atlantic seaboard had
turned on their lights to guide her in.

The last thing she had intended was for others to worry unneces-
sarily or to risk their lives searching for her. She vowed to make sure it
never happened again.

Bad weather plagued her again during her five-hour flight to Miami the
next day. Customs held her up for another ninety minutes. When she
stepped from the customs office with her clearance papers, it was as if
she had finally passed all the tests and the gods had waved their magic
wand. Bright sunshine. A slight breeze. Heavenly weather for flying.

It was hard not to feel a twinge of anxiety as she ventured out alone
over the Straits of Florida. As it happened, it was the easiest stretch of
her journey. She landed at Havana's airport at 4.47 pm, having taken
two hours and seventeen minutes to fly from Miami. She had also
set two records: the first person to fly from Pittsburgh to Cuba and the
first woman to fly from Florida to Cuba.

As she climbed from the top of her cabin, she could hear cheers and
cries of 'Bravo!' from the waiting crowd. An airport official brought her
a special welcoming cocktail. As she accepted it, she said with a laugh,
'I've come a long way for this!' Then she offered a toast to Havana and
its people.

Many American newspapers published pictures of her waving to
the crowd and accepting the welcoming cocktail. Many also mentioned

that another record-breaking attempt had commenced. Ruth Nichols had set off from New York for Los Angeles with the goal of breaking Chubbie's hard-won transcontinental record.

Chubbie's plan to return to Pittsburgh two days later had to be abandoned, not because of the weather or the political situation, which had quietened down to some extent, but because American customs was being obstructive. Its officials pointed out that she had originally entered America on a six-month visitor's permit and it had been extended six times. Why should they do so a seventh time? She finally managed to convince them to reissue her entry visa.

Meanwhile, she remained apprehensive about the sea crossing, having had so many bad experiences over water. She mentioned to a journalist that she'd had a premonition her plane would go down. She couldn't reassure herself that her plane was sound, particularly as it didn't have all the necessary instruments to deal with difficult weather or to alert searchers in the event of trouble. Frankly, she said in a moment of exasperation, it was an un-airworthy crate that no one else would fly.

Still, she wasn't going to let the premonition deter her. She didn't want to seem like a coward.

When other aviators asked why she was so determined to complete her flight, she explained, 'I am trying to put myself over as a commercial pilot. If I can make a flight like this in an old ship without any of the usual equipment, it ought to be an easy matter to get some company interested in using me as a regular pilot.'

People told her she was brave, but she disagreed. 'Everyone gives me credit for being brave and for making a go of it and I never let them think otherwise. But, really, I am afraid, desperately afraid when I'm over water or mountains or rough country. I got lost in the Alleghenies not long ago and the fog seemed to hang over me like a death shroud. I have felt many times like giving it up because I know it's eventually going to get me. But I can't. People would think me a coward. I guess I've just got to keep on until it does get me. Life at its best is short anyway so I guess I have no complaint coming.'

During her customs-enforced delay, the window of fine weather closed. Wednesday's planned departure had to be cancelled, Thursday's as well. Instead of spending Thanksgiving in Pittsburgh, she was invited to the home of W.D. Pawley, president of Cuba's primary airline, the Compañía Nacional Cubana de Aviación.

During the afternoon, she admitted to Pawley and another aviator that she didn't relish the thought of the next day's water crossing. They had heard the same concern expressed by other pilots of single-engine planes and proposed that she wait until later in the day and follow a Pan American plane across the strait. She demurred. 'I will feel alright when the sun shines tomorrow,' she told them optimistically, 'and will make the trip safely.'

The weather forecast was better the next day, although it predicted a strong headwind during her water crossing. She dismissed the recommendations that she again delay her flight. Her Pittsburgh sponsors were keen for her to return so as to maintain public interest in the flight, particularly as she was carrying a letter from General Machado to Pittsburgh's mayor. And, after the interminable weather-induced delays at Pittsburgh, she didn't want to risk any more 'Cautious Lady' jibes.

At 9.11 am on Friday, 28 November 1930, Chubbie took off from Havana in her flame-red Bullet and headed out over the deep blue waters of the Florida Strait.

Chapter Twenty-Eight

The Miami authorities refused to worry. A Havana to Miami crossing usually took two hours so Mrs Miller's plane should have arrived between 11 and 11.30 am. However, that same day a Pan American Airways pilot had been propelled across the strait by a strong tail-wind to achieve a record-setting one hour and thirty-five minute flight from Miami to Havana. Since that tail-wind was her head-wind, it could delay her plane until midday.

But noon came and went without any sighting of the Bullet, not at Key West or Miami or anywhere in-between. One o'clock passed. As the clock neared 2 pm, the Miami authorities accepted the worst: Mrs Miller was missing. With less than four hours until nightfall, it was time to activate a search.

Pan American officials ordered one of its pilots to search the East Florida coastline between Miami and Key West, while the pilot of a passenger plane was told to leave his scheduled course and search the west coast. Officials also questioned pilots who had flown near her flight path.

One reported seeing the Bullet when it was about twenty-five minutes out of Havana. Not only was it flying slowly because of the stiff

217

headwinds, it was flying low, which had troubled the Pan American pilot because of the poor flying conditions and rough sea.

When Havana's aviation authorities heard the report, they expressed surprise that she had been flying so low. Before she had set out, they had told her to climb to 8000 feet to escape the headwinds and had no idea why she hadn't done so or where she could be.

Federal customs agents had their suspicions. They hadn't wanted to give the Australian aviator yet another re-entry visa. Could she be carrying illegal contraband: alcohol, humans, dope? They contacted all the Florida airports to see if she had landed somewhere unannounced in order to slip past the mandatory custom checks.

In the meantime, Pawley in Havana dispatched aircraft to search the Cuban coastline and to follow her route to Miami. Miami's marine base ordered a seaplane to search as far west as the Dry Tortugas, which would take the pilot across the uninhabited Marquesas Keys, the only other sizeable islands in the Florida Strait. Every available plane belonging to private owners, the coastguard and the United States Navy set out to scour the Florida coastline and the sea between Miami and Havana.

The Key West naval station and Miami's Tropical Radio station broadcast radio messages every hour, asking ships in the Gulf of Mexico and the Atlantic Ocean to look out for a downed plane or traces of wreckage. Coastguard patrols based at Miami and Key West headed out to conduct their own searches. Even the Florida East Coast Railway staff were ordered to keep a look-out as they crossed the waters between the keys. Everything was being done that could possibly be done.

As the afternoon's light dimmed, the search planes returned to their bases for the night. By 7 pm, the reports were grim. Mrs Miller carried only nine hours of fuel, so her tanks would have long run dry. She had flown from Havana into what proved to be the worst storm of the season, one that had unexpectedly swept through the strait soon after her departure. If she'd been forced down while travelling over the strait, she would have faced serious problems. Her high-speed land plane would be extremely difficult to ditch safely onto any body of water, particularly the white-caps that had covered the Florida Strait. The Bullet would probably have lived up to its name and shot straight down to the ocean floor.

If she had somehow managed to land on the surface, the Bullet wouldn't have remained afloat for long even with the buoyancy of empty fuel tanks—if they hadn't been damaged upon landing. Even a stout seaplane wouldn't have stayed afloat for long on those waters because the winds had whipped the sea into a frenzy. She had already expressed doubts about her ability to inflate her rubber lifeboat, even in the best of situations. And if the Bullet had indeed sunk carrying her with it, the Gulf Stream would carry away the wreckage and her fate would never be known.

While nightfall limited any airborne activities, water vessels didn't give up the search. As dawn broke with no sign of her plane or person, only the most optimistic dared hope she might still be alive. Nonetheless, planes and boats from both sides of the strait headed out again to continue the search.

In Havana, her colleagues were cursing themselves. They knew that her plane lacked any navigation instruments except a compass and that she had set her course for Key West without allowing for the boisterous winds that could push her north-west. Without a drift indicator, she could have been blown off course into the Gulf of Mexico, where there was nothing to land on but water. And her concerns about her lack of instruments and the state of her plane could have spawned a festering fear that acted as a mental hazard if she encountered trouble.

With the clarity of hindsight, they asked themselves why they hadn't stopped her—forcibly if necessary—from beginning her flight.

Her sponsors and American friends, though, refused to consider the worst. She was an experienced pilot used to dealing with emergencies, and she carried a small supply of food and water, enough to keep her alive for a few days. Perhaps she had landed somewhere else in Florida, in a place with no outside communication. The remote islands in the Florida Keys, for example. There were 1700 of them, mostly unpopulated, and she might have become confused when she flew among them. Or the Florida Everglades, west of Miami. The large shallow lake contained thousands of thicket-covered islets— and alligators. Or she might have landed successfully in the water and been picked up by a boat that had no radio.

When other airmen were asked for their expert opinions, they tried to be tactful. Her plane's fast landing speed would require a much longer landing strip than anything that could be found in the smaller keys or the Everglades. Her chances of landing safely in any of those places— or at sea—were slim indeed. And while she always wore a parachute, it would be of limited help if she had bailed out over the water.

Then a pressman for Havana's *Diario de la Marina* newspaper revealed that she'd told him, just before her departure, that if the weather conditions were bad, she might not stop at Miami but instead continue as far northwards as possible. Since she had more hours of fuel than was required for the sea crossing, she might have travelled further into continental America than anyone had expected and landed in some out-of-the-way place that made contact with the rest of the world difficult. She had been presumed missing just a week earlier, during her flight to Havana. Perhaps she had been similarly remiss in failing to advise others of her safety.

No one mentioned the other possibility: that she had travelled further north than anyone expected and had been forced down—or crashed—in such an out-of-the-way place that no one would ever find her.

Her mother, who was visiting from Australia and staying in Chubbie's New York apartment, told the press, 'I am very anxious about my daughter but I shall not give up hope that she is safe.' When asked about Chubbie's alleged premonition, she dismissed it out of hand. 'My daughter is not morbid and did not fear anything before leaving here.'

Ruth Nichols, on her transcontinental record attempt, was scanning newspapers at her landing places, hoping to read that her friend had been found alive. Laura Ingalls, the one-time transcontinental record holder, was in Miami planning an endurance flight and had experienced the lousy weather conditions firsthand. She told pressmen it would be a grievous mistake to stop searching, and she reminded everyone that some missing aviators had been discovered alive after three or four days.

Bill, too, refused to consider the worst. 'She is far too plucky a little woman and too much of a flier to have gone down on the flight from Havana,' he advised the journalists. He said that he wouldn't accept she was gone until he found either a crashed plane or floating wreckage.

He ensconced himself in the *Pittsburgh Press* office the night of her disappearance so he would instantly hear any reports that came through. He told the pressmen that he had complete confidence in her abilities as an aviator, provided she received enough warning of an impending disaster. If so, she could have ditched her plane beside one of the many vessels that crossed the Gulf Stream, or she might have landed on one of the many keys. He had flown the stretch himself, so he knew that the keys were low and sandy with jagged coral outcroppings. While no plane could land on them intact, a skilled pilot like Chubbie could pancake in with little or no personal injury. If she had indeed come down on one of the barren keys, it shouldn't take long to spot her. Hopefully, once dawn's light allowed the search to continue, they would soon receive word of her survival.

Gale force winds, poor visibility and high seas battered the search zone on Saturday. Despite the risk to their own lives, pilots and seamen alike continued their search.

Bill headed south to join them. He asked his Pittsburgh Airways pilot to stop in Washington overnight so he could drum up support from the navy and war departments. After successful meetings, he retired to a hotel and tried to sleep.

At midnight, he gave up and returned to the Naval Air Station where the biplane was parked. Although it had no lights and wasn't supposed to be flown at night, he couldn't bear to waste any more search time. He had taught Chubbie to fly and understood the way she thought and reacted, both as a person and as a pilot. If anyone could find her at this late stage, it was him.

He swung the propeller and listened for the reassuring thrum. All he had to do was to get the plane off the ground and he would be halfway to Miami by daylight.

The propeller swung loosely; the engine failed to fire.

He woke the officer in charge and begged for his help. Aware of the tragic circumstances, the officer roused six sailors from their beds. In the night-time gloom, they inspected the troublesome motor and repaired a leaking fuel tank. When they turned to Bill and silently pleaded to be allowed to return to their beds, he begged them to crank the propeller so he could take off. The engine still refused to fire.

The sailors swung the propeller over and over again as Bill paced the field, tearing at his hair like a madman. Seeing him in such a frenzy of grief and stress—more like an anguished husband than a business partner—they kept cranking. At 5 am, a Pittsburgh Airways pilot arrived at the airport and found Bill looking almost insane with grief. The pilot refused to allow him to fly the airline's plane to Miami. Bill was stranded.

Meanwhile, a Colorado newspaper report had been picked up by the nation's press. 'The Bullet plane in which Mrs J.M. Keith Miller disappeared was known here as a "jinx craft", revealed a Colorado Springs journalist, whose colleagues had seen firsthand the disastrous consequences of the Bullet's accreditation test flights. 'Two test pilots lost their lives in crashes with it during experimental work more than a year ago. The ship was reconditioned, fitted with larger fuel tanks and presented to Mrs Keith Miller by an aviation company.'

In fact, Chubbie's Bullet wasn't one of the four crashed planes but an identical model. Still, the journalist's point was clear. The buffeting from the gale-force winds might have pushed her plane into the same lethal spin that had proved so disastrous for the test pilots. Her plane might have been as fast as a bullet, but it was also just as deadly.

Other newspapers were repeating Chubbie's comments about her plane being an 'un-airworthy crate'. During her unexpected stopover on her flight to Cuba, she had told journalists that her plane had been an abandoned wreck and was difficult to fly. She said that on her turbulent flight from Pittsburgh, she had wanted to remove her heavy coat, but the plane was so unstable she couldn't take her hands off the controls.

Aviators who had flown low-wing monoplanes knew about their instability issues. In fact, future aviation magazines would offer suggestions for changes in wing design to overcome this serious problem.

As for her ability to successfully parachute out, she'd told journalists that the extra fuel tanks made it almost impossible for a parachute to be used. They asked why she carried one.

'It makes people feel better.'

Late on Sunday, the search operation's leader, Karl Voelter, advised the press that he was winding the operation back. 'Further search for Mrs Keith Miller is useless. We have scoured every inch of territory to the south-east and west of Florida Peninsula, also the islands to the southward. We have flown low over swamps, glades and keys. The land is desolate, the winds are strong and the waters are running high.' He said that, if she had come down in the sea, too much time had passed for her survival to be likely. If she had come down in the sea and had reached land, she had probably died of exposure. And if she had safely come down on land, they would have received word from her by now.

He added that Captain Lancaster had wired to say he was coming to Miami to assist in the search. 'I will do all he asks of me,' Voelter told the press, 'but the case seems hopeless.'

Back in Washington, Bill's anguish was so great that the navy took pity on him, providing a plane and pilot to fly him to Miami. Darkness forced them down at Georgetown, South Carolina, on Sunday night. When they stopped at Jacksonville for refueling on Monday morning, he told the press that he remained confident she would still be found.

His haggard looks belied his words.

He said that he hoped to reach Miami that afternoon, although poor weather conditions might delay him until the following day.

No one mentioned that by then she would have been missing for four days.

As hope of Chubbie's survival was abandoned by all but her relatives and close friends, President Machado prepared messages of con-dolences to send to Pittsburgh's mayor and the British government. In Los Angeles, Ruth Nichols completed her transcontinental flight in a record-smashing seventeen hours; however, her delight at booting Chubbie from the record books was marred by sadness at her friend's disappearance and probable death.

The nation—indeed the world—began mourning the plucky aviator. 'A pall of sorrow has fallen on the United States public with the realisa-tion that there is little hope of finding the Australian airwoman alive,' lamented one journalist.

Another grieved: 'There is not one who reads of the disappearance of the woman but who makes a mental picture of the tragic end which searchers have said she met somewhere along the treacherous route from Cuba to Florida. There is not one but who feels a tightening of the heartstrings as they think of the lone woman and her un-airworthy plane plunging into the mountainous-like waves which were lashed into fury by a gale that prevailed that day—who thinks of her in her utter helplessness and despair as she realised that she had made the take-off to death, that port from which no pilot ever returns.'

Then at 5.20 pm on Monday, 1 December, Chubbie's mother received a telegram: 'Safe. Notify friends. Love Chubbie.'

Chapter Twenty-Nine

When Chubbie took off from Havana on Friday morning, 28 November, the weather forecasts were fair—better than those for the previous few days, at least. Wispy clouds trailed high in the Caribbean sky; however, lower down, headwinds tried to push her back onto Cuban soil.

She steered towards the twin lighthouses of Key West and Sand Key, a guide for planes crossing the strait, a guard to protect ships. From there, she intended to follow the Florida East Coast Railroad— the steel rope stringing together the sea-shells of the Florida Keys. The railway tracks spanned the sea between the keys, making it look from the air as if the trains floated on water. Once the railway tracks reached the mainland, she would follow the coastline up to Miami, reducing the amount of time she had to spend over the unforgiving water.

The distance from Havana to Key West was only a hundred miles— about an hour at cruising speed in normal weather conditions, much slower with this implacable headwind. But as the Bullet ate up the miles, she felt a change in wind direction. A blustering easterly nudged her sideways, a wind that hadn't been mentioned in the weather forecast. She used her right rudder to counteract the westward drift, fearing that the air current might push her towards the landless Gulf of Mexico.

By the ninety-minute mark, the Florida Keys should have long been visible. Instead, all she could see were wind-whipped waves. Thinking she must have drifted further west than she had expected and was looking at the stormy waters of the Gulf, she continued to bear right, calculating that this would eventually bring her over the Florida peninsula.

The wind increasingly buffeted her plane, knocking it around as if it were a dodgem car in a sideshow. She wrestled to keep it upright, fighting the low-wing instability issue that wanted to flip it over. Her feet grew numb, her shoulders tense.

Another hour passed without her seeing any land or boats or other clues as to where she might be. Anxiety crept through her. She wondered if her compass was malfunctioning—but how could she check when there were no navigation features to guide her?

She pushed her worries aside and continued to fly in the same direction for yet another hour. Still nothing.

Although visibility remained fair, a brigade of battleship-grey clouds now trooped towards her. Big, angry, determined clouds. The wind howled as it increased to gale force level, pounding at her plane. The sea frothed and churned beneath her, a deadly choppiness for a land plane heading towards its point of no return.

She thought about returning to Cuba. She started to turn. Stopped. Dithered. It was easier to keep on flying.

Onwards the Bullet droned. At the four-hour mark, a rush of panic ran through her when she realised she could have travelled all the way from Cuba to Miami and back again in the hours she'd been flying. Where was she? She peered around her again. Nothing breached the sky's desolate grey except for the massing clouds. Nothing ploughed through the white-capped waters. She felt very alone.

She pulled back her joystick and climbed to 7000 feet, hoping the altitude would offer a glimpse of more distant land. All she could see were more storm clouds scowling at the heaving ocean.

She tapped her compass, feeling increasingly uncertain about its accuracy. If it wasn't working, where was she? She checked her maps. She was obviously flying over a huge body of water, so there were only two options: the Gulf of Mexico to the west of Cuba or the Atlantic Ocean to the east. Whichever it was, the large expanses of blueness on her map indicated that more miles of sea lay between her and landfall than she had fuel left in her rapidly emptying tanks.

A feeling of despair enveloped her. She thought about diving to her death to end the torment. For a moment, she dropped the Bullet's nose towards the whitecaps. Then that stubborn streak of optimism that had always driven her into the sky reminded her that while she had fuel, she had hope. She decided to trust her compass and keep flying in the same direction.

Minutes ticked by—agonisingly slowly when she looked towards the empty horizon, frighteningly fast when she thought about the engine guzzling her remaining fuel. Unless she found a landing place soon, her engine would cut out and her plane would fall from the sky.

Then she spotted it. A line in the distant ocean. She had flown over enough water stretches to recognise it: the demarcation zone between the deep turquoise ocean water and the lighter greenish waters that surround land formations. She looked at her chart. In the Florida Bay area, it noted, 'Water three to six feet deep around the tip of Florida.' That's where she must be.

She spotted two small sailboats at anchor. Dropping so low she almost skimmed the wave-tops, she flew around them, shouting, 'Which way to Miami?' The dark-skinned occupants looked at her blankly, then turned to each other with the internationally recognisable shrug of incomprehension. When they looked back at her, they waved, as if she had merely tossed them a greeting, as if she was exhibiting the human desire to connect that afflicts strangers encountering each other in the middle of nowhere.

Dismissing this effort to get her bearings as futile, she continued on the same compass course. Another interminable hour passed. Then she saw land.

Minutes passed before she could compose herself enough to think about anything other than that she would live.

She looked at her map and compared it with the approaching terrain. The wide curve of coastline resembled the tip of Florida. She didn't know why it had taken her so many hours to get there but, according to her maps, that's where she must be.

Hugging the shoreline, she followed its southern curve. A lush greenness lay beneath her, a dense covering of palm trees and sinuous vines and thick tropical undergrowth partly submerged in swamps and lakes. It looked like the Florida landscape. She looked around trying to spot any of the Florida Keys to help plot her map position, but she couldn't see any of them. She looked for signs of civilisation— people, buildings, roads—but couldn't see any of those either. She kept glancing down at her map, then out of her cockpit windows looking for any distinctive matching features. There was nothing. It was strange indeed.

She flew for another ninety minutes, following the southern curve until it turned into the eastern coastline, then following that coastline northwards, as if it would take her to Miami. She had been in the air for nearly seven hours by this time and her battles with the elements had consumed far more fuel than normal weather conditions. Her fuel tanks were critically low. She had to find somewhere to land soon or her plane would do it for her.

Spotting thatched cottages set in a small clearing, she circled the village looking for a suitable landing place. Nothing was obvious. She circled again and again. After her fourth attempt she admitted to herself that her luck was out.

She crawled along the coastline for another ten minutes. The voracious tropical plants snaked down to the water's edge, leaving no open areas suitable for landing. Any moment now her engine would splutter as her tanks surrendered the last drops. She decided to return to the village and find somewhere to land. At least there, if the landing was a disaster, someone might come to her rescue.

She scanned the beach near the village. The swaying trees showed that the tide was into the wind so she couldn't use the beach as a runway. She peered out each of her windows, hoping to spot somewhere suitable. Bad options. Worse options. It looked like her only choice was to pancake in. She told herself that the one advantage of empty fuel tanks was the reduced risk of fire in the event of a crash.

Coming in from the sea, she turned her plane towards the coastline. Drawing on every ounce of her remaining courage, she pointed the nose towards a section of treeless undergrowth above the sandy waterline. With almost full power on, she stalled the aircraft. Then she pancaked onto the sand and into the thickly entwined vegetation.

The Bullet's forward progression stopped suddenly, as if she had thumped into an invisible wall. The plane's continued momentum forced the tail up . . . and up. If it kept rising, it would somersault over its nose. She clung to the cockpit and willed it down.

Just before the tail reached the critical ninety-degree angle, the momentum eased. The plane slammed down onto the spongy undergrowth and settled there.

She checked herself, barely able to believe she was on the ground and uninjured. Climbing out of the cockpit, she looked around her at the verdant lushness, which exuded the sickly sweet smell of tropical fruit and decay.

Suddenly, a group of dark-skinned people swarmed towards her. The shock of their unexpected arrival and their appearance—they didn't look like Americans—was one jolt too many for her overwrought senses. Images of cannibals feasting on her body flashed through her mind. Then their words filtered through. They were speaking a strangely accented dialect of English.

'Where am I?' she asked.

'Andros Island,' they said.

She had never heard of it. 'Who does it belong to?'

'King George.'

'Well, I am one of King George's subjects too!' she announced happily, as if their political connection was a form of physical protection, as if that one final barrier to her safety had been surmounted.

She discovered that somehow she had been swept east to the Bahamas, the British-occupied archipelago of 700 islands and cays (keys) that act as a barrier between the Florida Strait and the Atlantic Ocean. She had landed near Kemp's Bay on the largest island. The Bahamas wasn't marked on her map, which explained why she had thought she was seeing the Florida coastline. She later discovered that it was about 300 miles north-east of Havana and 200 miles south-east of Miami.

The locals were friendly and keen to offer their assistance. She asked if some of the men would help her tie down the plane. She always carried screw pickets and ropes to secure it in blustery conditions. As the tempest continued to rage, she was worried that a strong gust might catch its wings and flip it over, adding more injuries to the damage from the brutal landing.

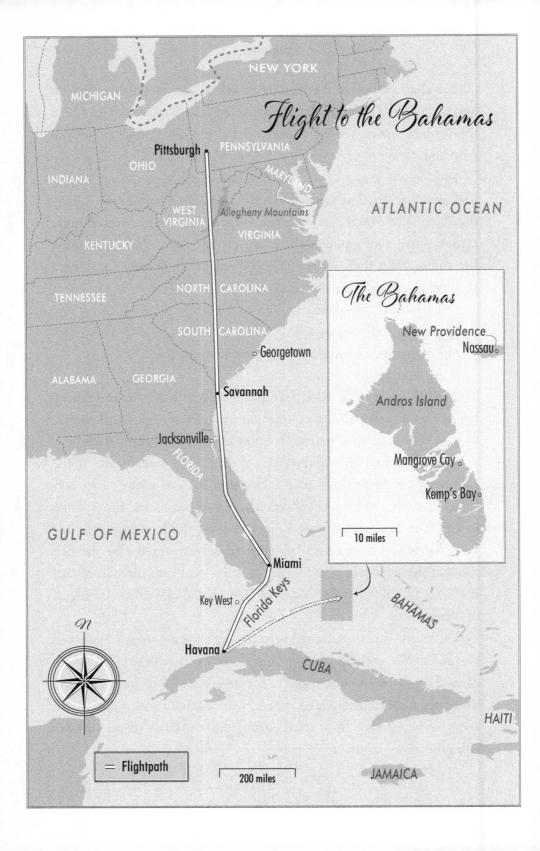

She directed the men to lie on the plane while she screwed the pickets into the dirt and sand. Then she circled the plane with the ropes and tied them to the pickets. As she did so, her quick inspection revealed that the Bullet would require extensive repairs. Still, so long as the locals didn't poke and prod it, as had happened previously with the *Red Rose*, it should be safe enough until she was rescued.

She asked how she could contact America. She needed to advise Bill and her mother and friends of her safety and to alert the authorities so they could recall the inevitable search parties. The locals said that the island had a telegraph station. Relieved, she asked them to point it out. They told her it was sixteen miles away. When she enquired how to get there, she learnt that there were no automobiles or bicycles or horses in the village—or even roads for that matter. She would have to walk.

One of the men agreed to act as her guide. She collected all her valuable possessions—passport, money, maps—and placed them in her briefcase. Around 4.30 pm, they started their journey.

For the first three miles, they trudged along ivory beaches with sand crunching beneath her shoes. The sun was slipping behind the island to the west, its soft golden rays still lighting their way, but lengthening shadows warned of darkness ahead.

The sandy beaches gave way to long stretches littered with sharp rocks and shingle. They stumbled across the rough terrain and climbed over boulders and recently felled palm trees. The headwind was so strong it was like walking into the invisible force field of a repelling magnet. If she hadn't been so desperate to contact the outside world, she would have remained in the village until the weather conditions improved.

They continued to push forwards, their bodies bending with the effort, making little headway. Wind gusts whipped her hair across her face, lashing it against her skin like pine needles. Sand slipped inside her shoes, blistering her heels. Soon, each step was agony. Recollecting that she had pliers in her brief case, she sat down and cut the heels from her shoes, hoping it would ease the difficulty of walking across the coarse surfaces.

The sun slipped behind the hills. Before long, darkness engulfed them. Each tree became a huge moving shadow, each boulder a black void. With the gloom came a strange visceral fear that clutched at her insides. It reminded her that she didn't know the big man who was guiding her, that she couldn't tell if he was really taking her to the telegraph station or if he would find a suitable spot to steal her money and dispose of her body. Or otherwise. As he continued plodding along in front of her, unthreateningly, she told herself not to be silly. She kept walking in his footsteps.

A headland now blocked their way. In the spears of moonlight that filtered through the clouds and wildly waving trees, the man guided her up the sloping hillside and directed her along the cliff edge. The wind continued to batter them as they lurched along the makeshift path. Below them, the waves, white with froth, surged against the headland.

Fear still had her in its grasp. She was so close to the edge it wouldn't take much to push her over. Her body would be smashed against the cliff then swept out to sea. The plane could easily be dismantled. No one would ever know what had happened to her.

The man turned towards her. As she stared at him in shock, he pointed to a spot where the cliff had subsided. He said that if she wanted to continue her journey, they would have to get down to the beach. He would lower her over the edge and she was to slide down the rocky slope to the shore below.

She grasped his rough hand and clambered over the edge; then she half-scrambled, half-slid down the twenty-foot slope to the sandy beach. She waited for him to join her.

He directed her around the bottom of another headland. They splashed through shallow water and across rock-pools. On the other side, he helped her climb another cliff. By the time she reached the top she was drenched and filthy, another misery added to her increasing list of woes.

She struggled on. The blisters on her feet burst. Glass-like specks of sand ground into the wounds. She tied a handkerchief around each foot to protect them. Then she stood up and started walking again, putting one foot in front of the other like a mindless robot.

Around midnight, they reached a small habitation, a bar on a beach. Her guide said that it belonged to his brother-in-law and that he would go inside and wake the man.

She sank onto the beach, exhausted. She had been fighting the elements for almost fifteen hours. Her feet were so swollen and sore she didn't think she could take another step. And she was desperately thirsty. She would give anything for a drink of water.

The men came out with a hurricane lamp. The wind promptly blew it out. They told her to come with them into the shelter. The wind slammed the door shut before she could get there. The men rammed their shoulders against the door and pushed against the built-up sand, making an opening wide enough for her to slip through.

Her host was a dark-skinned man who described himself as a Scotsman. She begged him for a glass of water. He didn't have any— only Bacardi Rum and Holland's Gin. She started on the gin, then moved onto the rum. It eased her aches and calmed her frazzled nerves.

The bar proved to be a two-room hut. Her host invited her into the second room to rest. The hut had no lights, so he guided her to the bed.

She lay down and was just dropping off to sleep when she felt a movement by her side. Every fear she had suppressed throughout the horrific day flooded through her again. As her fumbling fingers searched for a match, she wondered what sort of creepy-crawlies were found on Andros Island: snakes? . . . spiders? . . . scorpions?

In the tiny flare of the lit match, she looked around the room. On the bed beside her lay a sleeping baby. Next to the baby lay its mother, her skin so dark she was almost invisible in the gloom. Four children slept on the floor nearby. Calmed by the sight of them, she lay down again and slept.

At dawn, her host brought her a bowl of water and said she could use it for washing. He handed her another item as well: his own toothbrush. Not wishing to hurt his feelings, she thanked him and tucked it—unused—behind the basin. Then she said that she was keen to get going again. She had been gone for nearly twenty-four hours and her family would be fretting.

He explained that to get to the telegraph station she would need to travel a further few miles to the shoreline, then across three miles of water to Mangrove Cay. Andros comprised two large islands and she was on the southern-most. The telegraph station lay on a cay between the islands.

When she tried to walk, her feet were so sore she could barely put them to the ground. Her host lifted her onto the back of a horse and said that his brother-in-law would travel with her to the bight, then return with the horse. It would be up to her to convince a boat owner to take her across the water to Mangrove Cay.

Once they reached the coastline, she looked at the water with dismay. Three miles of storm-tossed sea greeted her. She tentatively asked the locals if anyone would take her across. They looked at the menacing sea, then back at her as if she were mad. Escorting her into a hut, they told her to wait there until the weather improved.

Locals gathered around her, chattering about her, pointing and staring. Hours passed. Increasingly anxious at the thought of lives being risked in search operations—and irritated at being treated as a spectacle—she took out some money and offered it to anyone who was willing to ferry her to the other side. It wasn't enough for them to risk their lives. She waved around more money . . . and kept adding to the bundle until a couple of men held out their hands.

She knew she was risking her own life and theirs by attempting the crossing. The boat could be swamped. Or the men might head out a short distance, toss her overboard, take her money and say she had fallen overboard. More was at stake, though, than her own life. It had been her decision, her own choice, to fly across the Florida Strait. She could hardly decide now that her own life was more important than those of the men out searching for her.

The boat plunged through the turbulent seas, waves smashing over the sides, drenching her, terrifying her. She told herself she was nearly there, that the message would soon be sent. When they pulled into the shallow waters, she leapt from the boat—and screamed. She had nearly stepped on a stingray. The men laughed at her and then pointed to a path, saying that it would take her to the British Commissioner's house. Shipping their oars, they turned towards the sea again.

They didn't tell her it was a three-mile walk. Only the knowledge that she was so close drove her to take step after painful step.

The commissioner, Mr Forsyth, looked startled to see her at his tiny colonial outpost. He asked who she was and what she was doing there. It took a while to explain.

After hearing of her trials, he gave her a stiff drink and said that his wife would dress her feet and help her to bed. She told him that her first priority was to send a telegraph message to report that she was safe. That's when he revealed that his post was a wireless station rather than a telegraph office, and that the radio was out of commission. It had broken down some weeks previously and he hadn't yet had it repaired, being unable to see much value in these newfangled things. The island had no other means of communication with the outside world.

Wearily, she asked for the location of the nearest telegraph station. He said that it was at Nassau, the capital of the Bahamas, which lay on the island of New Providence some fifty miles away by sea. A mail boat usually ran between Andros and Nassau; however, all trips had been cancelled for the past couple of days because of the storm and rough seas. She would be unable to reach the telegraph station until the weather cleared.

Kindhearted Mrs Forsyth brought bowls of disinfectant-laced water and bathed and bandaged her feet, then handed her a nightie and led her to the guest room. Chubbie slid between the cool sheets and slept the sleep of the exhausted.

The following morning, Sunday, another visitor arrived at the commissioner's house. Only two other Europeans lived on the tiny British outpost and this one happened to be a fellow Australian. He told the Forsyths that he had heard of Chubbie's sudden arrival and wanted to meet her.

Percy Cavill was his name. He had once been a famous swimmer, the first Australian to win an international race using the Australian Crawl swimming stroke. After his swimming career was over, he had spent the next fifteen years in America teaching this swimming style. Currently, he worked as a boat builder and tarpon-fishing guide in the Bahamas.

Chubbie explained her predicament, saying that it had now been forty-eight hours since anyone had heard from her and that it was urgent she inform them of her safety. Cavill said that he owned a small sailing boat and was willing to brave the rough seas and take her to Nassau.

Mr Forsyth had spent too long being lord of all he surveyed. He refused to allow her to leave. It was too dangerous, he said. He would be the one blamed if anything went wrong.

Chubbie wouldn't let him boss her around. She politely suggested that she should at least walk down to the beach with Cavill to see his boat. Forsyth grudgingly agreed, but insisted on accompanying them.

Cavill's boat proved to be a twenty-footer powered by a single-cylinder engine. As they inspected the boat, he said to her, 'Come and look at this. This is pretty nifty, don't you think?'

She looked at him and saw that his eyes were fixed on her own, as if he were trying to tell her something. Grasping his meaning, she scrambled on board. He pulled up the anchor. Off they sailed, leaving Mr Forsyth standing on the beach, shaking his fists and screaming, 'I forbid it! I forbid it!'

As she turned to face the sea, she saw a chilling sight. Her previous day's crossing had been frightening, but at least she had known that only three miles of water separated her from safety. Now she was venturing into the frenzied waters of the open ocean. She wasn't surprised that the mail-boat captains had refused to leave port.

As Cavill set his course, she clung to the main sheet. The boat cut through the waves, sending up sheets of spray that stung like nettles. Bruise-coloured storm clouds massed and dumped heavy raindrops, plump wet missiles that soaked through everything. Then another squall hit them, and another.

Once she had her sea legs, she left the main sheet's protection and offered to assist him. As the water boiled around them, she helped him grip the tiller, and hung off the sides when necessary, and bailed.

Late in the afternoon, they reached an area where huge waves crashed over jagged reefs. For a couple of hours, Cavill attempted to navigate through six miles of surf. After darkness fell, he decided it was too risky to keep going in the dim moonlight. It would be best if they took shelter in a cove until dawn.

Using a log of wood he found on the beach, he built a fire in the boat's grate and brewed an excellent cup of tea. Chubbie was amused at his resourcefulness, deciding it was a typical Australian characteristic. She gulped down the tea along with some bully beef and bread. She had barely eaten since Thanksgiving and her stomach ached with hunger.

They set sail again after dawn woke them, spending further hours battling the savage seas. At last, shortly after 3 pm, they reached Nassau. For the first time in three-and-a-half days, she was able to communicate with the outside world. She sent telegrams to her mother and Bill and Aerial Enterprises advising them of her safety.

As she waited for Bill to arrive in Nassau, she began drafting an account of her adventures. 'The story of how I passed through this black ordeal fills me with retrospective horror as I chronicle it,' she wrote. 'That I am here, safe and sound, to write this narrative of the most dramatic encounter a lone woman ever waged in the air is as profound a mystery to me as it is to those who gave me up for lost.'

Chapter Thirty

Brave and courageous? Or foolish? In the days after her disappearance, when the world mourned her probable death, editorials and opinion pieces questioned her actions in flying across the strait that day.

Some saw the bravery. Others, believing she had been sacrificed to the sea, declared it a 'needless death', a 'useless death'.

The editor of Charleston's *Daily Mail* compared her actions unfavourably with those of America's greatest male aviators, Charles Lindbergh and Richard Byrd. He claimed that these men had triumphed because they were fully conscious of the dangers and took the utmost precautions to guard against them. He obviously had a short memory. Lindbergh's flight would have been judged the epitome of recklessness if he hadn't successfully completed the crossing.

How foolhardy was Chubbie's venture? All she had attempted to do was to fly across a hundred-mile stretch of boat-dotted water during daylight hours on an air route regularly flown by passenger and mail planes, a route she had previously flown herself. The visibility was good—'perfect' according to local aviators who searched for her—so she didn't need blind-flying instruments (as they later tried to tell the press). The weather forecasts didn't predict the gale that eventuated, merely a strong headwind whose effects could be minimised at a high altitude. And while a radio would have been helpful once she landed and learnt her location, it couldn't tell her or anyone else where she was while lost over the sea.

Of course, most of the condemnatory arguments focused on the statements she had reportedly made about her 'premonition of death' and her plane's airworthiness, along with the poor weather conditions that many claimed should have grounded her flight. When she later heard the talk about her premonitions, she expressed her astonishment and dismissed it as journalistic fiction.

In all probability, a grumble of frustration and natural concern was sensationalised by a journalist eager for good copy.

She also dismissed the remarks about her plane's airworthiness, reminding the press that it had carried her in record-breaking time more than 5000 miles from the Atlantic to the Pacific and back—and also to a safe Bahamas landing. As for the poor weather forecast, it hadn't in fact been unfavourable. Rather, the conditions had deteriorated during the crossing.

Locals in Key West and Miami supported her statement but, by then, few were listening.

Her resurrection had unleashed a new torrent of criticism, this time from some who had previously refrained from speaking ill of the seemingly dead. 'We cannot ascribe much sympathy to Mrs Keith Miller,' was the *Jefferson City Post-Tribune*'s harsh judgement, while Brooklyn's *Daily Eagle* warned: 'Luck such as hers does not always hold.'

Her reappearance also sparked a new series of questions. When an eighty-mile wind was blowing from the east at ground level and a forty-five-mile wind from the south at 3000 feet, how on earth had she been blown east to the Bahamas?

And what was this about wanting a fee for her story?

As she rested in Nassau, rumours began to spread that she had delayed giving a full account of her dramatic disappearance because Bill was demanding a fee for her story. The press and public didn't like it. One moment the world was mourning the woman's death; the next, she had popped up and wanted money to tell her tale. It was a slap in the face.

El Paso's *Evening Post* was disgusted: 'Before the thrill of the news that she was safe had ceased to vibrate, her manager was asking for bids. Lives have been risked in the hunt for her. The wires had tingled with the accounts of that search. The whole world had grown anxious. The news that she was safe was good news. But the details—they were withheld from the anxious world. For they were for sale. A typical sign of these commercialised times.'

But a bigger issue was also at stake, the article continued. What if searchers, who had previously been happy to risk their own lives, put a price on their services before they set off on a rescue mission? And what if the general public became calloused—what if they became suspicious that disappearances were merely income-generating opportunities—and ceased to be worried. It wouldn't be ideal for any future missing aviators.

In fact, cynical eyes had already begun to narrow. And cynical brains had listed the oddities. Aviation experts were puzzled as to how she'd found herself east in the Bahamas when the prevailing winds should have pushed her north or west. Her friends and family had been adamant she'd be found alive and well. And the Nassau press had reported that she seemed 'unmoved' by her experience and that both she and her plane were uninjured.

The first allegation that her disappearance had been a publicity stunt was levelled by a journalist at a news conference Bill organised on the morning after she resurfaced. Horrified, Bill told the pressmen that he would radio Chubbie to refuse all offers.

It was too late. The daggers of innuendo were now sledgehammers of open accusation. And, as Kingsford Smith had learnt, the press was more interested in sensationalism and sales than in truthfulness.

Under the heading 'Without Wetting Her Feet', the editor of Canonsburg's *Daily Notes* began by expressing the public's pleasure that Mrs Miller hadn't perished. Then came the sting of its journalistic venom. The American people were wondering if they had been 'taken in' by a well-planned and cleverly executed publicity stunt. Her trip from Pittsburgh to Havana and back again would have generated $1000 in income and only a brief newspaper mention because the flight achieved nothing for the woman or for aeronautical science. When she disappeared, though, she gained press attention all over the world. And when she reappeared, she was urged to accept $5000 for her story. 'Whether it was all by accident or design, the fact remains that the Australian aviatrix went through the "hazardous" experience without damaging her plane and without getting her feet wet,' the journalist asserted, without bothering to check his facts. After reminding the public that she, by her own admission, was flying a 'junkyard' plane, the journalist concluded caustically, 'It was a stunt flight from beginning to end and foolhardy in the extreme, and the questionable manner in which it is climaxed will mean extra dollars for the woman, at the expense of the warm-hearted sentiment of the American people.'

Chubbie was appalled. From Nassau, she dashed off a letter to the press, saying, 'As an experienced flyer, I feel ashamed to think I failed to reach my objective. Those who suggested that I might for publicity purposes do such a thing are despicable. I hope that my reputation as an aviator is good enough to refute such a claim.' She said that the press themselves had asked Bill for a price for her story, rather than Bill offering to sell it to them, and she had ended up accepting one of the offers because she needed the money. And if the press could see her plane's location and her blistered feet, they would have no doubt whatsoever that she was telling the truth.

Some locals came to her rescue. A Miami newsman told the world that Andros Island was hardly the spot for a publicity coup. 'I can't imagine publicist Steve Hannagan, for instance, trying to persuade Sadie Glutz, the only woman to hang by her toes from a parachute and now seeking a movie contract, to fly her plane over 200 miles of strange water and set down in a clump of mangrove roots, all for the benefit of newspaper space. No more can I imagine Mrs Keith Miller taking that chance for the opportunity of selling "my own story" of the adventure to the amalgamated press for $2000. Or for the dubious distinction of being known as a foolish flier and a worse navigator.'

Search leader Karl Voelter dismissed the charge with a single word: 'Nutty!' He told the press that he had travelled to Andros Island with Mrs Keith Miller and Captain Lancaster and had conducted his own investigation. Andros was a remote island with no communication facilities and no landing place, so it was the last place anyone planning a publicity stunt would have chosen. More importantly, the island wasn't even marked on her maps. He knew because he had looked at them. So how could she navigate towards something that, according to her maps, wasn't even there? He had tested the Bullet's tanks and could report that the plane truly was out of fuel. As for her landing site, the only reason she had survived was because of her great skill as a pilot, a skill he could personally attest to because he had flown against her the previous year in the Ford Reliability Tour.

He didn't mention that she had beaten him.

The press asked about the wind direction. He said that, yes, there had been an easterly rather than a westerly wind. But it was important to remember that she was a land pilot not a sea pilot. Seaplane pilots could easily understand how a land pilot slipped off course on an over-water hop, particularly during a gale-force wind. 'Her story is perfectly plausible,' he concluded. As a pilot himself, he could only shake his head in wonder at her survival. 'The angels must have helped her.'

'Have you noticed how Mrs Keith Miller has been dropped from the front page?' wrote a snarky journalistic pen on 12 December 1930. 'Getting lost is not so hot even in the Bahamas.'

The national press reports had petered out after the publicity stunt claims. At least she hadn't faced the vitriol hurled at Kingsford Smith during the Coffee Royal Affair.

The press briefly mentioned a near-disaster when she eventually took off from Andros in the repaired Bullet. She had met up with Bill again when Karl Voelter flew him to Nassau in an amphibian. All three of them continued to Andros to inspect the Bullet's damage then flew to Miami to obtain dope fabric, needles, oil and fuel. When they arrived back at Andros, the locals transported the goods ashore on boats. She and Bill lay under the wings for most of the night using torchlight to guide them as they stitched and doped the badly torn fabric. A low tide allowed her to take-off for Miami the next morning. During the journey though, one of the motor's rocker-arms fell into the sea, crippling the engine. Her stomach churned for the entire trip to Miami.

After the repairs were completed in Miami, she flew off for Washington via a refueling stop at Jacksonville. Few spectators were watching when she sped down Jacksonville's runway on 14 December. Her plane rose thirty to forty feet into the air then faltered.

Trainee pilots were always told that if their engine quits on take-off they should continue in the same direction rather than attempt to change course. Chubbie looked ahead and saw a fence and a huge row of trees. A second runway headed off at a right-angle from her own.

She booted the rudder and silently implored the Bullet to respond quickly. A moment after it turned, her plane hit the ground.

'Thus ended the jinx plane,' summed up Pennsylvania's *News Herald*. 'The plucky little woman can be thankful she's alive.'

The plucky little woman was reminded how lucky she truly was when she heard that Claire Fahy, the Powder Puff Derbyist with the 'acid-ruptured' bracing wires, had died the same week after her own plane fell out of the sky from a similar altitude.

In the aftermath, Chubbie had to return to Pittsburgh by the humble train. She still held President Machado's letter to Pittsburgh's mayor and was determined to deliver it as a matter of pride. She also needed to negotiate with Aerial Enterprises, who were baulking at paying her.

As soon as she received a mutually satisfactory payout, she headed back to New York to seek medical attention. There she was diagnosed with kidney damage caused by the crash and was admitted to hospital for treatment.

Most of America's press showed little interest in the humiliating ending to her previously celebrated flight. Only one of the three news services even mentioned—albeit briefly—the Jacksonville crash.

It was a heartbreaking reminder that fame can blossom slowly—and yet wilt very quickly.

Chapter Thirty-One

The Dow Jones Industrial Average was America's litmus test, a daily indicator of the robustness of its economy. In September 1929, it had reached a healthy high of 381 points. A month later, the stock market had collapsed.

As the Dow bounced around throughout 1930, other indicators provided a more graphic gauge of the country's economic woes. Only one in thirty had been unemployed in 1929 when Herbert Hoover became president, backed by a huge swell of public support. A year later, that figure had risen to one in twelve. Chubbie and Bill were not alone in their struggle to find work.

In October 1930, as Chubbie set her transcontinental records, the Dow plunged below fifty per cent of its 1929 peak. While her reputation was being trashed after the Bahamas incident, the Dow dropped to the forty per cent mark.

It was not an ideal time to have the public turn against her.

Despite her mortifying experience and the serious economic downturn, Chubbie's dreams hadn't diminished. As she recovered from her injuries, and as the Dow clawed its way back up to the fifty per cent mark, she continued making plans and seeking sponsors for a solo Atlantic flight.

In April 1931, she was devastated to hear that Ruth Nichols was about to tackle the arduous passage herself. But when Ruth crashed before leaving Canada, Chubbie had no time to reactivate her own plans. The window of opportunity determined by the weather was narrow. Moreover, sponsorship was proving increasingly difficult to obtain. The Dow was falling again and the American people were questioning the value of pilots risking their lives—and taxpayers' money when things went amiss—in activities that did nothing to alleviate the national suffering.

As the summer sun tried to warm America's cold worried soul, Chubbie was invited to join the Redpath Chautauqua speaking tour, a popular adult movement aimed at educating, entertaining and spiritually enlightening its audiences. A large tent was erected outside each circuit town for a week and the locals would flock to hear musicians, comedians, lecturers and religious evangelists. Two or three acts were scheduled for each day of the six-day program, with each act moving to the next town immediately after it performed.

Chubbie was to tell her 'thrilling story of adventure'—her tales of the *Red Rose*'s flight and her Bahamas disappearance—on the fifth afternoon of each six-day program. Afterwards, she was supposed to give an exhibition of aerobatics and then fly to the next town; however, this plan had to be abandoned because the makeshift landing fields proved too small.

Just as the tour commenced, Keith lodged divorce papers. He had repeatedly asked her when she was returning home, a question she had always evaded. Eventually he demanded formal notice that she preferred her career to married life. She told the press that she was still very fond of him, so she had given him the notice he required.

The timing, though, was dreadful. The Chautauqua organisers were largely religious fundamentalists, horrified at even the mention of divorce. She hated to think what their reaction would be if her adultery also hit the newspaper headlines.

One pressman continued digging. He discovered that she hadn't lived with her husband since she and Bill had made the *Red Rose* flight. He tracked Bill down and found him alone at her Roosevelt Hotel apartment in New York.

Bill usually lived at New York's Army and Navy Club. He and Chubbie had always maintained the fiction that they were business associates and close—but not too close—friends. Any moments of intimacy were snatched between business meetings. So it was only by chance that Bill was apartment-sitting when the eagle-eyed reporter caught up with him.

Bill admitted that they had expected Keith to lodge divorce papers sooner or later.

'Do you plan to marry her after the legal obstacles have been removed?' the nosy pressman asked bluntly.

'I couldn't very well answer that right now,' Bill hedged.

As the days passed and the newspapers remained free of any scandalous headlines, Chubbie was able to laugh off her separation as a 'divorce of convenience' granted by a kind husband to allow her to continue her aviation career.

Other hiccups occurred during the Chautauqua tour. A pleasurable summer swim left her with an ear infection and an abscess that needed to be lanced in hospital under a general anaesthetic. Determined to fulfil her speaking commitments, she discharged herself the following morning, despite the pain and jaw stiffness, and made it to the next town for that afternoon's talk. A couple of towns later, her hotel burnt down.

The eighty or so guests of Fort Plain's Hotel Grant could only be thankful that the fire started near the room of a person with quick reflexes and an almost sixth sense for danger. It was around 3.30 am when Chubbie's sensitive nose smelled smoke. Spotting flames coming from an adjacent storeroom, she raced along the corridors of the four-storey hotel triggering fire alarms, banging on doors and yelling for everyone to flee. The billowing smoke trapped residents on the fourth-floor until firemen shot out the glass with rifle fire and carried them down ladders. Everyone escaped the fire although the hotel itself was destroyed and nearby shops damaged.

Chubbie's modest declarations that her efforts were minimal were ignored by the townsfolk and press. They considered her a heroine, whose quick wit and bravery had averted a tragedy. She was an even greater attraction in the final month of the Chautauqua tour.

Meanwhile, few were attempting to rescue those suffering the ill effects of the worsening economic depression, including Herbert Hoover himself and his 'hear nothing, see nothing, do nothing government'. As the year dragged on and winter's chill approached, unemployment doubled to one in six and continued worsening in a country with no unemployment insurance and minimal public relief.

Banks failed by the thousands. Families abandoned homes when they could no longer pay the rent and moved into shantytowns, which appeared all over the country. These ramshackle communities—built of tents, packing crates and flattened tin cans—became known as Hoovervilles, while the newspapers wrapped around the inhabitants' thin shivering bodies became known as Hoover blankets. Herbert Hoover himself would be swept out in a tsunami of public disgust at the 1932 elections.

In September 1931, as the Dow slumped to below thirty per cent of its 1929 peak, Chubbie announced plans to try to beat Ruth Nichols' transcontinental record, flying in the company of a Hollywood actress. A few weeks later, appendix surgery in Los Angeles and the need for a long period of recuperation forced her to abandon her flight plans.

By the end of 1931, the Dow had dropped to below twenty per cent of its high of 381 points. As the New Year dawned, it continued falling towards the ten per cent mark.

While market seers, economists, business leaders and government officials tried to convince themselves that it couldn't get much worse, ever present was a frightening thought: what would happen if the Dow continued plummeting all the way to zero?

Part Three
NIGHTMARES

Chapter Thirty-Two

No jobs. No goals. No future prospects.

As the Christmas of 1931 approached, Chubbie and Bill's hopeful refrain that 'Things will surely get better soon' had transformed into 'What if it doesn't?' And if it didn't, how were they to support themselves? They couldn't just give up their flying aspirations and accept any old job. There were few available.

Hearing that air races were to be held in Miami from 7 January 1932, Bill approached his friend Gentry Shelton Junior, the charming black sheep of a wealthy St Louis family. They had previously talked about establishing an aviation business together, using Gentry's currently leased-out plane. Lured by the $10,000 prize pot, they decided that Gentry would repossess his plane and fly it to Miami for Bill and Chubbie to race and that he would attempt to obtain a second plane from his father for the same purpose. After the races, they would explore the possibility of establishing an air service based in Miami.

Chubbie and Bill drove Bill's Lincoln from Los Angeles to Miami, arriving shortly before Christmas. There, surrounded by blue skies and balmy air, with the rhythmic thump of waves on the shore and the heady scent of night-blooming jasmine, they decided to settle.

Early in the new year, they moved into a two-storey stucco house at 2321 South-West Twenty-First Terrace, about five miles south-west of downtown Miami, which they rented in Chubbie's name. Chubbie chose the large upstairs bedroom, which contained two single beds and an ensuite bathroom. Bill took one of the beds on the top-floor sleeping porch, which had once been an open balcony on the eastern side of the house but was now closed off and glassed in. They hoped that Gentry would move in as well, so they could split the expenses. But Gentry didn't appear—and nor did his plane. It had crashed, while still under lease, killing the two pilots. He was unable to obtain another.

They attended the air races as frustrated spectators, and partied at night with their fly-in, fly-out aviation friends. Afterwards, reality struck them. Dwindling bank accounts. A landlady who was pestering them for the remaining advance rental. And no jobs in aviation, or even a plane to find contract work with.

Desperation was setting in when Gentry phoned to say he had obtained a plane, but couldn't yet make his way to Miami. They decided that Bill would travel to New York to collect it.

The Curtiss Robin wasn't new, nor in the best condition, but it was better than nothing. Bill had almost completed his flight preparations when he returned to his New York hotel on 3 February to find two telegrams from Chubbie asking that he telephone her. It was important, she said. But when he tried to reach her, she didn't answer.

'Am in a cold sweat,' he scrawled in his diary between attempts to phone her. 'What can it be? This urgent request to telephone Chubbie has knocked me flat.'

Over the previous few months, he had grown increasingly concerned about her wellbeing. She seemed so despondent, so distant. Her happiness at acquiring the Miami house had been pleasing. She had also been her vibrant bubbly self during the races, standing around in her coveralls and high heels with a cigarette dangling from her fingers as she chatted in her delightful Australian accent to her devoted followers.

But her despair—their despair—had crept back as January slid by with no word from Gentry. The most obvious sign of her unhappiness was her drinking. Tipsy while ferrying a friend back to his Miami hotel, she had bumped the Lincoln into a Buick. Bill, sober in the back seat, had claimed he was the driver to save her from embarrassment. He was arrested for drunken driving and spent an hour in gaol, then was fined $50 and given a suspended sentence.

He continued phoning her from his hotel, hoping that her drinking hadn't caused further problems. 'God, if anything has happened to her, I will suffer as I have never suffered in my whole life.' Then he tried to reassure himself: 'It cannot be bad otherwise she would not be out until one.'

At long last, he reached her. She had good news, it turned out. A group called Latin American Airways had approached her about a possible business partnership so she suggested that he return to Miami straight away. 'The man says money is no object,' she added as a clincher.

'Well, if the man says money is no object, ask him to send me $100,' he replied flippantly.

Captain Mark G. Tancrel and J.F. Russell greeted Bill when he landed at Miami airport on 7 February. They launched into a discussion about their aviation plans, saying that they hoped to leave for Mexico straight away to begin operations. Among other activities, their airline would run cash belonging to Chinese men in Mexico.

When Bill expressed concern about border crossings because of his British passport, they assured him that all of his flights would be within Mexico.

Caught up in the excitement and enthusiasm of a new venture—and the prospect of money in their pockets and food on their table—he and Chubbie went the next day to the office of attorney Ernest M. Huston and signed the documents making them partners in Latin American Airways.

Immediately afterwards, Bill felt a niggling concern about his new partners' intentions. Had he and Chubbie unwittingly signed up for a smuggling operation? That night, he jotted in his diary, 'Doubtful of Tancrel, a terrible story teller (all lies).' He asked a Washington friend to verify Tancrel's naval career, recognising that if Tancrel was lying about that, he was probably lying about the airline's objectives as well.

As he waited for an answer, the airline's plans neared completion. Russell headed to Mexico to complete the necessary paperwork and to build up the business. Bill and Tancrel—and Gentry Shelton, when he arrived in Miami ten days after the signing—met or telephoned daily to continue their own preparations. When Tancrel learnt that Bill and Chubbie were almost destitute, that they were resorting to stealing chickens to eat, he lent Bill another $50 to tide him over, then a further $50. Each payment was like a golden rope that bound Bill ever more tightly to the suspect operation.

Chubbie had her doubts about the airline as well; however, she was too busy with a potential money-making venture of her own to spend time worrying about it.

At a Miami party, she had met a university lecturer named Mrs Ida Clyde Clarke, a one-time journalist who had written books and articles about women's suffrage. When Mrs Clarke heard about Chubbie's adventures, she suggested that Chubbie write an auto-biography. Chubbie mentioned that she had sold some of her accounts to newspapers but had failed to sell any recent articles and was unsure if she was capable of crafting an entire book. Mrs Clarke said that her son Haden was a journalist and could perhaps assist as a ghostwriter. She organised a meeting between them.

Haden proved to be a good-looking man, tall, with a full head of dark wavy slicked-down hair and sultry blue eyes. He said that he was thirty-one and had a degree from Columbia University. He had worked as an associate editor for *Good Housekeeping* magazine and recently for a New Orleans newspaper. He was articulate, erudite, personable and charming—and she didn't like him at all. But she liked his mother and she knew that she needed a professional writer's help if she was to maximise her chances of attracting a publisher.

Once the airline contract was signed, she invited Haden to the house to meet Bill and to discuss terms. They agreed to a fifty–fifty royalty split between her and Haden. They also agreed that the unemployed writer would move in with them while crafting her story.

Charles Haden Clarke joined the household three days later, on 12 February 1932.

Most friendships develop slowly, but the occasional connection between kindred spirits can propel a relationship to the next level. The rare dynamic in the Miami household in February 1932 was like a rela-tionship rocket-booster. The outcome would prove both spectacular and catastrophic.

Bill welcomed Haden to his sleeping porch and directed him to the spare bed, which lay only three-and-a-half feet from his own. When they retired each night they found that night-time's gloom, combined with their need for openness, generated an instant intimacy. Within days they were best mates and were spending most of their time together.

Meanwhile, Bill remained concerned about the airline operation, especially after he learned that Tancrel's name was not on Washington's list of naval officers. When he challenged Tancrel, the 'captain' pulled out government correspondence referring to him as a Lieutenant Commander in the United States Naval Reserve and claimed that the fire at Washington's bureau of records had destroyed his paperwork. Unable to prove that Tancrel was a liar and lacking the funds to repay the loaned money, Bill realised that he had little choice but to meet his contractual obligations and fly with Tancrel to Mexico.

The night before he left Miami, he had a long talk with Haden, revealing for the first time that he and Chubbie had been intimate for nearly five years and hoped one day to marry. He also expressed concern about Chubbie's drinking, saying that she sometimes drank so much she behaved rashly. Haden promised to take care of her and to protect her from herself.

On 6 March 1932, with Gentry and Tancrel accompanying him, Bill began his journey to Arizona, leaving Chubbie and Haden alone together in the Miami house.

Chubbie was glad to see Bill fly away. She was annoyed with him. Over the past couple of years, she had struggled with their relationship. Income-wise, nothing he did seemed to work out. The Miami air races had been a classic example. They had travelled 3000 miles on his mate's promise to send planes, but the planes hadn't materialised and they had been left stranded.

She had long realised that little came to fruition unless she was the driving force. And when she did activate a plan, he could still undermine her hard work. She had engaged Haden to write her life story and yet, instead of letting him do so, Bill had monopolised the fellow, taking him on long rambling walks and to business meetings and social gatherings. And Haden had followed him around like a devoted puppy.

Not only was she unable to get on with her book, the pair had left her to do all the housework, as if her only responsibility was to cook and clean and care for them. She had snapped at Bill, 'He's living here at my expense to write my book and you clear out together for the day. What's the idea? This is not a free-for-all place. I'm paying all the rent and keeping it going.' Yet still they pottered off together.

Frustration and disenchantment had cooled her feelings for Bill. He sometimes complained that his darling Chubbie seemed different, distant. He was right. She was sick of struggling to survive. She wanted to get married again. She wanted someone to look after her. Having obtained her own divorce, she was free to marry; but Bill wasn't—and wasn't ever likely to be. Kiki had made that clear. So they could never settle down together as a normal married couple. She would never be free of the fear that their adulterous relationship would be publicly exposed—which would have little effect on Bill's reputation or career but would destroy her own. She still loved him as a friend and business partner, but she was no longer in love with him. She couldn't tell him, though—not yet, anyway. Times were too tough and their lives too closely entwined.

Other men had shown an interest in her over the years. Some had even proposed marriage. But Bill was always hovering and he shooed them away. He was still passionately devoted to her, a devotion that seemed increasingly like a smothering pillow.

Now he was gone, she hoped that Haden would settle down to write her story, although she had her doubts about him as well. When she had been able to catch his attention and provide information for the story, he took no notes and seemed to do nothing with it. She had been forced to have it out with him. 'Look, when is this book going to get started? You have been here three weeks and I haven't seen a page yet.'

'Everything will be alright,' he soothed. 'It will come to me. I'm just waiting for the inspiration.'

He often talked about how he would spend his earnings, failing to grasp that there wouldn't be any royalty payments unless he composed a good book. When he at last proffered some pages, she realised with dismay that they were inadequate. She tried to write them herself, but her construction was too disjointed.

Haden made a second attempt but never seemed to get going. She would hear his typewriter clacking but the noise soon died away. On one occasion, she headed upstairs to the sleeping porch and found the typewriter sitting idle on a table at the end of Haden's bed as he smoked and gazed out the window. When she asked how much he had done, he said, 'I can't write to order. I've got to get the inspiration to get the thing going. I know how it ought to go but it hasn't come to me yet.'

She felt let down by the men in her life and by the world in general.

Bill had estimated that it would take him three or four days to fly from Miami to Nogales, Arizona, one of the many southern towns that straddled the Mexican border. He was wrong. Gale-force winds, flooded landing fields, engine trouble, bent propeller blades, snow and numerous forced landings delayed them for weeks.

He heard little from Chubbie during this frustrating period, which was itself a source of disappointment and concern. Each day he penned her a letter containing detailed descriptions of his day's activities, and sometimes he telephoned or telegraphed as well. In each letter he expressed his affection. On 18 March he wrote: 'I miss and long for you, my sweetheart. I lay in my bed at night and pray you are not suffering too great hardship. I want to have you in my arms again, Chub.' In his diary that night, he expressed his anguish at her long silences and unaffectionate responses: 'Tonight I am more than just worried. I am plumb crazy, all because of no news of Chubbie.' Ten days later he added, 'Letter from Haden Clarke and Chubbie. Very disappointing. Looks as though Chub just dashed off a note as a sort of duty. Haden a little more enlightening. Hope he is keeping his promise to me, feel sure he is. But Chubbie—Hell.'

To add to his problems, his business partners had revealed their true intentions. They wanted him to smuggle Chinese men and drugs from Mexico into America. He had promised Chubbie he wouldn't participate in a smuggling operation; however, he was worried about their finances so he decided to sound out Haden on the quiet.

'You know I am devoted to Chubbie,' he wrote on 21 March. He explained Russell's plan and asked Haden to subtly assess Chubbie's thoughts because he was worried he would lose her if he returned to Miami in a penniless condition. He would do anything—risk everything—to keep her.

Bill received a telegram from them four days later, telling him not to join Russell. While their financial situation was difficult, it didn't warrant such recklessness. 'You are in doghouse on chain if you ignore this,' was its droll conclusion.

Haden followed up with a detailed letter explaining why it would be foolish for Bill to take part. He concluded, 'Bill, I can't begin to express my appreciation for the friendship you have repeatedly shown for me. To say that the feeling is mutual is putting it mildly. Nothing in the world would make me happier than to do everything in my power for you and Chubbie.'

Bill had expressed similar thoughts in a letter to Chubbie written that same day: 'Thank Haden for me for his kindness and for anything he has done for you. I somehow felt I could trust him more than anyone else I have met for a long time. I hope this turns out to be so.'

Latin American Airways was almost broke by the time Bill reached Nogales, Arizona, on 29 March. The next day Russell and Tancrel pressured him to fly smuggling runs to help replenish the company's funds. 'Within three months we will have $100,000 apiece,' Russell said temptingly.

Bill's response was simple and to the point. 'I'm going back to Miami.'

When Gentry—the plane's owner—said that he would accompany Bill, it looked for a moment as if the airline would collapse. Then Russell reminded them that they had no money to finance their return trip to Miami. They would have to stick with him until the airline could pay them.

Carrying Russell and a legal paying passenger—a woman—Bill flew to Los Angeles on 1 April. There Russell approached his former business partners about investing in the airline. When his plan failed, he advised Bill that smuggling seemed their only solution. He added, 'There is no need for you to go back to Miami. Haden Clarke has taken your place. What you need is some quick money and then you can go back and get rid of Clarke.'

Bill reeled in shock, as if Russell had just punched him in the stomach. Then, as a look of disbelief crossed Bill's face, Russell pulled out two letters from his wife, a Miami resident, and pointed to the relevant parts.

One said, 'Chubbie and Clarke came round tonight. They were all ginned up. I really think that Clarke has gained Chubbie's affections and Bill lost them.'

The other said, 'Was round at Chubbie's tonight. She and Clarke got all ginned up together. Don't tell Bill, but I believe she is being well satisfied.'

'I don't believe it,' Bill declared. 'I know Chubbie and I trust her.'

But in his diary that night, he fretted, 'Mental agony!!! Hell!'

The next day he wired her every cent he could raise. Receiving no response, he tried to phone but still hadn't reached her by 4 am. 'Ill with nervous worry,' read his diary entry.

Meanwhile, when Russell told Bill of a new money-making plan, its duplicity—along with Russell's smugness—was the final straw. Bill told him he would take their paying passenger back to Nogales the next day, and that Russell could accompany them if he was at the airport. Afterwards, he would return to Miami.

That night, Bill finally reached Chubbie on the phone. The timing was unfortunate. The background chatter and laughter indicated she was socialising. Bill told her that Russell had received a letter from his wife containing some disturbing news. 'Is everything all right?' he asked, listening carefully not just to her words but to her tone. Her voice seemed cold when she replied that it was.

After she handed the phone to Haden, Bill asked him the same question. Haden replied, 'Certainly.' When Bill enquired if he had kept his promise, Haden assured him that he had but then rang off quickly.

Upon Bill's arrival at Los Angeles' Metropolitan Airport the following morning, a federal officer approached him and asked questions about the airline's activities. When the man mentioned that his colleagues planned to talk to Tancrel and Russell as well, Bill decided to instantly sever his connection with the airline. He flew back to Arizona without collecting Russell. In Nogales, he told Tancrel that he was finished with Latin American Airways: 'Tancrel, you may be just a fool but Russell is a crook.'

His plans for an immediate departure were stymied when the plane's landing gear broke on take-off, delaying the flight until money arrived from some of Bill's friends to pay for repairs. In that night's letter to Chubbie, he said, 'Have been through hell, sweetie, but see daylight at last. Russell and Tancrel may try to be vindictive. Take no notice of anything until I get back. Mrs R. wrote Russell, but I told R.: "You don't know Chubbie. To hell with what you may say or think."'

On 9 April, he wired Chubbie but her cool response worried him. He lamented in his diary, 'If only she would say something nice such as, "Don't worry, I still love you."'

A night's sleep didn't improve the situation. 'Awaken with misgivings. Suffer the tortures of the damned! Ways and means have to be found today to get on east—east is where my life lies, everything I hold dear is there. If it's gone from me, I will end this life. I can't stand the strain much longer.'

During the phone call, Chubbie had told Bill that letters would be waiting for him in St Louis. In Bill's next letter, he expressed his eagerness to hear what she had written. 'Is it good news or bad news? I don't know whether I can stand any more shocks. Tell Haden I am not taking any notice of any scandal. I know in my heart that he would not go behind my back at a time like this.'

At last, on 12 April he and Gentry took off for St Louis, where they planned to discuss business possibilities with Gentry's father. When they arrived on 15 April, Bill found four letters waiting for him, two each from Chubbie and Haden.

The day afterwards, his diary entries ceased.

Chapter Thirty-Three

Chubbie hadn't intended it to happen. She had just wanted her autobiography written. But after Bill left, everything changed.

Haden seemed to notice her for the first time. When they were invited to a party, he would ask what she was planning to wear. If she dismissively said something like, 'Oh, just the old black', he would respond, 'No, I would like you to wear the one with the rose on. I like you in that.' He would suggest a colour that might suit her or a different hair style. Once he straightened her hair with water and gave it an Eton crop, then stood back and said, with a smile in his eyes, 'I rather like that.'

She wasn't used to a man treating her in such a way. Bill was a man's man. He barely noticed what she wore. To him she was just a beloved face in a pilot's coverall. Haden was different. He seemed to actually see her, not just as a pilot and adventurer, but as a woman. It was intimate and strangely appealing.

Still, she was annoyed at his inability to get on with the book. Bill had indirectly asked how it was going when he wrote in one of his letters, 'You will probably have put in some really constructive work on the book.' Haden had admitted in his response that he was disappointed with his progress; however, he was determined to have three chapters ready for his mother to show publishers when she went to New York around 20 March.

Chubbie still had her doubts. 'Don't say anything to Haden,' she complained to Bill, 'but I'm very sceptical about the book being written. He hasn't done one paragraph so far.' In a later letter, she added, 'Am writing very hard so Haden will have all the material he needs for the book. He is without doubt the laziest, slowest writer I have ever seen, but for God's sake don't tell him I said so or he will walk out and leave me alone. He wrote the first chapter (which is very short) but it is incorrect, as he would not take the trouble to read over that stuff I wrote two years ago. The only thing seems to be for me to write the whole thing and have him rewrite it, so this I am doing.'

Spring brought a sense of hope for a new and better life. The first few chapters started to come together and they both felt confident of finding a publisher. One night, a few weeks after Bill's departure, she and Haden visited friends and drank too much. The next morning she found Haden asleep across the foot of her bed. Embarrassed, she slipped out of her room and didn't mention the incident all day. But a sexual tension existed between them that hadn't been present before.

That night they visited other friends and enjoyed some home-brew. When they returned home late in the evening, Haden said that it was too hot to go inside. They plopped down on the grass and talked. As the moon cast its romantic glow over them and as spring's perfumes filled the night air, he said that he knew what he'd done the night before. Then he leaned over and kissed her and said that he loved her.

They spent the night together in Haden's bed. The next day, he asked her to marry him. She said yes.

Chapter Thirty-Four

'Hello, darling. I've missed you,' was Bill's surprisingly affectionate greeting to Chubbie when she and Haden picked him up from Miami airport shortly before 7 pm on Wednesday, 20 April.

Chubbie knew that Bill had received their letters when he arrived in St Louis. Aware that he would read hers first, she had broken the news gently: 'The inconceivable has happened . . .' It broke her heart to tell him, but, 'I know that your one thought has been for my happiness, and feel you will take it in the right way.'

Haden's letters attempted to justify his behaviour. He said that he had never wanted to harm or hurt Bill. 'I did my damnedest to make friendship kill my love for Chubbie, but it was a losing fight from the very beginning. We both tried to talk each other out of it, but we could convince neither each other nor ourselves.'

He said that he had wired his estranged wife asking for an immediate divorce; they would marry as soon as it was granted. He promised to do everything in his power to make her happy and concluded with a warning: 'Please think it all over sanely, Bill, and try to see your way clear to help us get it over with as smoothly as possible. If you do lose your head, I'm afraid I can do nothing but meet you halfway. It would break Chubbie's heart if either of us did anything violent, but the decision regarding this is entirely up to you.'

He and Chubbie had been delighted to receive Bill's telegram of 18 April: 'Am no dog in manger but hold your horses, kids, until I arrive. Insist on being best man and best friends of you both for life. Happiness of you is my happiness. Hope to arrive tomorrow night or Wednesday latest. Love.'

Bill followed the 'Hello, darling' with a kiss for Chubbie. Then he turned to Haden and said, 'Hello, old man' as if nothing had happened in the intervening weeks, as if the man he had asked to protect the love of his life hadn't committed a Judas-like betrayal.

They piled into the Lincoln's front seat and headed home, stopping to buy cigarettes along the way. Bill gave Haden a $5 bill to pay for them and told him to keep the change—as if he were tipping a helpful waiter.

Continuing their journey, Bill said, 'I'm nearly dead for a drink,' and asked if they had any liquor in the house. Chubbie said that they hadn't because Haden wasn't drinking. When Bill asked why, Haden remained silent. Chubbie explained that it was for medical reasons, that his doctor had ordered him to abstain two weeks previously and she was supporting him by doing the same.

Just before they reached the house, Bill at last acknowledged the seemingly unmentionable. He turned to Chubbie and asked if she knew her own mind. Had she decided to marry Haden after having a few too many drinks or was their love a true thing?

'Yes, it is true. I want to marry Haden.'

'Your happiness is foremost with me, whatever happens,' he reminded her. He then asked Haden pointedly, 'Are you sure you can make Chubbie happy?'

'Damn sure!' was Haden's response.

Bill urged Chubbie to wait four weeks so she would know for certain. When she agreed to the delay, he said that he wanted to help them financially. He would give her a cheque for $1000 on her wedding day.

She was astonished. She knew he had no money. Latin American Airways owed him a couple of hundred dollars, but he was unlikely to ever be reimbursed. She asked how he would obtain such a large sum.

He responded firmly, 'I'll arrange it. Don't question me about it. You'll get it on your wedding day.' She didn't push the issue, thankful he appeared to have accepted the situation gracefully.

They chatted idly as they ate dinner and, for a moment, it seemed like old times again. Then, as if he could hold it in no longer, Bill turned to his rival and said bitterly, 'Haden, old chap. I trusted you and you haven't acted as a gentleman.'

In a world where men of good breeding aspired to be considered gentlemen, it was a nasty slur. Haden stood up so violently that his chair flew back against the wall. 'I resent that,' he shouted. 'I am a gentleman!'

Bill pushed his own chair back from the table, prepared to respond in kind if Haden's anger turned physical. Before long, however, Haden calmed down and admitted, 'I guess you are right.'

They continued their meal, the air now sizzling with hostility. Afterwards, as Chubbie washed the dishes, Bill came in and made a wry comment about the situation—one woman and two men—adding with a rueful laugh, 'This is a mess, isn't it?' She couldn't help laughing as well.

Haden stormed into the kitchen, complaining, 'The captain is trying to talk you out of it.' Turning to his rival, he declared, 'Bill, I won't have you trying to break down my wagon.' He then told Bill that he mustn't talk to Chubbie alone.

Chubbie and Bill protested, with Bill exasperatedly saying that he'd known Chubbie for five years so it was natural that he would want to talk to her alone. Haden was unbending. After further angry words, Bill said, 'I'll give you a year to make her happy and, if you haven't, I'll swear by God that I'll come back and take her away from you.'

Sick of them snarling at each other like dogs fighting over a piece of meat, Chubbie sent them out to buy cigarettes, shedding tears of misery while they were gone.

On their return, Bill flipped through his pile of mail, stopping when he saw some letters from his insurance company, the National Air Pilots Association.

Looking over, Chubbie said, 'They're through. The company went bust the first of the month.'

'What?' Bill said sharply, as if horrified at the revelation.

She gazed at him in surprise. Companies were collapsing all the time. Why did he seem so concerned? As her eyes searched his for an answer, her mind clicked through the possibilities. The $1000 wedding gift. 'Are you planning to crash your plane and kill yourself?' she asked accusingly.

He denied the charge.

She wasn't deceived. She knew him too well. 'I know that's where you were planning to get the $1000.'

'No one would have ever known,' he admitted. 'Ships go into a spin and no one can tell anything about it.'

For a moment there was silence. What could they say? Then Chubbie changed the subject. The tension eased as she and Bill talked shop about his recent flights and Gentry's latest money-making idea. Haden grew increasingly resentful at being left out. When he demanded to speak privately with Chubbie, Bill left them alone and took the dog for a drive.

Bill's reappearance in their lives had intensified Haden's plans for a speedy marriage: he now suggested that they marry before his divorce was finalised, saying that everything would be fine if he stayed away from California. But Chubbie had no interest in breaking the law. Moreover, she had just promised Bill to wait a month.

When Bill returned, he said that he'd had time to think about their situation and had decided to leave.

'Leave for where?' Chubbie demanded to know.

'I'll stay in a hotel tonight, and then go back to St Louis, make some money and send it back to you kids.'

Chubbie begged him not to go although it was clear that Haden was pleased with the decision. When Chubbie continued to plead with him, Bill agreed to stay for now. He then said that he was tired and he retired to the sleeping porch leaving Chubbie and Haden alone downstairs.

Having seen Bill's emotional pain, yet his willingness to give them what they wanted, to even help them financially by doing something so awful as killing himself, Chubbie was confronted by the depth of her betrayal. In despair, she burst out, 'I wish we could go and end it all!'

'Yes, I wish we could too,' Haden responded. They sat there in silence for a moment, thinking about life and love. He told her how much he wanted her, how he hated having to sleep apart. Then he announced, 'I want you to lock your door.'

She said that she never locked her door, that she kept it open for the fresh air. He entreated her to do as he asked. 'I don't want that son of a bitch to come into your room and try to talk you out of marrying me.' Then he too retired to bed.

When she eventually headed upstairs, she went to the sleeping porch rather than to her own room. She found a pyjama-clad Bill sitting near the foot of his bed looking at his letters. Haden was seated on his own bed. She said that she had come to collect the alarm clock. As Bill handed it to her, he asked her to wake him when it went off as he had lots to do in the morning.

Turning to leave, she said, 'Good night, chaps.' Bill didn't answer. He was reading a letter. Concerned that he thought she was ousting him from her life forever, she said good night again and gave him a shaky smile. This time he responded.

She looked over at Haden. He frowned at her. She went to her room and locked the door as Haden had requested. As she wound the alarm clock and placed it beside her bed, she noticed that it was 12.45 am. Climbing into bed, she began reading a long detective novelette in a magazine.

It was hard to concentrate. Part of her was listening to the voices in the nearby room. She heard Haden go to the bathroom, then she heard laughter from the two of them on his return. Her tension eased. As the voices died away, she fell asleep.

She had just left alone two men—rivals for her affections—who had each professed such a passionate love for her that they were willing to kill themselves.

She hadn't considered the other possibility. Who would have?

Chapter Thirty-Five

Latin American Airways attorney Ernest Huston was woken from a deep sleep by the ominous trilling of the telephone. A groggy look at the clock indicated that it was nearing 3 am on Thursday morning, 21 April.

Chubbie was on the line. She sounded hysterical. 'Haden Clarke has shot himself!' She begged him to call a doctor and to come to the house immediately.

Huston phoned the central telephone operator and requested that an ambulance and doctor be dispatched to Mrs Miller's house. He dressed and drove there, through streets that were almost empty in these darkest hours before the dawn.

The ambulance was waiting outside when he arrived, but there was no sign of the doctor's car. As he walked along the moonlit front path, he could hear an eerie moaning from inside the house, a noise that raised the hairs on the back of his neck and triggered a visceral urge to flee. Chubbie opened the door, looking white-faced and distraught. 'Thank God you are here!' She pounded up the stairs, expecting him to follow.

On the landing, they met an equally shocked-looking Bill. He exclaimed, 'It's terrible, isn't it.' Then he turned and led him to the sleeping porch, while Chubbie returned downstairs to wait for the doctor.

The meaty odour of fresh blood hit him as he stepped into the room. The same spine-chilling moans, louder now, drew him towards a bed set against the far wall. The noises suggested that Haden was in excruciating pain but, from close up, it was clear that he was unconscious.

Blood was everywhere, matting his dark hair, running down his once good-looking face, washing over his neck and onto his pillow. A gun lay on the bed near his waist, partly concealed by his restless body.

Bill said, 'Haden left these' and handed him two notes that had been sitting on the table. One was addressed to Chubbie and signed Haden. It said:

Chubbie, The economic situation is such I can't go through with it. Comfort mother in her sorrow. You have Bill, he is the whitest man I know.

The other, signed H, was addressed to Bill and said:

Bill, I can't make the grade. Tell Chubbie of our talk. My advise is never leave her again.

Huston read the notes then passed them back to Bill. They stayed for a moment looking down at the gravely wounded lad and then headed downstairs to speak to Chubbie.

Still no sign of the doctor. Huston called the operator and asked if she had contacted a physician. The woman said that he was on his way.

They waited silently, trying to come to grips with the enormity of what had happened. Chubbie asked what they should do about the notes. She was concerned about a scandal if they became public. Bill suggested

276

tearing them up. Huston dismissed the idea. Donning his attorney's hat, he said that the notes must be kept. They might be important.

Charles P. Ditsler, the ambulance driver for W.L. Philbrick's Funeral Home, was waiting impatiently. When he had arrived at the house and discovered that Clarke was still alive, he had told Clarke's house-mates that the fellow must be taken to the hospital immediately. Mrs Miller—Chubbie, as they called her—objected, saying that a doctor was on the way. Ditsler agreed to wait. If a doctor was coming, it would be best to have his authorisation before moving the critically injured man.

When the doctor didn't appear, Chubbie phoned Clarke's physician and said, 'Doctor, Haden has shot himself. He's bleeding terribly. Can you come right away?'

Another five minutes passed. Ten. When there was still no sign of either doctor, Ditsler requested permission to use the telephone. He wanted his superior, O.C. Yeargin, to come to the house and autho-rise Clarke's removal to the hospital. As he dialled the number, Chubbie asked if he was calling the police. 'It is not my duty,' he told her and returned to his call.

By the time Yeargin arrived, Ditsler had been waiting for nearly forty minutes, unable to do anything while he listened to the ghastly moans. Neither of the two doctors had appeared, despite further calls. After Yeargin provided the necessary authorisation, Ditsler and his offsider picked Clarke up, one clutching him under the arms, the other holding him by the legs. They bundled him down the stairs and out to the ambulance, then drove him to Jackson Memorial Hospital, ten miles away in north-west Miami.

Haden's physician, Dr Carlton Deederer hadn't been able to find the house among the myriad streets and terraces with similar names. Around 3.30 am, he returned home and phoned the physicians' exchange, asking for directions. He finally reached the place just after the ambulance had sped off. Collecting the two aviators, he took them to the hospital, leaving Attorney Huston sitting in his own car outside the house in case the police showed up.

When he entered the hospital, the pungent odour of disinfectant greeted him. The nursing staff took him to see Haden. He found the lad still unconscious, still moaning. He removed Haden's blood-saturated bandages and inspected his injuries. The right side of his head was bleeding and his hair was matted with congealed blood. He separated the hair and located the entrance wound. Continuing his search, he found the bullet's exit wound on the left side of Haden's head.

From the bullet's trajectory through Haden's brain, it was clear that he wouldn't survive his devastating injuries. If his family wanted to say their goodbyes, they would need to do so immediately.

Police emergency officer, Earl S. Hudson, had received a call from the hospital advising him of the gunshot victim's admission. Finding the two aviators waiting tensely outside the emergency room, he asked what had happened. They said that Haden Clarke had shot himself. Hudson, who knew Haden personally and had heard him speak of Chubbie and Bill, asked why the fellow had done such a thing. Bill said that Haden had contracted a contagious disease and that it was preying heavily on his mind.

Hudson had rules to follow for gunshot cases. He told the aviators they were to return to their home with him so he and his colleague could search the property.

When they arrived back at the house, Attorney Huston stepped from his parked car and joined them. Bill escorted them to the sleeping porch and showed them Haden's bed. Hudson placed a handkerchief over the gun—a Colt .38—and picked it up. He searched for the bullet in the bedding and around the bed, but couldn't find it.

After exploring the cottage, he asked if Haden had left a suicide note. Chubbie gave him the note addressed to Bill. When Hudson said that the ambulance officer had mentioned two notes, she protested that one was addressed to her personally but handed it over anyway.

After he completed his search and said that he was ready to return them to the hospital, Chubbie begged to be allowed to go to the Everglades Hotel so she could talk to Haden's mother. When they reached the hotel and asked for Mrs Clarke, they were told she had received a call from the hospital and would be downstairs in a moment.

Dr Deederer had also arrived at the hotel by the time Haden's mother entered the lobby. He was Mrs Clarke's doctor as well as her son's and he started telling her about Haden's condition, detail by gruesome detail.

She interrupted him, saying 'I don't want to hear it.' Then she asked bleakly, 'Is there any chance?' Gravely Dr Deederer reported that there was no chance of him surviving, that his injuries were too severe. She said that if her son wasn't going to live, she saw no need to go to the hospital to see him.

Before she returned to her quarters, Officer Hudson showed her the typewritten note addressed to Chubbie, the one with the full signature. Mrs Clarke inspected it. She said that she wasn't sure if the signature was her son's; however, she knew he was worried about money. He had told her so the previous day. In view of their conversation and the notes, she thought it likely that he had taken his own life.

Hudson took the aviators back to the hospital. But before they could see Haden, two investigators from the state attorney's office approached them. They were to be taken to the courthouse for questioning.

Haden Clarke died at 11.20 that morning, alone, without his mother or fiancée to kiss him goodbye.

Chapter Thirty-Six

State Attorney N. Vernon Hawthorne had no intention of assigning such a high-profile case to an underling. His tenure was in the hands of the voting public so he would leave nothing to chance in a case that would surely generate international publicity.

He and his team recognised that there were three possible causes of Haden Clarke's death: accident, suicide or homicide. They soon eliminated 'accident' as a possibility. It wasn't as if Clarke was drunk or was hunting in the Everglades.

Supporting a hypothesis of suicide were Clarke's two notes along with his housemates' statements that he had shot himself. Significantly, his housemates' accounts of the evening were essentially the same—similar enough to be consistent yet different enough to indicate that the pair hadn't rehearsed them. Additionally, there was Mrs Clarke's remark that her son had complained of financial difficulties.

However, Mrs Clarke had also said that she wasn't sure if the signature on the farewell note was her son's. They would need to compare the notes with Haden's correspondence to obtain clarification.

If it was homicide, there were four possible perpetrators: Captain Lancaster, Mrs Miller, the two of them, or a person or persons unknown. When Hawthorne's team found no evidence to support a hypothesis of homicide, they told the hovering pressmen that the two notes pointed conclusively to suicide.

But as the day progressed, his investigators read eye-opening papers taken from Mrs Miller's house. Love letters between the three residents. Letters detailing Lancaster's involvement in a smuggling operation.

Hawthorne told the press later that day, 'We are positive there was a love triangle behind this thing, but whether it was murder or suicide, we do not yet know.' When asked about his murder suspicions, he said that he didn't suspect Mrs Miller because her story rang true. However, he said nothing about Lancaster, except to add that the two aviators were being kept in custody overnight for further questioning.

By mid afternoon, news of the shooting death had spread across the country. Little was said about the victim, apart from the erroneous description of him as an aviator. What hooked the public's interest—and later filled the nation's headlines—was the involvement of Mrs Miller, who had been a household name since her dramatic disappearance in the Bahamas.

Locked in Miami's gaol, Chubbie was unaware that her name was being publicly bandied about as a suspect in a possible murder, although it was clear from the investigators' questions that they were considering the possibility that she or Bill had killed Haden. For hour after hour she was besieged with questions: about the love-triangle, the events of the previous evening, her discovery of her blood-covered fiancé. Over and over she repeated her answers until she was stumbling over her words, traumatised, heartsick, exhausted. They seemed to believe her when she said she didn't shoot Haden—she loved him!—but did they believe

Bill? She hadn't seen him since they reached the county gaol and court-house. They had been interrogated and incarcerated separately.

That evening, she was released to attend Haden's funeral, escorted by a deputy. As she slipped into the chapel via a side entrance, Haden's mother looked up and saw her. For a moment, she gazed at the older woman, who looked bereft and bewildered, as if she couldn't comprehend what had happened. Then she slipped into Mrs Clarke's embrace and the two of them wept.

She wasn't allowed to attend Haden's burial the next morning. She wouldn't discover until much later that the state attorney had allowed Haden's remains to be embalmed and buried without ordering an autopsy.

Although Hawthorne told the press on Friday that he still remained guided by Mrs Clarke's belief that her son had committed suicide, it turned out that Mrs Clarke herself was less certain. Dr Deederer had told her that neither he nor the embalmer had found any trace of powder burns or marks on Haden's head or body, indicating that the shot was not fired at close range. The doctor had also found evidence of a probable basal fracture of the skull, which was unlikely to have been caused by the bullet because the fracture was about three inches from the bullet's path. Additionally, he had found bruises above Haden's right ear, while the embalmer had found a bruise on Haden's shoulder. These were possibly caused by blows from a knuckle or gun butt and raised the possibility that there had been a struggle before the shot was fired.

Based on this new information, Mrs Clarke told the *Miami Daily News* that she no longer accepted without reservation that her son had killed himself. Indeed, in the hours since his death, she had remembered that he'd always had an aversion to suicide and was afraid of firearms. Even as a little boy, he had refused to play with toy guns. She told the pressmen, 'When Captain Lancaster ran out of money during a recent trip to Mexico, he telegraphed back that he was going to pawn his pistol. Haden told me he hoped fervently that Lancaster wouldn't bring the damn thing back.' She added that she would accept a verdict of suicide if the authorities so decided but currently found such a theory incomprehensible.

Mrs Clarke and Dr Deederer were in attendance when Hawthorne held a press conference that Friday evening. He reported that the investigation was ongoing and proceeded to describe Dr Deederer's discoveries. He then talked about the handwriting analysis, saying that the experts had found nine points of difference between the signature 'Haden' on one of the suicide notes and other specimens of Clarke's handwriting. For confirmation, they were awaiting a letter Clarke had sent his brother the day before his death. They had also found differences in phraseology and spellings. Notably, the word *advice* had been spelt *advise* in one of the suicide notes, yet the university-educated writer always spelt the word correctly. And the suicide notes omitted the space usually found at the end of a typewritten sentence, a space always found in Clarke's typewritten prose. Significantly, when Lancaster was asked to type a series of sentences, he omitted that same space and typed the word *advice* as *advise*.

Lancaster's pillow was another source of concern. Lancaster had told the investigators he was asleep when Clarke shot himself, yet his pillowslip was smooth in the police photographs. When asked why it wasn't rumpled, Lancaster had said that either the ambulance man or the physician must have smoothed it. Yet these men had signed statements vowing they hadn't touched the pillow.

And a blood-stained pencil had been found on the sleeping porch.

While Hawthorne didn't say anything more about the blood-stained pencil, it wasn't hard for the reporters to work out its significance.

If this was the pencil that had signed the suicide notes, how could it be blood-stained? Unless the hand that signed the notes had done so after Clarke had been shot.

Hawthorne chose not to disclose one more finding. The ballistics expert had been unable to find any usable fingerprints on the gun Lancaster had admitted bringing back to Miami with him, the gun that had shot Haden. It had been wiped clean.

While Hawthorne continued to hold the aviators in custody, he granted permission for Chubbie to communicate with the press. She issued a statement saying that she had loved Haden with all her heart and soul, and was proud they were to have been married.

The next day Miami discovered that a local resident had taken issue with Chubbie's appropriation of Haden's affections. A young attractive blonde woman entered the state attorney's office and claimed that she, rather than Mrs Miller, was Haden Clarke's fiancée. Her name was Peggy Brown and she had come to help them determine whether Haden had killed himself or had been slain.

When Hawthorne's team investigated her claims, they discovered that she had been seen repeatedly in Haden's company. She was also the sister-in-law of Officer Hudson, the policeman dispatched to Mrs Miller's house after the shooting. Could this simple 'suicide' get any more complicated?

Hawthorne released Chubbie at 4 pm on Saturday afternoon, two-and-a-half days after the shooting. Mrs Clarke's solicitor, James H. Lathero, collected her and took her to the Everglades Hotel, where the three of them discussed her future. Mrs Clarke raised the possibility of taking over the ghost-writing task herself. In the short term, though, they decided that Chubbie would stay overnight at the hotel and return to her home the next day.

Bill joined them at the hotel later that evening. After being released from Hawthorne's custody, he had been detained by federal authorities for questioning about Latin American Airways. The authorities later told the press that he had helped them in their enquiries and they were convinced he wasn't a party to the smuggling conspiracy.

Chubbie took him to see Haden's mother.

Bill moved over to her and placed his arm around her shoulders. Looking squarely into her eyes, he said, 'Mrs Clarke, I want to tell you that I didn't kill your son.'

'I am glad to hear you say that,' she answered.

She would later report the conversation to the press.

Chubbie and Bill returned to their house the following day. It looked as if a tornado had swept through. All their letters and personal papers were missing and a telegram from Haden's wife was lying crumpled on the floor. As they cleaned up the mess, they could only hope that the question of murder had been laid to rest and that they were not only picking up the pieces of their shambolic home, but also of their lives.

Despite releasing Chubbie and Bill, Hawthorne had too many concerns about the case to announce that the matter was settled. So when he heard that J.V. Haring, an international expert on forgeries and fraudulent documents, was wintering at his Florida home, he asked him to examine the suicide notes and determine if they were genuine.

For four days Haring studied the two notes along with other samples of Haden's correspondence. His verdict was summarised in two words: 'Palpable forgeries.'

On Monday, 2 May, Hawthorne summoned the two aviators and advised them of Haring's conclusion. He added that if they had anything else to tell him, it was time to do so.

After a moment's silence, Bill began to speak.

Bill informed Hawthorne that he had previously told the absolute truth about Haden's death with the exception of his statements about the two suicide notes. He declared, in what became his written voluntary statement, 'The incidents connected with these two notes are the only incidents which I feel were unworthy, foolish and cowardly of any part I may have played in the investigation.'

He said that, shortly after his release from custody, he had gone to Attorney Lathero's house and had told him that he had written the suicide notes—but he hadn't killed Haden. He asked if Lathero would represent him if it proved necessary. When Lathero agreed to do so, he enquired if he should tell the state attorney or if Lathero would do it for him. Lathero advised him, as attorney to client, that he shouldn't reveal the information at this time, because Hawthorne might consider it his duty to hold him. Bill agreed to delay doing so, but said that he wouldn't leave Miami without telling Hawthorne the entire truth. To Hawthorne himself, he added that Mr Lathero would be able to verify the conversation.

Asked about the suicide notes, Bill responded, 'When I switched on the light in the room and found Haden Clarke had shot himself, I suppose I was a little panicky. When the full seriousness of the situation sunk in, my first thought was "Chubbie will think I am responsible". I did not know how seriously Haden was injured. I thought he might die. I sat down at the typewriter and typed the two notes. I typed them as I honestly thought Haden would dictate such notes. They used expressions he had used to me that night in a talk we had earlier in the evening. I picked up a pencil, which was by the side of the type-writer, and went back to the bed where Haden was lying. I spoke to him. I begged him to sign the two notes I had written. He made no sound other than a heavy breathing and gurgling.'

Bill talked about rousing Chubbie and calling for help and showing her the notes. He asked her to return them to him after she read them, because he wanted to destroy them, but she refused to hand them over. He then forgot about them until the policeman brought up the subject.

'From then on they weighed very heavily on my mind. I realised that they would weigh heavily against me were I suspected of taking the life of Haden Clarke. I can only say that I wrote them in the first place with honesty of purpose, as had Clarke recovered sufficiently to sign them, it would have had the effect of setting Chubbie's mind at ease concerning his wound. Through events over which I had no control, the contents of those notes became common property.'

He closed with the avowal, 'I did not kill him. In no way have I willingly been a reason for his death.'

With such an admission, Hawthorne knew that if he could establish grounds for motive, means and opportunity he could indict Bill for murder. Opportunity was easy enough. Bill had admitted that he was in the room when Clarke was shot.

In an attempt to establish means, Hawthorne asked if he had purchased the gun that shot Clarke.

Bill admitted that he had.

'Where and when did you purchase it?'

'In St Louis, having first gone to the sheriff and obtained his permission to purchase a gun of that type. I told the sheriff that I wanted to purchase a gun to replace one which had been lost by me, and he gave me a certificate of permission.'

When Hawthorne asked about the gun he had lost, Bill said that Attorney Huston had lent it to him just before he left Miami.

This brought them to the question of motive. Hawthorne asked about his discovery that Chubbie had fallen in love with Haden.

'I had been told insinuating things by J.F. Russell on the west coast, and I had read letters in St Louis from Chubbie and Clarke, which were honest and straightforward, and told me the exact situation. But I had definitely decided before I returned to Miami that if such love between the two was honest, that I would help them in any way possible for, to me, Chubbie's happiness was the most important thing.'

Hawthorne read out Bill's diary entry written on 9 April, in which he talked about his concerns about Chubbie's affections and whether Haden could be trusted. The entry also said, 'Thank goodness for one thing—I have made a firm resolution to end all this mental strain— have it out! Then work for a common good!' Hawthorne asked if this entry indicated any malice towards Haden.

'It did not. If I had come to Miami and found that Haden had behaved towards Chubbie in a manner that was dastardly, I would have born malice, but when I arrived at Miami I found nothing to indicate this. He may have behaved to me in a manner that was not the way of a gentleman, but this was of secondary consideration, for the affection between them seemed to be mutual and sincere.'

With the evidence in Bill's own words of his passion for Chubbie, his purchase of the gun that shot Clarke, and his forgery of the suicide notes, Hawthorne charged him with first-degree murder.

Chapter Thirty-Seven

The press had already heard the news by the time a haggard Chubbie emerged from the state attorney's office that afternoon. When they demanded to know what she thought about Lancaster's arrest, she said, 'I am absolutely confident everything will come out all right. I know the truth will be learned and that Captain Lancaster will be cleared. He is innocent and I know it.'

Bill gave permission for the press to interview him. They were taken to his ten-by-eight-foot cell on the twenty-second floor of the Miami-Dade County Courthouse. Almost cruelly, his window overlooked the quintessence of freedom: white sandy beaches, foaming waves, boats. At least it didn't overlook an airfield.

They found him sitting calmly on his cot with two pictures of his beloved pinned to the wall. They asked how he felt about his arrest for murder.

'It came as a great shock to me, the fact that a technical charge of murder has been made against me. I am absolutely innocent, and I know that the outcome will prove this.'

When they asked what would happen if he was indicted, he said, 'I should like to act as my own attorney if I am brought to trial. Of course, I know it is not possible to defend myself but I know'—and he thumped a clenched fist on his shoulder in emphasis—'that I can convince twelve reasonable men that I am innocent of the boy's death.' Then he glanced at the two pictures on the wall as if silently swearing the same to the woman he loved.

Despite Bill's declarations of innocence, the evidence continued to pile up against him and was presented to the grand jury hearing his case. The St Louis paperwork associated with his gun purchase revealed that he had purchased the gun on 19 April, only thirty-six hours before Clarke was shot. His reason for the purchase? Far from telling the sheriff that he wanted to replace a borrowed gun he'd lost, he had said he was buying it to carry on transcontinental flights. An Oregon newspaper summed up the general reaction to the news: 'Coil tightens for Lancaster.'

Fearing that the coil had already tightened too far, Chubbie set about finding funds and retaining counsel. Lathero recommended James M. Carson, an eminent attorney who had long been prominent in South Florida's legal and political circles.

When she arrived at Carson's office, she felt intimidated by the big man looming over her with his bushy eyebrows and round owl-like glasses. She asked if he would consider defending Bill—if he was indicted by the grand jury, of course.

'I wouldn't touch it,' was the decisive response. 'He's as guilty as hell.'

'No, you're wrong there. I know you're wrong,' she cried. When he looked sceptical, she begged, 'All I ask you to do is to go down and see him in the gaol and form your own opinion because I am quite sure that when you meet him you will feel as I do that he couldn't have done it. He is not a coward.'

She left his office with the promise that he would consider her entreaty. He had no need to make a decision until the grand jury announced its finding.

As Chubbie and Bill waited nervously for the grand jury's report, Haden's mother told the press that she had asked Hawthorne to exhume her son's body. She wanted to know for certain whether Haden had been struck before his death. Hawthorne said that he would order a disinterment only if he thought it necessary.

Mrs Clarke also told the press that Bill had said to her, three days after her son's death, 'Sometimes I think I did kill Haden.' And she claimed he had said, 'Mrs Clarke, I want you to say you know I did not kill your son.' Her response had been, 'I hope I may be able to say that someday, Captain, but I don't know whether you killed Haden or not. The circumstances are very strong.'

There were remarkable differences between these statements and her reports about their conversations after Bill's release from custody. At that time, she made no mention of any remark along the lines of, 'sometimes he thought he killed Haden'. Perhaps it was being recollected out of context, the gist being that he'd been asked the question so many times during his interrogation that the authorities had almost made him think he *had* killed Haden. Bill's other words to her—by her own account—had been, 'I want to tell you that I did not kill your son.'

It raised the question as to whether a murder indictment might distort other people's memories as well, whether minds that now viewed events through the prism of a murder charge might transform passing comments or actions into evidence of guilt or wrongdoing.

On Monday, 9 May, Chubbie heard the dreaded news. The grand jury had indicted Bill for first-degree murder.

It was like a nightmare she couldn't awaken from.

Florida law allowed bail at the court's discretion; however, the judge appointed to preside over Bill's case refused to allow it. No one was surprised. A British aviator was a flight risk if ever there was one.

Two pieces of good news surfaced. Bill's father sent a small sum through the British Embassy to assist with defence costs. And Carson agreed to represent him.

'It's going to be tricky,' Carson told Chubbie. 'We have got to get him off but it is not going to be easy because of that damned note. He shouldn't have done that.'

In Carson's conversations with Bill before his arraignment, he suggested applying to the court for a disinterment to allow Haden's body to be autopsied. His medical expert had advised that an autopsy might provide conclusive evidence of suicide . . . or conclusive evidence that the death wasn't a suicide. Did Bill want him to pursue the matter?

The medical commission performed the autopsy on Tuesday, 31 May. Carson received their report a short time later. In the aftermath, he decided not to request a dismissal of the charges against Bill.

Chubbie and Bill were forced to accept the harsh reality. Bill would have to face the whim of a jury. And, if the jury decided against him, he would soon afterwards be strapped to the electric chair.

Chapter Thirty-Eight

James Carson was concerned. A critical witness, the acclaimed Miami neurologist Dr Percy L. Dodge, was in Boston suffering heart trouble. Dodge was supposed to testify in Bill's trial—which was starting that day—about the physical evidence associated with self-inflicted gunshot wounds. He also had psychological and neurological insights to offer about men like Haden Clarke. However, Dodge's medical problems would prevent him from testifying unless the trial judge, Justice Henry F. Atkinson, could be convinced to allow a continuance.

Carson didn't like his chances of persuading the judge because the trial had already been delayed several times. The previous day, Monday, 1 August, the spacious criminal courtroom on the sixth floor of Miami-Dade's County Courthouse had been prepared for the trial. For the first time in county history, three international news services had been granted permission to install telegraph instruments in the courtroom itself. The jury pool and witnesses had also been summoned. These costs alone would deter the judge from acceding to the defence's wishes.

Carson and Lathero entered the courtroom with their client accompanying them. Bill was dressed in a dark brown suit, grey shirt and tan tie as if it were a normal business day, but his gaol-house pallor betrayed him. As he spotted the press, he switched on an easy-going, not-a-care-in-the-world smile, telling the journalists he was calmly confident of an acquittal. However, his lighthearted mask dropped away as he walked to the defence table, replaced by a look of haunted trepidation.

Chubbie looked even more nervous than Bill, if that was possible. She was elegantly dressed in a white silk dress and hat, with matching white shoes brightened with yellow insteps. When the press asked for her photograph, she stared blindly in front of her with tightly clenched lips, incapable of releasing the bright smile that normally captivated press and public alike.

The elderly white-haired judge took his seat at the bench and indicated that he was ready to proceed. Carson introduced his motion asking for a continuance to 15 September. He explained that without Dodge's testimony Captain Lancaster could not safely go to trial.

Judge Atkinson denied the motion.

Carson had already told Bill and Chubbie that the trial would be an uphill battle. Dodge's absence left the defence at a serious disadvantage.

For the next two and a half hours, Carson and the prosecution questioned the jury pool. Carson enquired if revelations of moral laxity or sordid living would influence the men's opinions. He also asked them to affirm that they wouldn't hold Lancaster's British citizenship against him (juries tended to treat foreigners less favourably). Hawthorne, with the electric chair in his sights, asked if the men had any compunctions about capital punishment—and bade goodbye to those who had. Ultimately, a panel of salesmen, merchants, contractors, farmers and a meter-checker was sworn in by the judge and settled to hear the opening statements.

The news that the woman at the heart of the love triangle was to testify brought hordes of spectators to the sixth-floor lobby early on Wednesday morning. The state was to commence its case-in-chief and attempt to prove that Bill had not only killed Haden but had acted with premeditation. As soon as the doors opened at 9 am, dozens rushed into the courtroom. When all available seats were filled, the deputies slammed shut the steel grille barriers, locking out hundreds of people, most of whom were women.

Justice Atkinson took his seat on the bench at 9.30 am. As the sound of scraping chairs and rustling skirts died away, the state called its first witness, Ernest Huston, the Latin American Airways attorney Chubbie had telephoned immediately after the shooting.

Hawthorne asked him to describe the events of the morning of 21 April and then questioned him about his conversation with Lancaster regarding the gun that shot Clarke.

'On the way to the Everglades Hotel, I asked Lancaster if it was the gun which I had loaned him. He said that it was not.' Huston paused at that point and asked how much he could reveal of their conversations because of client–attorney privilege.

Carson interjected to say that Huston could answer any and every question. The defence was determined to show the court that Bill had no secrets.

Hawthorne enquired if Lancaster had said anything about the gun that shot Haden.

'He asked me if it would be all right if he said that it was my gun. I said, "No, it would not." He then said would it be all right if he said that the gun belonged to the Latin American Airways and I said, "No."'

'Was either you or Latin American Airways indebted to Lancaster at that time?'

'I most certainly was not.'

'Was the Latin American Airways?'

'I don't know.'

In Carson's opening statement he had said that Huston, as secretary and treasurer of Latin American Airways, had owed Bill $250 and that Bill had purchased the replacement revolver to ensure that Huston didn't use the missing gun as a pretext for non-payment. Yet Huston had just told the court that he didn't owe Bill any money.

Huston had been one of the first to visit the sleeping porch after the shooting so Hawthorne wanted confirmation of the room's appearance at that time. Handing Huston some pictures taken by the police photographer, he asked if they accurately depicted the sleeping porch on his arrival. Huston said that they didn't. Not completely. In the photograph, Lancaster's pillow was smooth. When he had entered the sleeping porch, it was mussed.

Hawthorne had previously told the press that Lancaster's claim to be asleep when he had heard the shot was refuted by the evidence of his smooth pillow, and that his excuse that an ambulance man or physician must have smoothed it was refuted by the men themselves. Carson, in his cross-examination, asked Huston to repeat his comments about the mussed pillow, although he didn't enquire if he knew how it had been smoothed. He had another witness who would provide the explanation.

He returned Huston's attention to the subject of the gun, asking about the model he had lent Lancaster.

'A .38 calibre Colt.'

'Like this?' Carson picked up the gun that shot Haden.

'Yes.'

'When you loaned the gun to Lancaster did you loan him any cartridges?'

Huston agreed that he had.

Carson then asked him to tell the court about his conversation with Bill in the aftermath of Haden's death. What had Bill said regarding the gun?

'I had previously told him that my gun had belonged to a friend of mine and that I cared a great deal about it and wanted it back. Lancaster said that he would take the best care of it and if anything happened to it he would replace it. On the way to the hospital he said that he had pawned it and had replaced it.'

'Did he say that it was the gun he replaced which had been used by Clarke?'

'Yes, he did.'

The state's argument that Bill had purchased the gun between the time he received confirmation about Haden's betrayal and the time he returned to Miami had been one of its strongest pieces of evidence suggesting premeditation. Huston's testimony had critically weakened the foundations of this argument.

Carson had a third point he wanted Huston to clarify. In Hawthorne's opening statement, he had claimed that Bill had repeatedly asked, 'Do you think Haden will be able to talk again?' as if Bill had desperately hoped that Clarke *wouldn't* talk so he couldn't reveal who had shot him. Carson asked Huston, 'Do you remember Lancaster on April 21 saying that he wished to God that Haden could speak so he could tell why he did it?'

'He said that.'

'And at this time Haden Clarke was alive.'

'He was.'

Hawthorne's next witness, ambulance driver Charles Ditsler, also told the court that Lancaster had asked him if Clarke would ever speak again and that his response had been that it seemed unlikely.

Ditsler then talked about the delay in taking Clarke to the hospital and how he and his fellow ambulance officer eventually carried the unconscious body down the stairs and out to the ambulance.

Hawthorne asked, 'Did Haden Clarke's body strike the wall or bannister while being carried to the ambulance?'

'I'm not sure,' was the response.

It wasn't the answer Hawthorne had hoped for. It provided the reasonable doubt the defence required to dismiss any claim that the bruise on Clarke's arm resulted from a physical altercation with his killer.

Emergency Officer Earl S. Hudson followed Ditsler to the stand. Hawthorne questioned him about his encounters with the two aviators then asked, 'Did Lancaster say anything on the way back to the house?'

'Yes. He asked if the boy had any chance of coming to long enough to say anything.'

'Was anything said about the gun?'

Hudson reported that Lancaster told him it belonged to some airways company he had worked for, that he had laid it by the typewriter and that Clarke had been playing with it on the bed before they went to sleep.

Under cross-examination, Carson elicited from him that Lancaster had actually asked if Clarke would speak again *so he could explain how it happened*. Carson had now drawn the same critical amplification from two of the state's witnesses.

He then asked Hudson, 'Did you discuss with Lancaster the matter of Haden Clarke's attempted suicide and did he assign any reason for the act?'

'The only reason he gave was that Haden Clarke had contracted a contagious disease and that it was preying heavily on his mind.'

While Hudson's last answer—that Haden had been playing with the gun—raised the possibility of an accidental death, it was the curious reference to Haden's contagious disease that would linger in the jurors' minds. This was the first argument presented to the court to support the suicide defence.

Chapter Thirty-Nine

Carson was a canny lawyer with an enviable reputation he was determined to retain. After assessing the evidence in Bill's case, he had realised there was only one way to obtain an acquittal. 'I am afraid we have got to make you a scarlet woman,' he had told Chubbie. 'Can you take it?'

Could she expose her private life to a salacious and judgemental public? It was a horrifying thought. She had spent the last five years doing everything possible to hide it. She had little choice, though, under the circumstances. She told him she would do anything she could—everything she could—to keep Bill from the electric chair.

As the trial date loomed, he told her his plan. While *he* couldn't talk to the press about the case, she could—and Bill as well. If they could nudge the pendulum of public opinion in Bill's favour, it might mean the difference between life and death. That being the case, he had organised for the International News Service to interview them and for their signed statements to be published immediately after the trial's commencement.

The jurors wouldn't read them, of course. In such an important trial, they would be sequestered. However, the public would pore over them, the public who would stream into the courtroom each day to hear the witnesses' testimonies. And the public's mood would soon be felt by everyone in the courtroom, including the jurors.

'Slim, white-faced Mrs Keith Miller looked little like the "chubby" of Captain Lancaster's lovesick diary,' observed a reporter when he spotted her in the courthouse on the trial's second day. The pressman assumed she was white-faced because of the ordeal she was about to endure. In fact, it had already begun.

Chubbie's International News Service statement was to be printed on the front page of the *Miami Daily News* that day. She had begun the statement by saying that she was just a witness in the trial, however, 'I shall, in a sense, be a defendant because necessarily the irregularities of my private life must be exposed to the public gaze.' She added that, knowing Bill as well as she did, she was certain he was innocent and shouldn't have been accused or indicted; however, since he had no choice but to face a jury, she must help establish his innocence even if it was at the expense of her own reputation.

It had been mortifying to reveal to the journalist the details of her alcohol consumption and love life. The thought of repeating this information in open court was terrifying. Yet she had to do so. She owed it to Bill. But when this nightmare was over, she would rethink her future. She fervently told the public, 'My drinking days are over.'

When Chubbie walked towards the witness stand, clad in mourning black, a frisson of excitement filled the courtroom. Men and women rose from their seats to stare and point and gossip, forcing the bailiffs to call the court to order.

Hawthorne informed the court that she would be testifying as a court witness rather than a state witness. 'I have reason to believe and do believe,' he told the judge, 'that she will, as far as possible, testify on behalf of the defendant and that she will attempt to give testimony prejudicial to the state's interest.'

A clever statement from a clever prosecutor, he was hoping to undermine the value of anything she said that was at odds with the prosecution's stated position.

Hawthorne began by asking her about the four months in Miami that had preceded Haden's death. The spectators leaned forward in their seats, eager to hear every word from the softly spoken aviator. He then enquired, 'Were you engaged to be married to Captain Lancaster?'

'You can't be engaged to a person who is married,' she replied spiritedly. She admitted, though, that she had long intended to marry him and still had the same intention when he left Miami on 6 March—until she and Haden had fallen in love and had sent him the letters telling him so.

Hawthorne drew from her that neither Haden nor Bill were divorced yet both were engaged to her at the same time. It made her seem like a hussy. Worse, it undermined her credibility even further. Who would trust the word of such a woman?

He then asked, 'Did you write with the same affectionate terms to Lancaster after the affair with Haden Clarke as you did in the past?'

She looked shamefaced when she admitted that she had. To her embarrassment, Hawthorne's team would later read many of her letters to the court.

Hawthorne asked about their flying experiences together, making it clear that they had been partners in life and love for many years. He then enquired, 'And haven't you insisted since Haden Clarke's death that Bill couldn't have killed him?'

'I just know Bill couldn't do it.'

'And when you learnt that the authorities had detained him, didn't you tell me that if Lancaster was put in jail you would make a statement to the press and state that you killed Haden.'

'It sounds dramatic,' she said, lowering her head, 'but yes, I did say it.'

'Was that statement made for the purpose of helping Lancaster out of his difficulties?'

'Yes.'

It was clear why Hawthorne had called her as a court's witness, why he had indicated to the court that she might say anything to get Lancaster off.

Returning to the subject of her love for Haden, Hawthorne asked, 'Did you anticipate trouble when Lancaster received the letters?'

'No, I did not anticipate trouble. I knew that he would be upset.'

'What was his attitude when he arrived in Miami: pleased or displeased?'

'He was tired, ill and sad.'

When Hawthorne questioned her about the events of that evening, tears flooded her eyes as she described saying goodnight to the two men. Her voice shook so badly she appeared on the verge of a breakdown.

Hawthorne then asked what had happened when Bill knocked at her locked door.

'He said, "Come at once. Haden has shot himself." I said, "Don't be ridiculous, there isn't a pistol in the house." He said, "Yes there is. I brought one back with me."' She added that she went straight to the sleeping porch where she found her blood-covered fiancé moving his head from side to side and groaning.

The judge enquired if Haden's blood was fresh when she arrived at his bedside. She said that she couldn't remember.

Hawthorne questioned her about the notes and she told him that Bill had handed them to her and she had read them. Afterwards he had asked her to destroy them because there might be a scandal.

'What did you answer?'

'I said that I couldn't destroy them.'

Suddenly, Hawthorne thundered, 'Mrs Keith Miller, do you know who killed Haden Clarke?'

Pale and teary, she whispered, 'I am convinced in my own mind that Haden killed himself.'

'You stated, Mrs Keith Miller, that when Lancaster said that Haden had shot himself, you were surprised?'

'I was shocked.'

'Well, you might be shocked and not surprised. Were you surprised to hear that Haden was a suicide?'

'Yes, it surprised me. Yes.'

'When you came to my office, did you attempt to tell me your theory of why Haden committed suicide?'

'I believe I tried to tell you a number of theories.'

'Did you look on Haden as one who, if disappointed in life, might take his life?'

'Yes. He talked about suicide quite a bit.'

'In the presence of others?'

'Yes.' She added that he'd said that the surest way to commit suicide was to shoot oneself through the head just above and behind the right ear.

'Was Haden depressed when you told him good night on the night of the tragedy?'

'Yes. He told me that everything was much worse than he thought.'

'Was there any indication later that Haden and Bill were friendly?'

'Yes, I heard them laughing.'

'Please refresh your memory, Mrs Keith Miller,' Hawthorne remonstrated. 'Didn't you say in my office that you were uneasy until you heard laughter?'

'I had no fear of violence but it was most certainly a relief to know that they were getting along all right.'

Hawthorne told the court that he was introducing into evidence a slip of paper Chubbie had given him in May, offering reasons as to why Haden might have had suicidal intentions. He then read out Chubbie's words:

1. Remorse;
2. Doubt of Mrs Keith Miller and fear that the past five years with Lancaster would prove too strong a bond and that she might return to Lancaster;
3. Financial worry;
4. Doubt of his ability to write the book of Mrs Keith Miller's life as an aviator and to make money with his writings;
5. Intense sexual life suddenly discontinued, but the desire stronger than ever;
6. That Clarke was very young and that Mrs Keith Miller placed too much responsibility on him;
7. His physical condition; and
8. That he was temperamental and emotional and went from heights of joy to depths of despair.

When Hawthorne advised the judge a short time later that he had finished with the witness, some brows furrowed in surprise. A prosecutor intent upon convincing the jury that the victim had been murdered had left the jurors pondering eight reasons why the victim might have committed suicide.

Like any skilled trial attorney, Carson was adaptable. He made the most of Hawthorne's error of judgement. To reinforce the argument for suicide, he asked Chubbie to explain her eight reasons. She provided obvious explanations for the first four. She couldn't bring herself to elaborate on point five, the cessation of Haden's intense sexual life, which was the result of point seven, his physical condition. It was too personal, too intrusive.

Carson decided to introduce the subject indirectly by asking her to tell the jury about the beginning of their love affair. She mentioned Bill's departure, which left them alone together, then spoke hesitantly about the morning she found Haden asleep at the foot of her bed and the night they became lovers. Her voice broke and she kept pausing, trying to regain emotional control, as Carson's probing questions forced her to disclose intimate details. Among them was that their passion had increased until Haden's enforced celibacy two weeks before Bill's return.

Carson asked about their marriage plans and Haden's need to obtain a divorce. She said that he had written to his wife and asked for one.

'What happened next?'

'One night she telephoned from California. She said that she had been divorced last November and had remarried and that he could get married the next day if he wanted to.'

'Did you?'

'No. I wanted to see that the divorce papers were in order.'

'When was that?'

'The Saturday before April 20.'

Carson put into evidence a telegram sent by Haden's wife a few days later stating that it would be illegal for him to marry until she had obtained her final decree (Californian divorces had a one-year interlocutory period) and that the story of her romance and remarriage was imaginary. The telegram reached Miami on the morning of Tuesday, 19 April.

'What effect did the receipt of this telegram have on Clarke? Did it elevate or depress his spirits?'

'He flew into a violent rage and called her all kinds of names. He said, "Where am I going to get $100 to start divorce proceedings in Miami?"'

306

'But he tried to object when Bill wanted to postpone the wedding a month?'

Chubbie agreed that he had.

Carson was satisfied with the day's proceedings. Through Chubbie's testimony, he had expounded upon most of the reasons why Haden might have committed suicide, although he had ignored the 'malady' for the moment, a touchy subject best raised when it made a powerful point. He had also revealed a ninth reason why Haden might have committed suicide: his marital status. Unless Haden could finance a Miami divorce, he wouldn't be free until January 1933, allowing Chubbie nine months to change her mind—or Bill to change it for her.

He had finished the day by alerting the jurors to the date Haden received the telegram that wrecked his marriage plans: Tuesday, 19 April, the day before Bill returned to Miami. Hopefully, he had left the men wondering if its receipt might have acted as a switch that triggered a suicidal descent.

Chapter Forty

Dressed in a pale blue dress and small Panama hat, Chubbie seated herself in the witness stand the next day and gave Bill a tremulous smile. During her previous session, Hawthorne had thundered at her, trying to trick her into saying what he wanted to hear, but Carson's prying questions had been the more difficult to answer. For Bill's sake, she'd had to answer every intrusive question—an excruciating experience, worse than she had imagined. And it was about to begin again.

Carson returned to the subject of the divorce telegram, asking if she knew what had become of this critical piece of evidence because it wasn't among the items passed to him by the prosecution. She said that after Haden showed it to her she had left it on the living room table.

'When was the next time you saw it?'

'When Captain Lancaster and I were released from custody, I returned home and found it screwed up in a ball on the floor.'

'Who had been in charge of the house?'

'The police.'

Carson also drew from her that the carbon copy of only one of Haden's two explanatory letters to Bill was among the prosecution's bundle of evidence and that she had no idea what had happened to the other. He didn't elaborate on what this revealed in terms of the state's investigation. The jurors could reach their own conclusion.

Hawthorne continued his case-in-chief by having his assistant, Henry Jones, call Dr Carlton Deederer to the witness stand. The prosecution had heard Chubbie's revelation that Haden thought the most reliable suicide method was to shoot oneself through the head just above and behind the right ear. Jones asked Deederer to describe the location of the entrance wound in Clarke's head.

'The bullet entered halfway between the right eye and the hole in the right ear and nearly three inches away from the hole in the ear.'

Deederer had previously told the press that Clarke might have been beaten before he was shot. Yet the prosecution didn't question him about this claim, nor did the defence under cross-examination. Deederer had been present at the autopsy. Perhaps he had been forced to reassess his conclusions in the light of the evidence from Haden's remains.

Hawthorne introduced into evidence the statement Bill made on 2 May in which he admitted to forging the suicide notes. It was the most damaging piece of evidence the prosecution had presented so far and it was in Bill's own words.

The damning evidence continued when Hawthorne called Latin American Airways president, J.F. Russell, the man responsible for alerting Bill to Chubbie's transfer of affections. After questioning him about the airline's activities, Hawthorne enquired about his knowledge of Bill's relationship with Chubbie. Russell told the court about the night he showed Bill the letters from his wife.

'What did Lancaster do then?'

'He said, "Do you think I have been double-crossed? What do you think?" I said, "You can see for yourself." Russell then informed the jurors that Bill had paced the floor and bit his lip and said, "I'll get rid of him." Russell added, 'He must not have realised that I was there, for he checked himself and turned to me and said, "That sure is good of you, old man, to tell me this."

'Did Lancaster head for Miami shortly after this?'

'Very shortly, at ten or eleven o'clock the following day.'

Carson's cross-examination had barely commenced before the court adjourned for the day. The next morning, he asked Russell, 'Who was the man who stood by your side while you testified yesterday?' The man in question had been dressed in the distinctive uniform of a deputy United States marshal.

'I have no way of knowing,' Russell responded disingenuously.

The spectators laughed. The bailiffs called the court to order.

'Are you under guard?'

'I don't know,' he said, as if the marshal's role was open to doubt.

Again the spectators laughed.

'You said yesterday that your permanent address was someplace in Miami Beach. Where is your temporary address?'

'I have none.'

'Where did you come from when you came into this courtroom?'

'Twenty-one South.'

'Is that the jail section of this building?'

'So called.'

'Are you serving a sentence?'

'I'm supposed to be. I expect to be released soon.'

Bursts of laughter had continued to erupt from the spectators as they wondered how long the state's witness could slither away from admitting what was now obvious to all: that he was a convicted criminal imprisoned in the county gaol. His Latin American Airways roguery had caught up with him and he was serving a six-month federal sentence for conspiracy to smuggle aliens into the country.

'Did you ever serve any time in Leavenworth penitentiary?'

'Yes.'

'What were you sent there for?'

'Nothing.'

'Yes, I understand that,' said Carson dryly, to the spectators' amusement, 'but what was the charge?'

'For shipping a carload of hay from El Paso, Texas.'

'There were a few Syrians concealed in the hay, weren't there?'

'I didn't put them there,' was the coy response.

More chortling from the spectators forced the bailiffs to call for order.

Carson then asked pointedly, 'Did Lancaster know that you were in Leavenworth?'

'No, I don't believe he did,' Russell admitted.

Carson questioned him about the trip to Los Angeles, enquiring if he had any ill feelings towards Lancaster for abandoning him there after the federal authorities questioned him.

'I hold no feeling against Captain Lancaster.'

Carson then asked slyly, 'Do you know the man standing behind you?'

'I saw him this morning,' was the evasive response. As Russell slithered away from further questions about the deputy marshal guarding him, and as the spectators guffawed as if they were watching a real-life Laurel and Hardy routine, Carson delighted in the knowledge that this key witness for the prosecution had managed to destroy his own credibility.

Calling jailbird witnesses was always a roll of the dice, but Hawthorne hadn't expected this one to turn himself into a laughing stock. Who would remember the critical 'get rid of' evidence when it was trumped by the image of Russell blithely driving a hay-load of Syrians?

He held off calling his second jailbird witness. Instead, he had his team read out Bill's diary entries from January to April 1932, explaining that these provided the context for Russell's testimony.

In the *Miami Herald*'s report, the journalist remarked: 'The first word in the amazing diary kept faithfully day by day by Captain William Newton Lancaster was "Chubbie" and, throughout the scribbled volume, a deep, passionate devotion is etched in unmistakable terms for the woman flyer. Business matters, desperate struggles for funds to meet his and Chubbie's needs, inconsequential data—all are in the volume and, running like a golden thread in a sombre tapestry, are the words which reiterate his love.'

To Hawthorne though, Bill's words contained more than evidence of his love and devotion. The ecstasy when he heard from her, the despair when he didn't, suggested an obsessive love that grew desperate after Russell's revelations of her unfaithfulness. To read the April entries was like hearing the thoughts of a tortured soul as he descended into hell.

Hawthorne read out the surviving correspondence between the trio, including Haden's letter to Bill explaining his love for Chubbie and urging him not to lose his head and respond violently. Hawthorne followed this with Bill's telegram of 18 April, in which he insisted on being their best man and best friend.

When the court adjourned for the night, the jurors were left pondering the fact that, the day after Bill sent the friendly telegram, he had purchased the gun that had killed his rival only hours after his return.

Chapter Forty-One

As Latin American Airways partner Mark Tancrel walked to the witness stand on Saturday morning, Hawthorne's team hoped he wouldn't prove as slippery as his jailbird mate. No one wanted a repeat of the Russell debacle.

Tancrel was more forthcoming than his confederate, admitting from the start that he was in gaol under indictment for impersonating a United States naval officer. He testified that Bill had asked him if he'd seen Russell's letters mentioning Chubbie and Haden's relationship. He told the court that Bill had then said, 'I'll go back and get rid of that son of a bitch.'

'Who was he talking about?' Hawthorne asked, unaware that Bill was scribbling a note to his attorney, a note that Carson read with great interest.

'He was talking about Clarke.'

'Did Lancaster say how he intended to dispose of Clarke?'

'No, he just said that he was going to get rid of that son of a bitch.'

Hawthorne asked if Bill had ever mentioned his relationship with Haden.

'Yes. In El Paso we were in the same hotel room together.'

'What was the date of that conversation?'

'I believe it was March 19,' Tancrel said, which was only thirteen days after Bill left Miami. Tancrel declared that Bill was talking to a man named Joe Ince when he said something about not getting any letters from Chubbie and that he was concerned about her relationship with Haden. He told the court that Bill then said, 'I don't think Haden Clarke has double-crossed me but if he has, well, I've seen a lot of dead men and one more won't make any difference.'

'Do you know J.P. Moe?' Carson asked Tancrel under cross-examination.

'I don't know.'

'Don't you know that he is the deputy United States marshal who met you at the train?'

'I've seen him before,' Tancrel admitted.

'You know that he is the same man who brought Russell into the courtroom yesterday to testify?'

'I don't know if Russell was brought in to testify.'

Carson put aside the subject of Deputy Marshal Moe for the time being—the man himself would be questioned when the defence presented its case—and asked pointedly,

'How close is your cell to Russell's?'

'They put him in the same cell with me yesterday.'

A burst of laughter erupted from the spectators. It was happening again. Tancrel had initially seemed more open about his ignoble circumstances but the same shiftiness was now revealing itself. Did he really expect them to believe that he didn't know Russell had testified when they were sharing the same cell?

Having heard from Bill that Tancrel was a chronic liar, Carson asked him if he had told Bill that he'd been a captain in the United

States Navy—'No'—and had pulled out his paper hangers' union card to show Bill that he was a member—'No'—and had said that he'd hung thousands of square miles of wallpaper . . .

'Yes, I have,' Tancrel admitted defiantly. 'In my home I have hung thousands of miles of wallpaper.'

'Then you are a paperhanger?'

'No. I'm not a member of the paperhangers' union.'

'Yet you've hung thousands of miles of wallpaper?'

'Oh, not that many. No paperhanger in his lifetime could hang that much wallpaper. I've papered my own house many times.'

As Hawthorne listened to the spectators' chortles and realised that his second jailbird's testimony had also turned into a farce, Justice Atkinson halted the line of questioning as irrelevant.

With relief, Hawthorne called a more reliable witness, J.O. Barker, the man in charge of the police identification bureau. He asked if he had examined the gun for fingerprints.

Barker said that all he had found were some smudged fingerprints on the end of the barrel. He added that fingerprints would normally be found on the trigger and handle but that they would be absent if gloves were worn or if the fingerprints were exposed to water or gasoline.

While Barker didn't specifically state it, and Hawthorne didn't ask him to specifically state it, this fingerprint expert appeared to be suggesting that either the killer wore gloves or had wiped off the gun.

Under cross-examination, Carson asked if there was any blood on the gun when it was passed to him. Barker responded that there wasn't.

'Could blood have been wiped off without wiping fingerprints off the gun?'

'No.'

'Would you expect to find any fingerprints if the pistol had been wiped off?'

'Depends on what parts of the gun had been touched during the wiping process.'

Carson's questions also suggested that he too thought that the gun had been wiped off. But while a killer could—and likely would—wipe off fingerprints, a suicide, for obvious reasons, would not. Carson returned to his seat knowing that his line of questioning would leave the more thoughtful spectators wondering where he was heading. A future witness would provide the necessary clarification.

Hawthorne continued to focus on the forensic evidence when he called embalmer K.B. Bess to the stand and asked if he had observed powder burns on Clarke's head. Bess said that he hadn't seen any and that he had specifically looked for them because it was his funeral home's practice to carefully examine the wounds in gunshot deaths in case the staff were called to testify in court.

Hawthorne asked if he knew of any suicide cases from gunshot wounds in which there were no trace of powder burns.

'On the suicide cases reported to us, if it is a gunshot case, there are usually powder burns showing.'

'Do you recall ever seeing one where this was not true?'

'None that I can remember.'

Just before the Saturday session ended, Hawthorne recalled Officer Hudson and asked if there was blood on the gun when he found it on Clarke's bed. Hudson said that there was. Hawthorne asked what he had done with the gun.

'I placed a handkerchief over it and picked it up, placing it still wrapped into the pistol box, which I found on the table at the foot of Clarke's bed. Later I gave it to Barker, fingerprint man at police headquarters.'

Under cross-examination, Carson queried, 'You didn't put that gun in your pocket?'

'Yes, after placing it in the box.'

'Then you shoved the box in your pocket?'

'Yes.'

Carson returned to his seat knowing that, when court reconvened the following week, he would delight in revealing the truth.

Chapter Forty-Two

Despite the detailed trial reports published in the local newspapers, many south Floridians still wanted to hear the testimonies for themselves. The news that Chubbie would again be called to testify on Monday, 8 August, spurred hundreds towards the courthouse. They began congregating on the sixth floor at 6 am, leaving those who arrived a couple of hours later looking at the crowds in dismay. Many were left outside clamouring to get in after the courtroom doors closed.

Bill had been writing copious notes throughout the trial; however, as Chubbie walked to the witness stand, he stopped writing and gazed at her. He continued watching her, his pen still, as she began to testify.

Hawthorne again questioned her about the night of Clarke's death. His voice was hard and threatening, a deliberate ploy to put her under so much strain she might trip up and reveal something that implicated Bill. He then focused on the two notes, asking, 'What was your belief when you were shown the alleged suicide notes?'

'I had no belief.'

'Didn't you tell me in my office that you were positive that Bill didn't write them?'

'I don't remember saying that.'

'Didn't you assert that Lancaster's code of honour wouldn't have permitted him to write such notes?'

'Yes, I believe so.'

It was the first breach in the armour of her stated conviction that Bill couldn't commit such a crime. It revealed that she might not know her lover as well as she thought.

Hawthorne drew from her that she discovered the notes were forgeries when she asked Bill about them after their release from gaol. The prosecutor then enquired, 'If you had asked him if he had killed Haden Clarke and had received the answer yes, would that have surprised you more than the admission of the forgery?'

'Most decidedly.'

'Although you had stated to me previously that you were as positive Lancaster had not written the notes as you were that he had not killed Haden Clarke . . .'

Not a sound disturbed the courtroom as he waited for her response. She remained silent.

Hawthorne's voice increased to a thunder as he demanded, 'Do you still love Haden Clarke?'

'No,' she said, beginning to weep.

'Do you love Captain Lancaster?'

Tears poured down her face as she admitted, 'No.'

'When did your affection die for Captain Lancaster?'

'About two years ago.'

The spectators glanced at Bill and saw that he continued to watch her. She kept her own gaze averted.

'Did it die a natural death?'

'Yes. I am still intensely fond of him.'

'Then did you deliberately betray him in every letter, telegram and telephone message to him? Weren't you a traitor to him during all that time when he was sending every dollar he could beg, borrow or steal?'

'You don't understand the feeling which exists between Captain Lancaster and myself,' she protested, as tears continued to fall. 'We have been through hardships and misfortunes. What was mine was Bill's and what was Bill's was mine. We were pals, not ordinary friends. We trusted each other.'

'You no longer have love for the memory of Haden Clarke?'

'No.'

'Why?'

'I have been completely disillusioned.'

'By what?'

'Proofs.'

'Are you referring to his illness?'

'Yes, and other things.'

'Did he lie about his love for you?'

'No, I don't think so.'

'What then?'

'He lied to me about his age, his university degree. He told me that he had never had that malady before. He lied about things he had done.'

'The principal thing that killed your love for Haden Clarke was because he was a liar?'

'Yes.'

Hawthorne had her hooked and he went in for the kill. 'You said that you admire Captain Lancaster because he is honest and courageous.'

'Yes.'

'Did you know that Captain Lancaster went into court and was sentenced for a crime he did not commit to save you?'

It was a humiliating reference to her drunken automobile accident, when Bill had lied to protect her. She had no choice but to say yes. 'He always tried to save me, to help me.'

'At all costs?'

'Yes.'

'And you would protect and defend him?'

'Yes.'

'Didn't you make the statement that you would die for him?'

'Yes.'

'Would you lie for him now?'

'No,' she hurled back, 'because you would know that I was lying to you.'

The spectators burst out laughing. The judge rapped his gavel for order.

'Then one of the principal things you admire in Lancaster is his code of honour?'

'Yes. He is one of the finest men I ever knew.'

'He'd steal for you, wouldn't he? He stole chickens, in fact, didn't he?'

As Chubbie admitted with a laugh that he had, the comical juxta-position of fine man and chook-thief elicited another chuckle from the spectators.

'Did he steal rabbits?'

'Yes.'

'Did he steal ducks?'

'No . . . Yes, we did.'

The spectators laughed so loudly the bailiffs had to join the judge in calling for order.

Hawthorne changed the subject, turning to a more serious question. 'Did Haden Clarke fear trouble with Lancaster on the latter's return from the west?'

'No, he wasn't afraid of him.'

Hawthorne then asked if Clarke knew that Lancaster was a polo player and bronco buster and boxing champion. After these allusions to Bill's physical strength, he enquired again if Clarke was afraid of Lancaster. After Chubbie repeated that he wasn't, Hawthorne threw in a few more questions about her feelings for the two men but the spectators were laughing too readily by this time for him to make any serious impact. He surrendered her to Carson for cross-examination.

'Do you think more or less of a man who has violated his word of honour to you?' Carson asked.

'Less.'

It was time to introduce the subject of Haden's venereal disease. Carson did so indirectly, by asking for the names of the doctors she herself had seen. He then enquired bluntly, 'Do you have the malady?'

'No,' was her mortified response.

The point was made. Her honour, of sorts, was maintained.

Released from the stand soon afterwards, she stumbled from the courtroom sobbing hysterically, 'They're crucifying me, crucifying me!'

She had exposed herself in the most humiliating way to save Bill. She wouldn't know until the end of the trial whether it was worth it.

Carson recalled Police Officer Hudson and asked about the scrunched-up telegram from Clarke's wife found on the floor of Mrs Miller's house. Hudson claimed that he had passed it to the investigators on the morning of Clarke's death.

It wasn't hard to see where Carson was heading. Either Hudson was lying or one of the state's investigators had crumpled the telegram and tossed it aside. Whatever the situation, it was evidence of incompetence on the part of a state employee, an incompetence that was especially alarming when a man's life was at stake.

What was also clear was that Carson was whittling away at a case that had initially seemed cut-and-dried. So when Carson recalled a second state witness, Attorney Huston, everyone listened closely.

Carson drew Huston's attention to the time when he and the two aviators and Officer Hudson went to the sleeping porch. He then asked, 'When Officer Hudson took the pistol from the bed, after covering it with his handkerchief, what did he do with it?'

'Slipped it into his hip pocket.'

'He did not place it in a box?'

'He did not.'

'Was there blood on the gun?'

'It was running with blood.'

As Carson heard the spectators' murmurs of comprehension, he was reassured that they had put the pieces together. Police Officer Hudson had picked up the blood-soaked gun, wrapped it in his handkerchief, and stuffed it into his pocket—not into the gun box as he had claimed. When he later handed it to the ballistics expert, it was wiped clean of blood and fingerprints. Lancaster hadn't wiped off the fingerprints to hide his culpability, as the prosecution had intimated. It was the policeman himself who had destroyed this vital piece of evidence.

Hawthorne attempted to shake Huston's testimony, knowing that it had seriously undermined the state's case.

Huston didn't budge.

Chapter Forty-Three

Perception is everything.

Carson knew that in cases dominated by circumstantial evidence, a defendant's appearance and reputation could sway the jury. Jurors, being human, tend to favour those they like. Bill was an especially likeable fellow so Carson called him as his first witness for the defence.

He spent the next few hours introducing Bill to the court, tracing his air force career during the Great War and presenting a character reference from a commanding officer. He then tracked Bill's rise to international fame in the years that followed. Recognising that he would also have to confront issues that might argue Bill's lack of integrity, he mentioned his English wife and children in his questions about the Australian flight. Bill said that he and Chubbie had split their earnings three ways, sending one third to his wife—about $4000 or $5000—and dividing the remainder between themselves. He also told the court that he had been only twenty years of age when he had married Kiki, a widow with private means.

When Carson asked Bill to identify Kiki's religion, his response—
'Roman Catholic'—spoke volumes to an audience aware of the religion's
inflexible attitudes to divorce.

When the judge adjourned court for the day, the jurors had been
shown an honourable man, a war hero no less, a person unlikely to
commit such a heinous and cowardly deed as the cold-blooded murder
of a defenceless man.

Haden Clarke wasn't mentioned until the following morning when
Carson questioned Bill about their relationship. He asked him to read
entries from his diary showing that Haden was a drinker and also
elicited from him that Haden had a temper. He then raised the question
of Haden's integrity by asking Bill if he had told Haden the truth about
his relationship with Chubbie.

'I did on the last day before I left. I had a confessional talk with him
on the sun porch and told him things I haven't told him before.'

'What else was said?'

'I told him of Mrs Keith Miller's weaknesses as far as liquor was
concerned and asked him to keep on the water wagon and assist her
while I was away.'

'Were any promises made?'

'He promised to take care of her for me. He said, "Bill, I will take
care of her in such a way as to make you remember my friendship
forever."'

As the hours passed, Carson interrupted Bill's testimony to call
five character witnesses. Keith Bon, who had been Chubbie's host in
Singapore in 1928, said that he had travelled from France to testify
for his friend. He was joined by Captain Frank Upton, holder of
the Congressional Medal of Honor, Rex Gilmartin, commander of the
Aviation Post of the American Legion, Lieutenant A. Irving 'Bing'

Boyer, a former lieutenant in the Royal Flying Corps, and Clyde Pangborn, around-the-world flier. All attested to Bill's high reputation both in the American aviation industry and internationally. They also indicated that he was a calm-tempered, generous and honourable man.

Carson turned his attention again to Bill's character when he questioned him at length about Latin American Airways. He showed the court that Bill had abandoned the operation soon after receiving confirmation of his partners' lawless intentions. Carson then raised the subject of Russell's revelations about Chubbie's new relationship and asked, 'What did you say to Russell?'

'I wrote down what I said to him. It was: "I don't believe the statements. I know Chubbie and I trust her."'

Bill described his return trip to Nogales and his brief conversation with Tancrel during which he officially cut his ties with the airline. He told the court that he hadn't in fact said anything to Tancrel about Chubbie or Haden or their relationship at that time.

Carson asked about the letters he received from them in St Louis and how he had reacted. Bill said that he had shown them to Gentry and had then drunk a bottle of Scotch. 'I was very blue and behaved like a schoolboy.' By Saturday he was feeling a bit better. He discussed the situation with Gentry and his father and they all decided that he should fly to Miami to talk to Chubbie.

'You said you took steps the following Monday to purchase the pistol which was to replace the one loaned you by Huston?'

'Yes. It was a dishonest act, I admit, to pawn the pistol and then not redeem it. Huston had said that if the western venture wasn't a go he would try and help me when I came back. I wanted to replace the pistol and keep in his good graces.' He explained that Gentry's father had lent him $100 to assist him on the Miami trip, so he had used some of the money to purchase a replacement gun and box of cartridges. He set off from St Louis on Tuesday, 19 April, and spent the night in Nashville, Tennessee, where he loaded the pistol.

'Why did you load it in the hotel room?'

'I know of no reason except that the pistol Huston loaned me was loaded.' He would later add that he frequently carried firearms on his flights and that they were usually loaded. Unspoken was the obvious: that an unloaded gun was of little use in the event of trouble.

'Captain Lancaster, did you kill Haden Clarke?' thundered Carson.

The dramatic question broke through the early morning rustles as the spectators—hundreds of women again—settled to hear the day's testimonies. Everyone froze, their eyes on the defendant, as they waited for his answer.

In a clear, steady voice Bill said, 'I did not.' And so began his third day on the witness stand.

Carson had decided to begin the session by disposing of the claims made by one of the jailbird witnesses. Bill had sent him a note during Tancrel's testimony which provided proof that Tancrel was lying. 'Captain Lancaster,' Carson asked, 'did you ever tell Tancrel, when referring to Haden Clarke, that you would get rid of that "son of a bitch"?'

'Mr Carson, I have never ever referred to anyone as a "son of a bitch". In England, that word doesn't mean anything. The testimony of both Tancrel and Russell was a tissue of lies.'

'Well, what expression do you use as your swearword?'

'Do you want me to say it?' Bill enquired hesitantly.

'Yes.'

'Bastard.'

Carson resumed his questions about the evening of 20 April, asking if there had been any discussion about Haden's malady. Bill said that Haden had mentioned the problem after they retired to the sleeping porch, saying that he was suffering pain and that Bill wasn't to be alarmed and to think he was visiting Chubbie if he heard him walking around. He was often up five or six times a night.

Bill then hesitated and said to Carson, 'I didn't tell all of this conversation to Mr Hawthorne or Mr Jones when I was first arrested. I wanted to protect Haden's name and to keep his mother from knowing about the malady. I didn't think all this would come out. I do not want to tell of that conversation now and I will not unless it is absolutely necessary.'

'Captain Lancaster, the responsibility of this line of questioning rests with me,' Carson responded firmly and urged Bill to continue.

With obvious reluctance, Bill said, 'Haden told me that he had had the disease for some time and was getting relapses. He was almost in tears when he told me.'

'While you and Haden were talking that night, did Haden tell you of his intimate relations with Mrs Keith Miller?'

'Yes. The last talk I had with Haden, he was straight with me and told me many things.'

'Did he say anything about the permanence of his love for Mrs Keith Miller?'

'Yes. He was very frank. He said, "I have had many affairs in my life, but this time I am absolutely in love. I shall do everything in my power to make her happy. Now I have something to work for." ' Bill added that Haden's evident sincerity had impressed him.

'Did he discuss his age?'

'Yes. He told me that he wasn't thirty-one as he had previously said. He said he was twenty-six or twenty-seven. He asked me if I thought it would make any difference with Chubbie. I told him, "You must tell her." '

'Was there any discussion about his other false claims?'

'Only about the book. He said he didn't know whether he would be able to put the book over. I remember the phrase he used. He said he didn't know if he could make the grade. He said that he had slightly exaggerated his qualifications before and wanted to put it straight.'

'Did he talk about his finances?'

Bill said that Haden had talked at length about his financial difficulties, remarking that everyone had turned to writing because of the depression, making it even harder to make money.

Hawthorne asked about the outcome of the conversation.

'I told him that he must talk to Chubbie the next morning, that he must tell her what he had told me tonight, and that if she loved him she would overlook his mis-statement.' He added that Haden had been so frank and honest, and had appeared so very sorry, that he had started talking about his trip so as to ease the tension and Haden's distress. He mentioned that Haden had laughed when he'd said, 'Can you imagine a captain in the United States Navy bringing a paper-hanger's card out of his pocket and saying that he had laid thousands of miles of wallpaper?'

Carson continued his interrogation, eliciting from Bill that he'd had a bad trip from St Louis and was dog-tired and in desperate need of sleep. As he lay in bed yawning, he said to Haden that they should talk it over with Chubbie in the morning. 'I can remember his last words,' he told the court. 'He said, "Bill, you're the whitest man I ever met."'

'What happened next?'

'I was awakened by a noise, a bang. When I first came to, I think I had the impression that it was a window bang. I called out, "What's that, Haden?"'

'What did you then hear?'

'A sort of a gurgling was coming from Haden's bed. I switched on the light at the foot of my bed. Haden was lying on his bed. As soon as I looked at him I saw something bad had happened. There was blood running over his face.' Bill placed his hand under his right jaw to show the location.

'Did you see the pistol?'

'Not right away. I jumped from my bed and ran to his. I shook him by the shoulder. I said, "What have you done?" Haden didn't reply. Then I saw the pistol.'

Carson asked if the pistol was in Haden's hand.

'No. It was on the bed by his right hip.' Tears came to Bill's eyes and his voice shook as he described the position of Haden's arm and hand.

'When and where did you last see the pistol before you saw it by Haden's hip?'

'On the table between our beds. I had unpacked it from the cardboard box.' Bill explained that, after he mentioned he had an appointment with Huston the following morning, Haden had asked what he had done about Huston's gun. Bill told the court, 'I got the gun out of the box and showed it to him. He took it in his hand and I cautioned him that it was loaded. I can't remember if he put it in the box or if I did.'

'What did you do when you first saw the blood?'

'First, I caught him by the shoulder and I believe I said, "For Christ's sake, what have you done?" I looked in the hall through the door. There was no light there. I went back and asked him to speak to me. He was just moaning and moving his head from side to side. He was moving his legs a little. I looked around and I could see no notes nor anything to indicate what had happened.'

'When did you make the notes?'

'After trying to get him to speak to me the second time, I sat down on a chair at the typewriter. I don't know how long it took me, probably five minutes. I then took a pencil and the notes and went over to the bed and asked him to speak to me again. I asked him to sign the notes. He was just moaning and didn't speak. I shouted out, "Chubbie" and got no reply. Then I did something I shouldn't have done. I scribbled Haden on one of them and H on the other and put them on the table.'

'What did you do next?'

'I rushed through the hall and banged on Chubbie's door. There was a slight delay and the door opened. The room was in darkness. She asked me what was the matter and I told her that Haden had shot himself. I think she said, "Don't talk nonsense. There's no gun." I told her, "Yes there is. I brought one back for Huston." She ran into the sun parlour and took Haden's head on her lap. I went downstairs to telephone the doctor.'

'Then what happened?'

'I returned upstairs and found Chubbie holding Haden's head up. She asked me if I had phoned for the doctor. I told her I had and suggested that she call Haden's doctor, which she went downstairs to do. She came back upstairs and had a wash cloth which she wet and wiped the blood off his head.'

'Who arrived first?'

'The ambulance or Huston arrived about the same time. I met somebody at the door and took them upstairs.'

'Was there any discussion with the ambulance men?'

'Yes, we discussed if Haden's feet should be raised as they were striking the rails of the bed.'

'Did you do it?'

'I got the pillow from my bed and started to do it, but one man said, "Don't do that. The blood will run to his head."'

'What did you do with the pillow then?'

'I put it back on my bed.'

There were a few 'hmms' from spectators as they realised they had just heard the explanation for the unruffled pillow.

Bill also confirmed that he had asked if Haden was likely to speak again, because he wanted to know why he had shot himself. And he too had seen Officer Hudson put a handkerchief over the bloodied gun and put it into his hip pocket.

There was one final issue Carson thought the jury should hear about: Bill's treatment by the state attorney's office.

Bill told the court that he had chosen not to have Attorney Huston represent him during the days of questioning after Haden's death because he had elicited from Hawthorne that it was the state attorney's duty to protect the innocent as well as convict the guilty. He also said that the state attorney and his men had been fair to him and that he had told them the truth, except about the notes. 'They didn't ask me if I wrote them, and if they had, I probably would have said that I did not.' He added that he had tried to be fair to them as well and had told them about the belongings left in his plane.

'Were any exhibits now in this trial taken from the plane after you told Mr Hawthorne?'

'Yes, my diary.'

Chapter Forty-Four

Listening to the accused testify is always one of the most gripping moments in a criminal trial, first as he (or she) dutifully follows the defence's lead and, later, as he ducks and weaves in his attempts to escape the prosecutor's deadly blows. Spectators—again mostly women—pushed and shoved to get into the courtroom on the afternoon Hawthorne began Bill's cross-examination.

'Captain, the first question you answered this morning was if you killed Haden Clarke and I believe you answered in the negative?'

'Yes.'

'Then who did kill Haden Clarke?'

'Haden Clarke committed suicide.'

Hawthorne picked up the 'suicide notes' and asked if he had written them. Bill admitted that he had.

'Positive?'

'Yes.'

'Are you as positive as you were positive on April 22, when I questioned you, that you had not?'

'You never asked me if they were my work but, if you had, I would have said they were not.' He added that no one else in the state attorney's office had asked him either.

'Were you not told that two local men, experts, had examined the notes and had pronounced them forgeries?'

'I was.'

'Then what did you say?'

'I said, "Why not get more experts?"'

'Why?'

'I was anxious to see somebody and get some advice. I had acted the part of the lie to you in the beginning and I was anxious to put it straight.'

'That is not answering my question. What advice would you be seeking by getting other experts?'

'I wanted to put you off the scent,' Bill admitted.

'To further deceive me?'

'To further deceive you.'

Carson had known that the suicide notes were Bill's ticket to the electric chair. Bill's action in producing them wasn't the only problem; equally important was their effect on the jury's perception of him as a person. His deceitfulness, not only in producing the notes but in lying about them, was torpedoing much of the defence's efforts to present him as a man of integrity. While the defence had succeeded in weakening many of the state's other claims, this concrete evidence of Bill's duplicity—if not his criminality—would not go away. As Carson hid a grimace of frustration, the prosecution continued its interrogation.

Hawthorne directed Bill's attention to his gun purchase, asking if he had entered the store three times on the morning he bought it. His question suggested that Bill had been suspiciously hesitant about the purchase.

Bill explained that he'd gone to the shop the first day to make enquiries and had returned the second day to get the gun's numbers. After obtaining the necessary permit from the sheriff's office, he had then purchased the gun and cartridges with money Gentry's father had lent him.

Hawthorne questioned him about loading the gun on the night before he reached Miami. Bill repeated his previous response, that Huston had lent him a loaded gun and that he'd wanted to return it in the same condition.

Carson was relieved that Bill was holding his own again. The purchase and loading of the gun were critical to the state's premeditation argument and Bill had provided an innocent and adequate explanation for both. While the suicide notes remained a threatening presence, the jury couldn't convict him based on their existence alone. Unless the prosecution could prove premeditation, the jury couldn't find him guilty of first-degree murder, the only charge the state had laid against him.

The prosecutor, having failed to trap Bill into admitting to the physical evidence of premeditation, turned to the subject of Bill's state of mind at the time of Haden's death. 'When you left Tucson, according to your diary you were "suffering the tortures of the damned".'

'I had a lot on my mind.'

Hawthorne asked if his primary concern was the affair between Haden and Chubbie. Bill said that he was worried about the affair and whether Haden had taken advantage of her and hurt her; however, he was also worried about finding money to send Chubbie and to pay for food and plane repairs.

'What?' asked Hawthorne sceptically. 'Did you believe that Chubbie might have been the victim of a rapist?'

'Mr Hawthorne,' Bill replied with weary patience, 'I knew that Chubbie drank.'

'The reason you were so worried about Chubbie was because you loved her better than anything in the world, wasn't it?'

'Absolutely.'

Hawthorne turned his attention to the airline, asking Bill why he hadn't agreed to assist Russell and Tancrel in smuggling dope and Chinese men.

'Because the dope was against my principles. The Chinamen might not have been against my moral principles. I didn't do it because, first, I had promised Chubbie I wouldn't and, second, because I would've been violating the laws of the land in which I was a guest.'

'Would you do anything for Chubbie?'

Bill agreed that he would and, under further questioning, admitted that he had lied for her and stolen poultry for her.

'But you said you wouldn't violate the laws of this country?'

'Well, not the major laws.'

It was evident to the courtroom that Hawthorne's intent was to portray Bill as a criminal and a hypocrite, rather than the upright citizen presented by the defence. However, in such difficult economic times, when the government was doing little to help the people, few could blame the struggling aviators for stealing rabbits and chickens to keep themselves alive. Somehow it made them seem more human. Moreover, to hear this handsome man professing such love for his woman that he would do anything for her—including stealing—made him seem chivalrous and romantic.

As if Hawthorne realised that the mood in the courtroom was heading towards admiration rather than condemnation, he turned the court's attention to the subject of Bill's wife. Bill was forced to admit that they were still married, not separated. But when Hawthorne introduced the subject of his daughters, Carson was able to halt the line of questioning.

Hawthorne now asked, 'Did you ever tell Gentry Shelton that you had seen hundreds die under machine-gun fire and you wouldn't mind seeing another dead man?'

'No,' Bill responded.

Gentry wasn't available to confirm or deny the words Hawthorne claimed he had spoken. While he had promised Bill he would testify, he had soon realised that he too would find himself in legal trouble if he went to Florida because of his involvement in Latin American Airways.

Even so, Hawthorne continued questioning Bill about information Gentry had seemingly provided. 'Did you say in St Louis that you'd see Haden Clarke dead before he'd marry Chubbie?'

'I don't think so.' Then Bill hesitated and added, 'When I had that pint of Scotch that night I might have said such a thing. I remember some people told me not to worry. I remember I said that if Haden hurt Chubbie he'd have to answer to me.'

'Would you consider his intimacy with her a hurt?'

'Yes, I think I would,' Bill admitted. However, he explained that his anger had died away in Miami when he saw how much in love they were.

When Hawthorne questioned him further about his feelings regarding Chubbie and Haden's relationship, Bill said, 'Mr Hawthorne, before I went to sleep that night I knew that Haden Clarke would never marry Chubbie.'

'Why? Because he was going to commit suicide before morning?' Hawthorne asked sarcastically.

'No, because of the talk we had had. He had agreed to tell Chubbie all about our conversation and in my heart I knew that, if he didn't, I would tell her. If he or I told her, I knew she wouldn't marry him.'

'You went to bed with an entirely different picture as a result of that confidential talk with Haden Clarke, didn't you?'

Bill agreed that he had.

Recognising that Bill was still coming across as honest and likeable, Hawthorne focused again on the minutes after the shooting, turning the court's attention to the most morally questionable of Bill's admitted actions.

'In your stress and strain after the shooting, you wrote the notes before you called for a doctor?'

'I did.'

'You recognised he was dying, or thought he was, and wrote the notes before calling a doctor for him?'

Bill admitted, shame-faced, that he had.

Hawthorne reminded him that he had served in a war and had seen wounded men and must have known that the wound was dangerous. 'And you tried to make Haden sit up and write?'

'I didn't think much about it.'

'How long was it from the time the shot was fired to the time you called Mrs Keith Miller and showed her the notes?'

'Not more than eight minutes.'

'Would you mind rewriting the notes on this typewriter now?'

Haden's typewriter was placed on the court reporter's table and Bill was handed a sheet of paper and the notes. As he slid the paper into the typewriter, the clerk, attorneys and spectators pulled out their watches. The only sound in the room was the clicking of the typewriter keys as Bill reproduced the notes. As the carriage return zinged and he pulled out the second note, the clerk announced, 'Two minutes and a half.'

Bill was handed the 'death pencil'. Nobody bothered to time how long it took him to sign H to one note and Haden to the other.

Carson relaxed after Hawthorne had finished with Bill. Although his client had admitted to possibly making a threat against Haden while imbibing an entire bottle of Scotch, anyone who had been drunk themselves, or had witnessed a drunken episode, would likely accept that it was the type of outburst that usually horrified a sober self the next day. Other than that, the state hadn't been able to materially shake any of Bill's claims, despite hours of stressful public interrogation.

Moreover, far from coming across as a slimy weasel like his business partners, he had shown himself to be the decent man the defence had been trying to portray, marred only by the unfortunate suicide notes, for which he had offered a chagrined explanation.

But there was one more point that needed to be brought to the court's attention. Under redirect, Carson asked if Clarke had ever discussed the act of suicide with him.

'No, sir.'

'Did you hear of him discussing suicide with anyone else?'

'I learned after his death that he had.'

'But before the time of his death?'

'No.'

For the prosecution's charge of premeditation to stick, Carson knew that the evidence of Bill's gun purchase had to be backed up by strong evidence of ill-intent. Although he had shown that Bill had a sound reason for purchasing and loading the gun, and although he had undermined the evidence of ill-intent by exposing Bill's business partners as fools and liars, he needed a trustworthy source to convince the jurors to dismiss it altogether.

He called United States Marshal, J.P. Moe, the man who had escorted Mark Tancrel from the train station to Miami's gaol. He asked if Tancrel had mentioned Captain Lancaster during their journey and, if so, what he had said.

'I asked him if he would like to be put in the same cell with Lancaster. He said, "My god, don't do that. I'd kill him."'

'What else did Tancrel say?'

'He said that he was glad to get back and that he would do all he could to see Lancaster "burn".'

As a final act of witness destruction, Carson called Joseph Ince to the stand. Tancrel had sworn under oath that Ince was present when Bill had said that he'd 'seen a lot of dead men and one more won't make any difference'. Ince told the court that he had only spent one night with Bill and that his friend had said nothing of the sort. In fact, far from appearing doubtful or resentful of Haden, Bill had seemed glad that Clarke was in Miami looking after Chubbie.

Step by step Carson was eating away at the state's case. Whether it would save Bill from the electric chair, though, was still anyone's guess.

Chapter Forty-Five

Carson was surprised that the prosecution hadn't introduced any witnesses to show Haden as a living breathing person, as a beloved son or loving brother or dear friend, rather than just a dead body. Haden's mother had been subpoenaed yet hadn't appeared in court. Haden's brother, Beverly Clarke, had sat at the prosecutor's table every day, but hadn't been called to testify.

An objective observer could argue that there was no clear evidence that Haden had a particularly volatile and unstable temperament. And while Chubbie had mentioned conversations about suicide, under the circumstances this could hardly be considered proof that such conversations had taken place. As for Haden's malady, if the medical records of every man in the courtroom were exposed to public view, others would no doubt show evidence of unmentionable afflictions. Indeed, during the Great War, an average of 18,000 American servicemen had been sidelined for venereal diseases every single day.

Carson was now going to do what the state had failed to do: introduce the jury to the third person in this love triangle. He would do so by inviting some of Haden's friends to talk about him, people who had nothing to gain or lose by revealing the truth.

Great War veteran Richard Lavender told the court that he had been a buddy of Haden's, having met him in New Orleans the previous January while Haden was working there as a journalist. They soon became roommates and spent much of their time imbibing the local hooch. Haden also enjoyed marijuana cigarettes and had smoked a few dozen while they drank in New Orleans. Sometimes he even peddled the drug. Occasionally he got into fights, returning to their residence one night with skinned knuckles and a cut over his eye.

'Did Haden suffer from any disease?'

'Yes,' said Lavender, mentioning a word that none of the nation's press dared put into print.

'Did he say how long he had had it?'

'He said that it was an old case and that he had taken treatments two or three times.' Lavender added that Haden had made no effort to protect others, justifying such behaviour by saying, 'Somebody gave it to me and I don't care if I give it to somebody else.'

After Haden lost his job, they had decided to catch freight trains to Miami. At Jacksonville, Lavender collected two $12 cheques, his Veterans' Bureau payments for war injuries. At Daytona Beach, while he was asleep, Haden stole most of his remaining money and skedaddled.

Lavender told the court that he had been deeply depressed when he first met Haden, so much so that Haden thought he was going to kill himself. This had led to some memorable conversations on the subject, with Haden telling him the best way to commit suicide.

'What did Haden say?'

'He said the best method was to shoot yourself in the head as death came instantly and painlessly.'

Under cross-examination, Hawthorne asked if he had thought that Haden had suicidal tendencies.

'No. He thought I had.'

'Did he say he would ever commit suicide?' Hawthorne asked, instantly regretting the question when he heard the answer.

'He said if he ever got in a jam he would.'

'Was he very drunk at the time?'

'No, just normally so.'

Playwright Richard Richardson informed the court that he had known Haden for about a year and had seen him multiple times a week. They had often drunk together when they could obtain alcohol. Haden had also smoked marijuana and had mentioned where he obtained it in Miami.

'Did you ever hear him discuss methods of suicide?' Carson asked.

'Yes, on two occasions.' He told the court that on the most recent occasion they had been discussing a play he was writing and he had mentioned to Haden that his character was proving difficult to kill.

'Did Clarke explain an easy and sure method?'

'Yes, he said the best way was to shoot yourself in the head about here'—and he pointed to a spot above and a little behind the right ear.

'How long was that before he killed himself?'

'About three weeks.'

Restaurant proprietor Alma Throop testified that Haden was always depressed when she saw him earlier in the year, even when he was living with Mrs Miller. The cause was mainly his financial difficulties.

Other witnesses attested to his economic woes, including Harry Antrobus, credit manager for the South Florida Motor Sales Company. He had encountered Clarke at 1.30 pm on the afternoon of Tuesday, 19 April, and had told him that his car's repayments were overdue and that, unless he could make the necessary payment, it would be repossessed.

'What did Clarke say?'

'He said that he didn't know where to get the money and that he couldn't pay for the automobile. He said that there was nowhere for him to turn and he didn't know what to do. He was in a distressed state of mind.'

Carson then turned the court's attention to the subject of Haden's love life. The wife Haden had been trying to divorce, Kathryn Korn, had returned to her parents in California some years previously; however, Haden's files included letters from two other women who had written to him in the months before his death. One letter was from his Miami lover, Peggy Brown, saying that she had talked to her husband and that he wouldn't give her a divorce. The other three were from 'Virginia' in New York, who had sent him money and said, 'I know that you love me and we were made to be one.'

By the time Carson had finished with the subject, it was obvious to everyone that Clarke was a serial libertine with a wife in California— admittedly estranged—and simultaneous lovers in Florida and New York. And, after his Florida relationship had cooled, he had turned his charms on Chubbie, creating the love triangle that was responsible, one way or another, for his own death.

Chapter Forty-Six

Having devoted his attention to the living Haden, Carson turned to the dead man. It was time to explore the forensic evidence. Of course, the only reason they had any forensic evidence in the first place was because Bill had asked Carson to apply for a court order for the body to be exhumed and autopsied.

Carson asked Lathero to read the commission's report on the autopsy. Hawthorne objected, telling the judge that the report was part of the court record only and was not evidence that should be admitted to the jury.

Judge Atkinson overruled his objection.

When Lathero read out the report, it was clear that it didn't reach any conclusion as to how Clarke met his death, except for the obvious: that he was shot in the head. It provided no easy answer to the question 'Who killed Haden Clarke?' So why hadn't Hawthorne wanted the jurors to hear the contents of the autopsy commission's report?

Carson called Dr M.H. Tallman, who had served as chairman of the commission of surgeons and physicians that examined Haden's exhumed body. He began by establishing Tallman's medical credentials and then asked if he had brought with him any exhibits from the autopsy.

Tallman turned towards the square pasteboard box he had carried into the courtroom and lifted out a shiny ivory-yellow object. It took a moment for the audience to realise what it was. Then a collective gasp broke the silence. It was the upper half of a skull. Haden Clarke's skull.

A horrified hush descended on the courtroom. The jurors stared at Tallman's hands, then leaned forward almost compulsively to gaze at the exhibit. A female spectator fled from the room. The International News Service's Larry Smits remarked that the skull's production was a macabre act worthy of the imagination of the great Edgar Allan Poe himself.

The courtroom attendees weren't looking at Haden's face, of course—at his dark hair or eyes or fleshy nose or upper lip. Or his blood-spattered wounds. They were looking at his bony skull, which had been boiled in water to remove the decomposing flesh. Still, it was a ghastly sight they would remember for the remainder of the trial, if not the remainder of their lives. They hadn't been offered a picture of the living Haden with his movie-star good looks. All they knew was that he enjoyed drink, drugs and debauchery. And now these negative impressions were being glued to the image of a gruesome skull. It was courtroom theatre at its most audacious.

Carson briefly questioned Tallman then called his newly acquired expert to the witness stand. Albert H. Hamilton, senior member of the firm of Hamilton & Hamilton, ballistic experts and criminologists of Auburn, New York, had read accounts of the trial in his local newspaper. He had phoned Carson with suggestions regarding the evidence already submitted to the court and had offered to travel to Miami to testify. When Carson admitted that he had no funds to pay him, Hamilton said that he would pay his own way.

Hamilton told the court that he'd had forty-seven years' experience in the industry, this being his 296th case. He was employed only to the extent of examining the exhibits and making his report to his employer. The evidence he found determined whether he was then employed by the prosecution or defence. His previous cases? He had, for example, been called to testify in the Sacco and Vanzetti case.

Everyone remembered this 1920s case involving two Italian anarchists who had been convicted and executed for murder. It continued to be the subject of much controversy.

Carson asked, 'Is there any scientific way to determine the distance of the muzzle from the body?'

Hamilton said that there was a way, with some limitations. He had examined the exhibits and determined that Clarke's wound was what was called a contact shot. Three types of contact wounds existed: contact with the muzzle just touching the skin; loose contact, in which the muzzle presses slightly into the skin; and close contact, in which the muzzle is pushed against the body or, in the case of the head, the muzzle is pushed hard against the head and the head against the muzzle.

'When the gun *loosely* touches the skin and the shot is fired,' Hamilton explained, 'the bullet comes first. Behind it is a mixture of powder gases of a high temperature. They are on the base of the bullet. The moment the bullet base leaves the muzzle and enters the skin, with the slightly loosened contact, it lets the smoke shoot out and it is deposited on the outer surface of the skin. This reduces the pressure so when the bullet enters the head, the maximum force of the bullet doesn't enter the head.'

The courtroom was silent as the spectators hung on his every word.

'In close contact, there is no explosion until the bullet enters the scalp and the smoke deposit goes on the inner surface of the scalp.

If you peel down the scalp and examine it, you find a roseate while the outside is not marked. The hair on the head around the wound is not even singed. Expanding of gases in the skull pounds the brain to a pulp jelly, the skull itself is fractured, and in certain instances from eight to ten radiating fractures are found.'

As Hamilton provided his detailed yet comprehensible explanation, Carson couldn't believe his luck. He now asked, 'Is there any way to distinguish whether it is suicide or murder in a contact shot?'

'Yes, in certain cases. When the gun is one-hundredth of an inch away you can't tell, but the record made by this shot shows that the gun was in close contact with the head, and the head was exerting itself against the gun. My conclusion is that the hand which held the gun belongs to the same body as the head.'

Picking up the gun, Hamilton pushed the muzzle against his head. As the seconds dragged by, every eye in the courtroom focused on his forefinger. They saw it tug gently on the trigger. As they held their collective breaths, the finger tugged harder and the firing pin clicked.

Nothing happened, of course. The chamber was empty. However, as he fired the gun another four times, some of the spectators looked decidedly queasy.

Receiving permission to leave the witness stand, he picked up the skull and carried it over to the jury box. Holding it so that the right ear was facing the jurors, he pointed to the bullet's entrance wound and to the three radiating fractures surrounding it. He said that the bullet had entered the thinnest portion of the skull, where it was between two-sixteenths and three-sixteenths of an inch in thickness. Swivelling the skull, he pointed to five radiating fractures at the exit point. Then he reached out and handed the skull to one of the jurors.

'I knew upon examination,' Hamilton told the man who was gingerly holding the skull, 'that there was a tremendous explosion in the skull, striking in all directions. That told me that the gun was pressed very hard against the head and the head was pressed against the muzzle of the gun.' He added that the photographs, which were excellent, showed that Haden's hair wasn't even singed. As he spoke, he handed the skull to each of the jurors. After he collected it from the final juror, he put it back in its box on the exhibit table.

Picking up the gun again, he demonstrated how Haden had held the gun at the time of the shooting. 'I found it easy to pull the trigger without cocking the gun,' Hamilton advised the jurors. Using a protractor, he showed that the bullet was fired across the head with a slight backward angle of between three and six degrees, and that the bullet's upward trajectory was between ten and twelve degrees. He indicated that this was feasible from a self-inflicted wound.

Carson asked, 'Have you made up your mind finally, based on the exhibits, as to how he came to his death?'

'Yes I have. There is but one conclusion that could be arrived at from this examination. And that was that this shot was a self-inflicted, close, hard contact shot at the instant the gun was hard against the head and the head hard against the gun.'

'Was it suicide or homicide?' Carson asked, wanting his expert's conclusion to be as clear as possible for the jury.

'Absolutely homicide!' Hamilton announced.

As Hamilton sat back triumphantly, Carson's face blanched with shock. He jumped to his feet and stuttered, 'What did you say?'

The spectators saw Hamilton pause for a moment as if replaying his words. His eyes widened with horror. Laughing nervously, he said, 'I was thinking of something else'—as if such a claim could account for his appalling gaffe. He then took a deep breath and proclaimed, 'Absolutely suicide! There is not a scintilla of evidence to support a theory of homicide or murder.'

349

The press largely ignored Hamilton's slip-up. They were dazzled. Everyone was. The United Press correspondent declared him to be the 'ace card played by the defence'. The *Miami Herald* pointed out that most of the spectators and court attachés thought his testimony conclusive, which meant that many of the jurors would as well. Hawthorne would have his work cut out if he was to undermine the evidence of the defence's last-minute expert.

Commencing his cross-examination, Hawthorne said, 'I think you stated that the death of Haden Clarke without question was self-inflicted. But if you were asleep with your head on a pillow when someone touched your forehead with an object, and you were trying to come out of a sound sleep, would the effect not be the same?' As he said the words, he placed his finger on his temple and jerked his head towards his finger.

'These conditions wouldn't exist, Mr Hawthorne. You would not have the power to throw your head as you just did. I'd say it would be impossible and his feather pillow would offer a springy effect which would not allow sufficient pressure unless you have the consent of the head.' He added that, if a person awoke to find a gun being pushed into his or her head, the tendency would in fact be to pull away.

Having failed to undermine Hamilton's explanations of the evidence, Hawthorne set about attacking his reputation. He denounced him as a publicity-conscious attention-seeker. He then took him to task over some problems with the evidence in the Sacco and Vanzetti case. But he failed to breach Hamilton's smug self-confidence.

The forensic interrogations continued the following morning. Dr Donald F. Gowe, a second member of the autopsy commission, told the court he had conducted 184 autopsies in his years as a doctor. He testified about the commission's findings, including the radiating fractures in the skull. As a rule, he said, these types of fractures were not caused by the bullet itself but by gas explosions.

'Can you infer from your examination the distance of the muzzle of the pistol from the head?'

'I infer that the muzzle was close to the head.'

'Do you feel competent to express an opinion if the wound was self-inflicted or not?'

'I do not, not scientifically.'

'Based on probability?'

'Oh, yes, on probability.'

Hawthorne objected to the question and answer and the judge sustained the objection. But the damage was already done. One of the city's own medical experts had just told the court that he had reached the same conclusion as the defence's ballistics expert. And the other three members of the commission also informed the jurors that the gun was clearly in direct contact with the skull when it was fired.

In Hamilton's testimony, he had mentioned that another sign of a close contact wound was a powder roseate found on the skull around the wound entrance. Carson asked Dr Tallman if he had seen such a roseate on the skull. Tallman said that he had.

Having established by the testimony of these five witnesses that the gun was pressed so firmly to Clarke's head that the gases could only escape into the skull itself, Carson completed his forensic interrogations.

Hawthorne wasn't finished with Hamilton. He knew how powerful the ballistics expert's testimony had been. Even if he hadn't been able to gauge the courtroom mood, he had read the journalists' opinions. He recalled Hamilton and questioned him about his decision to testify. Hamilton told him that he had approached Carson because it was too late by then to approach Hawthorne himself.

'Why was it too late to come to me?'

'That's very simple. You should have had my report before going before the grand jury and seeking an indictment. Then this trial never would have occurred.'

Hawthorne asked what information in the witnesses' testimonies had led him to contact Carson.

'I thought that the undertaker's statements about the powder burns was misleading and would have a misleading effect on the jury. I thought Mr Carson ought to know.'

It was one of those moments when a prosecutor wished he could object to his own question and have it struck from the record—and from the minds of the jurors. He slid onto a new subject, asking Hamilton if the results of his examinations could be determined with mathematical certainty.

Hamilton picked up the skull and turned it from one side to the other as he made his calculations. Suddenly it slipped from his hands and flew up into the air. The spectators gasped. Hawthorne reached out and tried to grab it. He missed. Time seemed to slow as the skull descended. Hamilton snatched at it and managed to grab hold of it, juggling it a few times before hugging it to his chest like a football.

Thankful that his interrogation hadn't descended into a complete farce, Hawthorne briskly rubbed his hands together—a symbolic 'phew!' As the spectators laughed, the courtroom tension eased.

The prosecution's final forensic rebuttal witness was C.A. Peterson, who had conducted the state's ballistics tests. Hawthorne asked if he knew Doctor Hamilton.

'Only by his reputation.'

'Do you know his general reputation as an expert witness regarding his regard for truth and veracity?'

When Peterson acknowledged that he did, Hawthorne asked if his reputation was good or bad.

'Bad.'

Naturally, Carson didn't want such a damaging assessment of his key witness lingering in the jurors' minds over the weekend. He and Hawthorne proceeded to conduct a legal skirmish, each using their questions to Peterson to belittle the other's expert.

Three of Carson's final witnesses were called to rebut the claims that Hamilton had a poor reputation. One was Miami's own Francis Malone, city editor of the *Miami Daily News*, who had collaborated in writing a series of articles about Hamilton and believed that the man had a sound reputation.

Hawthorne's rebuttal witnesses included men who testified that Haden had thought there would be trouble when Bill came back. But could anyone truly think there wouldn't be trouble of some sort when a man cuckolded his best friend? Other witnesses said that Haden was a happy-go-lucky fellow who wasn't depressed and didn't seem to worry about anything at all, including his finances.

Noteworthy by its absence was any testimony from Haden's mother or his brother. Beverly Clarke continued to sit with the prosecutors while witnesses testified about his brother's temperament and emotional state. Towards the end of the trial, his mother sat among the courtroom spectators. Neither was called to resurrect the reputation of the dead ghostwriter.

Chapter Forty-Seven

The final battle now began, the tug-of-war between two implacable forces who were determined to show the jurors they had the
truth on their side. Hawthorne and his team had commenced the trial
thinking that the verdict was a foregone conclusion—if there ever
could be such a thing in a jury trial. Now, two weeks later, they knew it
would be a fight to the finish.

Carson was the first to offer his closing argument. He began by
telling the jury that the prosecution's case had continuously crumbled
as it was being presented and that he would show its collapse by examining its witnesses' statements.

The state had drawn from Attorney Huston that Bill had wanted
him to say that the gun that killed Haden Clarke was his own; however,
this clearly wasn't the sleight-of-hand intimated by the state because
Bill had purchased the gun as a replacement. Likewise, Huston's testimony that Bill had asked *if* Haden was likely to speak again was later
shown to be phrased differently, that Bill *hoped* Clarke would speak
again so he could explain why he did it.

Regarding Officer Hudson's testimony, Carson told the court that he had many concerns. The crumpled telegram. The blood-soaked gun that had been wiped off before being passed to the state's fingerprint expert.

As for Chubbie's testimony, he remarked, 'There are women—all doctors know it and books show it—who, due to some pathological condition, are utterly unable to live up to the standards of virtue and chastity which you and I have been taught to believe constitutes the crowning virtue of their sex. Here is a woman whose bravery and courage have caused to be fixed upon her the admiring eyes of all the world; but here also is a woman who suffers from some particular physical or mental or pathological defect that has made it necessary for her weakness to be brought forth in this courtroom and detailed fully and completely. And by reason of her matchless gallantry in this courtroom (no matter what her faults may be), her sordid story has gone out over the instruments you hear clicking behind me to be read, to be condemned perhaps, to be gloated over by those of sordid minds in the far corners of the world.'

Chubbie sat in the courtroom watching him, her face expressionless but for her tightly clenched lips.

Carson reminded the court that Chubbie's testimony had withstood attack from every angle, both in the courtroom and during the initial investigation. If the state attorney's office had found her guilty of telling any falsehoods they would have trotted them out during the trial.

'Now we come to the big bad boy, Mr J.F. Russell, around whom the state's case is very largely built.' He pointed out that the state's witness had divulged the details of Chubbie's new relationship in the hope of inducing Bill to smuggle Chinese men and dope into America. Bill, however, had not only refused to break the law, he had written in his diary that Russell and Tancrel were accordingly likely to be vindictive.

After reminding the jurors of Tancrel's lies, Carson declared, 'These crooks, these lousy bastards, to quote Captain Lancaster, who were trying to violate the laws of this country, are brought into this American courtroom in the name and by the authority of the State of Florida. And without their testimony, what have you got?'

He directed the jurors' attention to Undertaker Bess, who had testified that there were no powder marks on the outside of Clarke's head. Yet Dr Thomas, who was paid by the state to perform autopsies, had examined Clarke's body after his death and had found powder stains inside the wound. Dr Thomas had presented his written report to the grand jury, yet the state attorney had not called him to testify.

Having shown the collapse of the state's case, he turned his attention to the defence's case. He told the court that Bill didn't have to testify, yet he had not only done so, he had been calm, courteous and collected throughout his three days of testimony, offering no contradictions in any of his statements. His character witnesses included national and international heroes who had spent their own money travelling to Miami to testify for Bill—a stark contrast to the witnesses offered by the state. 'For the defendant, clean, brilliant and outstanding warbirds of the world, birds who come to us from the clean highways of the sky. Can you picture the contrast? In the case of the state, Russell and Tancrel, foul carrion birds, who come to us from cells where they are charged with the betrayal of your country and mine.'

As the courtroom clock ticked the final few minutes before the noon recess, he again read out the eight reasons provided by Chubbie as to why Haden might have committed suicide.

The reporters made a beeline for Chubbie during the break, keen to ask her how she felt after such a public thrashing of her reputation.

She told them, 'I am interested only in freeing old Bill. Nothing else matters to me.'

When the trial resumed, Carson discussed the testimonies of Richard Lavender and Richard Richardson, saying that they had introduced an element he would have preferred to leave out: Haden's character. Clearly, Haden was a man with a brilliant mind, a charming personality and an interesting imagination. However, he was also emotional, unstable and erratic. He said that Haden's enforced sobriety had made him face his many difficulties. On the night in question, he'd had to account to Bill for his treacherous conduct. And he had known that the following morning he would have to reveal to Chubbie information he had deliberately kept from her.

Carson added that the two people who knew him best—his mother and brother—were currently sitting in the courtroom. If the facts revealed to the court about Haden's character and temperament could have been disputed by anybody, these were the people to do so. Yet neither had testified.

Turning his attention to the forensic evidence, Carson reminded the court that Haden had been buried without his body being autopsied and that the only reason the court had forensic evidence to examine was because Lancaster himself had signed the autopsy request. 'If Bill Lancaster had known he was guilty, don't you suppose he would have been glad to have Haden Clarke lie undisturbed in the cemetery?'

The autopsy doctors had all testified that the gun's muzzle had been held tight against Clarke's skull and that the entire explosion of gases had taken place inside his skull. Their report had been on file in the court since 22 June so the prosecution could have read it and called any of the doctors to the witness stand. Instead, the prosecution had relied upon the testimony of Undertaker Bess—because, without Bess's testimony about the lack of powder marks, the state had no case against Lancaster.

The state had also claimed that a man wouldn't lie down to shoot himself, yet two such suicide deaths had occurred within the last couple of years in their own county alone. One had occurred only the week before the trial commenced, so the state attorney's office should have known about the case.

And there were other points that needed to be considered, including the most obvious. The state had charged Bill with premeditated murder yet surely a military man—a war veteran—would know of more efficient and successful ways to rid himself of a foe.

He offered an explanation for the forged notes. 'I don't think that Lancaster ever meant for those notes to be seen by anybody but Mrs Keith Miller.' He reminded the jury that Lancaster had asked her to destroy the notes but she had refused, and that he couldn't tell her why he wanted them destroyed because that would have defeated the purpose of the forgery in the first place. The state had tried to argue premeditation, but the fact that the notes were written after Haden was shot clearly undermined any such premeditation argument.

Finally, Carson told the jurors that it was their duty to consider the following points. 'First: where is the state's case? We have been over it step by step and it is gone. They have utterly and completely failed. Second: make an examination of the evidence; make an examination of the exhibits and interpret them for yourselves. Third: weigh the character of the witnesses on the one side and on the other. Compare the jailbirds of the state with the warbirds for the defence and have your verdict. Find the defendant not guilty. Send word back to old England, from whence we get our Common Law, that in American courts justice is administered in a high, fair and solemn fashion that our ancestors won on that soil by their blood.'

Chapter Forty-Eight

'Lancaster is guilty of violating four of the ten commandments: thou shalt not kill, steal, commit adultery and bear false witness, yet Mr Carson says this man's moral code shines like a star on a background of filth,' jeered Hawthorne as he presented the state's closing argument on Tuesday afternoon, 16 August.

After thirteen days of testimonies and arguments, the trial was in its home stretch. His own closing argument should finish before lunchtime on Wednesday. If they were lucky, they might have a verdict before they headed home for dinner.

He reminded the jurors of Carson's claim that the state's case was entirely circumstantial. 'I say that there is a threat on every page of this diary from beginning to end,' he thundered and threw the diary onto the table in front of Bill.

Bill stared at him tight-lipped and kept his gaze fixed firmly on him throughout his closing.

Hawthorne said that Carson had announced in his opening statement that he would prove that Clarke had committed suicide, that Clarke had consulted suicide experts and had told witnesses the exact position he would shoot himself if he was to commit suicide. 'Yet the state has proved to you that the red hot bullet from St Louis hit Clarke just where he said it never would.'

It was an important point, one of the strongest pieces of evidence suggesting that Clarke had not shot himself.

Carson had also told the jury that Dr Thomas, the county physician, had seen powder burns inside the entrance wound immediately after Clarke's death and had reported his finding to the state attorney's office and the grand jury. This was true, the prosecutor admitted. The state attorney's office had approved the exhumation order requested by the defence but the autopsy results had provided little more than additional front-page publicity. 'It provided more testimony about internal explosions, which has never been in dispute, and that the gun was held at close range, which has not been disputed, but which does not preclude the theory of murder.'

Those who had sat through the entire trial listened with astonishment. At no point had Hawthorne disclosed this information to the jury. Rather than calling the county physician or any of the autopsy doctors to testify, he had instead relied on the evidence of the embalmer who had testified to *not* seeing any powder marks, thereby indicating that it wasn't a close contact wound and that Clarke's death could not have been a suicide. Yet Hawthorne was now agreeing with the defence that it was indeed a close contact wound, albeit with the disclaimer—also previously unmentioned—that such a wound was not proof in itself that the death wasn't a murder. It was an extraordinary revelation in the dying hours of the trial.

Hawthorne then laid out much of the state's evidence, including Bill's purchase of the gun when Chubbie was starving and the fact that Bill had remembered to collect the gun from the plane but had forgotten his diary and other papers. After dwelling at length on his authorship of the suicide notes, Hawthorne reminded the jurors that Haden was himself a writer. Surely, if he was planning to kill himself, he would have sat down at his typewriter and penned his own farewell note.

Summarising Hamilton's testimony about the sealed contact wound, he said that it required pressure from both directions, head and gun. 'If Haden Clarke had his head on the pillow, pushed the gun down firmly on his head, and then pushed his head up against the gun, why you can't do it without straining every muscle in your body. It isn't reasonable. Why lie down and then rear up to meet the gun?'

He declared that there wasn't a single fact or circumstance in this case that, when the rule of common sense was applied, didn't point to Lancaster's guilt. 'Every page in this diary points to his guilt. Every human instinct causes a man to fight for the woman he loves.'

Just before lunch-time on Wednesday, he concluded, 'Within a very few minutes, the fate of William Newton Lancaster will rest entirely on your shoulders. What you do is a matter that must be settled with your conscience and your oath, guided by the rules of law which his honour will give you. Be careful, cautious, prayerful in your deliberations. Do not let sympathy or emotions play a part. Decide simply if Haden Clarke committed suicide or if William Newton Lancaster killed him.'

At 11.45 am, the jury retired to consider its verdict. Reports trickled out, then and later. The men started by choosing a jury foreman who ordered a ballot. Some of the jurors abstained from voting. They decided to order lunch—sandwiches, milk and coffee—before they hunkered down to consider the evidence.

For the next four hours, all was quiet. Then at 4.24 pm, the men came out to ask the judge two questions. At 4.44 pm, they filed into the jury box. The foreman stood as Justice Atkinson read the slip of paper handed to him. The judge asked him to announce their verdict.

The courtroom was so still and silent it seemed as though its occupants had been snap-frozen.

'Not guilty.'

Women wept and shrieked. A stout matron who had monopolised a front-row seat throughout the trial fell back in her chair gasping. Vainly, the court officials called for order.

Suddenly, as if everyone had been instantaneously gagged, the courtroom went silent again. All eyes turned towards Bill as he stepped towards the jury box, his hands clasping and unclasping nervously.

'Gentlemen,' he said to the twelve men staring back at him. 'You have been very patient with my case. You have had to listen during the long trial to many things. I want to thank you, gentlemen, from the bottom of my heart for your verdict. I will never forget what you have done for me.' Clicking his heels in a salute, he bowed and headed back towards the prosecutor's table.

The courtroom erupted again. Spectators surged forward, eager to shake his hand. Court officials and police officers struggled to hold them back. 'Order! Order in the court!' they cried. It was as if the courtroom had been miraculously transformed from a hall of justice into a carnival.

Pressmen tried to interview Bill over the hullabaloo. 'I am over-joyed and delighted that I have been found not guilty,' he told them. 'I have been convinced all along my innocence would be sustained. I will always be grateful to Mr Carson and Mr Lathero for their splendid defence of me.' He said that he would spend the next few days at Carson's home and get some much-needed rest before thinking about his future.

As the bailiffs and deputies and police officers regained control of the courtroom, Bill shook hands with the judge and jurors and posed for pictures with them. Hawthorne approached him and also shook his hand, saying, 'The performance of my duty to the best of my ability is sufficient compensation. The jury, the only agency provided by law to determine the issue, has rendered its verdict and I accept it.'

Chubbie wasn't in the courtroom at the moment the verdict was announced. She was waiting in a nearby office when someone opened the door and called out the news. Later, questioned by the press, she said with a trace of her old smile, 'I am delighted. I knew old Bill would come through.' She left the building soon afterwards, her only contact with him a phone call that evening to offer her congratulations.

Chubbie had had an inkling of what the verdict would be—as they all had. When the jurors approached the judge twenty minutes before they announced their verdict, they had asked for an elaboration of his instructions regarding reasonable doubt. They also asked for permission to view the exhibits again. It wasn't hard for the lawyers to grasp what was happening in the jury room. On one side of the scales of justice sat reasonable doubt. On the other sat the exhibits.

The scales were currently weighted towards acquittal, unless the jurors saw something in the exhibits that precluded such a verdict. Either side could refuse permission for the jurors to examine the exhibits without the jurors learning who had denied it. Carson opted for a refusal.

In the aftermath, the American press expressed more surprise at the behaviour of the female spectators than at the jury's verdict. A syndicated article asked if the women saw Lancaster as an avenging hero who took into his own hands the law of 'one man for one woman'. Another writer wondered if Lancaster's behaviour in court—that he was gentlemanly and courteous, seemingly candid and courageous— had won over the female spectators so completely that they behaved like love-struck fools.

Neither mentioned the growing cult of celebrity worship. Bill had been only a minor star, a barnacle clinging to Chubbie's ship, until his indictment for murder hit the nation's press. Chubbie's involvement—perhaps more so than Bill's—acted as a drawcard for Miami's star-struck women, who saw it as an opportunity to experience a personal connection with fame. As the trial progressed, they came to see Bill as more than just a celebrity. They saw a real man, an ordinary man in many ways, one who loved so passionately he would do anything for his woman, even kill himself. His love rival was a man without honour or nobility, a drunken, drug-addicted, diseased lecher.

Perception is everything.

Part Four

RESOLUTIONS

Chapter Forty-Nine

'Moral turpitude' was the explanation offered by many of the country's newspapers when they learnt that Chubbie and Bill were being kicked out of the country. It wasn't true. Moral fury probably accounted for the error, a feeling that struck a chord across the nation and allowed the mistake to spread.

The facts were quite different. They were both told on 7 October, six weeks after the trial finished, that if they didn't leave the country voluntarily within seven days they would face arrest and possible incarceration for violating immigration laws.

Chubbie's departure was ignominious, a stark contrast to her ceremonial arrival in the country four years previously, when she and Bill had been cheered in a ticker-tape parade and welcomed by the Mayor of Oakland. Tears welled in her eyes as she stood on the dock on 14 October 1932 farewelling her friends and the country she had long called home. At last she turned and headed up the gangway of the SS *American Banker*. Dogging her footsteps was a female officer dressed in the austere uniform and sturdy shoes of the United States Immigration Department. The woman pursued her into her cabin and stayed there until the ship was about to depart, determined to ensure that the Land of Opportunity was rid of the likes of her forever.

Five years to the day since she had flown from Croydon in the *Red Rose*, Chubbie was on her way back to England. She remained in her cabin throughout the voyage, refusing to be interviewed when the ship docked at Plymouth, keeping her blinds drawn so no one could see her. As the ship negotiated a lock on its journey up the Thames to London, a crewman threw out a rope ladder and helped her climb down to a small boat nudging the ship's side.

Bill was waiting on the foreshore with a car. He had arrived in Liverpool on the *Scythia* earlier that day, and had sped to London to assist her to evade the crowds and reporters waiting at the dock. He ferried her to her aunt's house at Hampstead, where she rested and spent time considering her options.

England in 1932 bore little resemblance to the place she had left five years earlier. It was as if, like her, it had been sucked dry of its life and colour and energy. Dull boring clothes. Dismal weather. Despair and destitution. And there seemed little prospect of any improvement in the near future.

At least she was able to find work of sorts. The *Daily Express* wanted to publish her life story. Its management employed a ghostwriter to work with her—an ironic and rather surreal experience under the circumstances. Finding the travelling from Hampstead too tiring, she rented a bedsit in Oxford Terrace off Edgware Road, not far from her previous accommodation in Baker Street. She was back where she had started.

Bill was struggling. Unable to find work, he was forced to live with his parents. He couldn't even sell his story. His *Red Rose* 'failure' was half a decade ago and he hadn't triumphed in any of his American ventures. If not for the murder trial publicity, few in Britain would have remembered his name. And while Britain was keen to hear from the famous Australian aviator—now a scarlet woman—its people remained wary about their own Bill Lancaster, as if his acquittal wasn't enough to fully convince them of his innocence.

One day he arrived at her bedsit looking brighter than normal, having had a promising job interview for a commercial pilot position. Chubbie wasn't surprised when he failed to get the job. Even if there hadn't been an abundance of experienced commercial pilots looking for work, the murder trial and smuggling connection clung albatross-like around his neck. Would clients or passengers really want to know that Bill Lancaster—the man tried for murder in Miami, the man booted out of America for smuggling—was flying the plane?

Bill's despondency returned, tinged now with desperation. 'I will have to do something spectacular to get back in again,' he told her. He examined world maps and considered his options. He decided to try to beat Amy (Johnson) Mollison's recent record of four days, six hours and fifty-four minutes from Croydon to Cape Town.

His long-suffering father purchased a plane for him, an Avro Avian called the *Southern Cross Minor*. Its previous owner, Charles Kingsford Smith, had attempted to beat Jim Mollison's Australia-to-England record in the plane but had been foiled because of illness.

Chubbie helped him with his preparations. As they plotted his course through Europe and Africa, she expressed great concern about his Sahara Desert crossing. They both knew that he'd had little night-flying experience and that the plane was not equipped with night-flying instruments. Any attempt to cross the Sahara at night would be fool-hardy in the extreme.

The news of Bill's attempt to break Amy Mollison's record broke in a *Daily Express* exclusive on Thursday, 6 April 1933, under the headline 'Captain Lancaster's "Come-Back"'. It said that the man who had recently stood in the dock charged with murder—but had been honourably acquitted without a stain on his character—was about to make a flying comeback in an attempt to restore his reputation.

The following details left any aviator readers with a shiver of fore-boding, however. 'I have been warned to expect very bad weather on parts of the route,' Bill had told the reporter, adding that he couldn't wait around for the weather conditions to improve because it would take months. He mentioned 'three nights of moonlight flying' without explaining what he would do if the moonlight disap-peared for any reason, and 'one night over the inhospitable Sahara, a distance of 1500 miles in one hop' even though night-time flying over the largely trackless desert was almost as risky as a water crossing. He expected to get only 'five hours sleep for the first three nights; after that I will be content with an hour—if I can get that', raising the pos-sibility of exhaustion-induced errors on his five-day flight. He said that, if he succeeded, he would owe everything to his parents because they had beggared themselves to finance the trip. And the clincher was: 'My machine is twenty miles per hour slower than that used by Mrs Mollison.' Why was he even bothering?

Chubbie could understand why he was bothering. Battered in every direction since the night of Haden's death, he felt like he was standing at the edge of an abyss and had no choice but to make the deadly leap.

She told him she wouldn't come to see him off. He accepted her decision, saying it was probably for the best because his parents would be there. Not surprisingly, the elderly couple blamed her for all of his misfortunes.

He came to her house a few days before the flight and took some photographs of her. He also asked for a loan of her watch.

'Don't be daft,' was her response as she looked at her tiny wrist-watch. 'This is so small you could never see the time on it. It'll only get in your way. Wear a big one that you can see, one with a luminous dial.'

She knew why he wanted it. She had worn it for years. Carrying it with him would make him feel as if he were holding a precious part of her—a good luck charm of sorts.

He was still passionately in love with her, still keen to marry her, still hopeful that Kiki might one day grant him his freedom. If he had been divorced, she probably would have married him. Even though the romance was long gone—for her at least—they were still best friends and it would have solved so many problems. While they weren't social pariahs, the widespread uncertainty about Bill's guilt, combined with her own scandalous revelations, had made them curiosities in London's social scene. Marriage would legitimise their relationship and provide proof that she truly believed in his innocence.

But Kiki refused to release him, despite everything. Clearly the woman had no intention of ever changing her mind. Since Chubbie still yearned for the security of a loving marriage, it had left her with few options. As the post-America months passed, she had realised she would have to cut her ties with him, start afresh without his hovering presence. She didn't say anything to him, though. Not when he was about to start such a hazardous flight.

Hearing that he would be at Lympne aerodrome for a few days before his flight, she travelled there on Friday, 7 April, for a final farewell. She was horrified at his appearance. Hollow eyes. Gaunt cheeks. He looked like a death's head. As she watched him, she had a worrying premonition: 'He's not going to make it.'

In the days that followed, she kept abreast of his activities through the *Express* coverage. Reportedly, all he was taking food-wise was a cold chicken, so he could chew on the bones when he was sleepy, some beef extract and two gallons of water, the latter a French Government requirement for those flying across the Sahara.

The *Express* journalist was at Lympne aerodrome long before dawn on Tuesday morning, 11 April. Chubbie read that Bill looked pale and nervous, and was in a desperate hurry to take off so he could reach Oran before nightfall. Weather forecasts showed that he faced a twenty-mile-an-hour headwind for most of his first leg, which would reduce his cruising speed to around eighty miles an hour, nearly forty miles slower than Amy's cruising speed. Even though his flight must now be an almost sleepless endurance marathon, he refused to delay it. He told the journalist that he had been promised a good position if he succeeded in breaking the record.

Only the *Express* journalist, a handful of airport officials and his parents—his teary invalid mother and his ill but recuperating father—were there to wave goodbye to his little blue plane as it raced across the airfield at 5.38 am and headed south into the mist.

Each day, Chubbie grabbed the newspapers and flipped through them, looking for reports about his flight. Wednesday's morning papers merely recorded his departure from England. She already knew his day's route. His plan was to fly 1100 miles south over France and Spain to the Mediterranean city of Oran, Algeria, where he would rest for a few hours and refuel.

The evening papers said that he had reached Oran at 9 pm the previous night, which meant that he was already four-and-a-half hours behind Amy at the end of his first leg. It was an appalling start to an already difficult flight. She wondered if he would consider abandoning the flight and starting again at a later time.

She soon learnt that he hadn't—despite losing even more time. A bureaucratic hiccup, of all things, was responsible. Aviators following the Transsaharienne Company's motor track were required to pay a 100,000 franc (£800) 'insurance' fee to the company to help defray possible rescue costs. She knew that Bill had paid the required fee, but the Oran officials told him they had no record of his payment. They said that he had two choices: to remain in Oran until they contacted the London agent or to pay the fee again. Since Bill had no spare money or time, he signed a statement saying that he would fly at his own risk and would not expect any rescue efforts to be undertaken if he disappeared along the way.

Thursday's morning papers ominously reported that he had departed from Oran after midnight on Tuesday night in a do-or-die dash across the desert. He couldn't have had more than an hour or two of sleep, if any at all. Chubbie knew from their carefully worked-out plan that he would fly 720 miles to Reggane in central Algeria, an oasis in the Sahara Desert that served as a French outpost. This would be the most difficult stretch of the journey, because he would have to navigate by dead reckoning alone.

The newspapers said that he had landed to check his location on Wednesday morning around 8.30 am and had discovered that he was at Adrar, eighty miles north of Reggane and slightly east of his direct route. Adrar also lay on the Transsaharienne's southerly motor track and had supplies of aviation fuel, so he had decided to fill his tanks and hop off from there to commence his Gao leg. He had previously told Chubbie that he expected the flight across the Sahara Desert to Gao to be relatively easy flying because he would cross in daylight with good visibility and would follow the motor track marked out by the Transsaharienne Company. Not only did the tyre marks remain visible because of the sand's stability, tiny 'houses'—four walls and an iron roof—were positioned beside the track every six-and-a-half miles to serve as aerial beacons.

Reportedly, when he left Adrar at 9.15 am on Wednesday, he flew into a sandstorm. Blinded by the granular fog, he drifted off his flight path and found himself at Aoulef, south-east of Adrar, around 11 am. Once he regained his bearings, he attempted to continue his journey. Again he found himself lost in the sandstorm. Again he had to land to get his bearings. Realising he no longer had enough fuel to comfortably reach Gao, he stopped at Reggane at 1 pm. It had taken him nearly four hours to fly a distance that should have taken only one.

Chubbie felt tense all day as she waited for Thursday's evening newspapers, hoping she would read that he had crossed the Sahara safely. All they said was that he had left Reggane the previous day to head south to Gao.

More detailed information soon surfaced. Chubbie learnt that he was exhausted when he arrived at Reggane after battling through the sandstorm. He had organised to have his plane refuelled and then rested for three hours, but he refused any food. Around 6 pm on Wednesday evening, when he had declared himself ready to resume his flight, the head of the Transsaharienne Reggane station tried to deter him. Monsieur Borel told him that the conditions were highly unsuitable for a desert crossing, that there was a strong north-west wind and no moon, so the darkness would prevent him from seeing the tyre marks and beacons on the track. He would be forced to rely on dead reckoning, an especially difficult form of navigation when he had no lights on his instrument panel to help him steer a compass course. It would be madness to take off under such conditions.

However, Bill had dismissed Borel's concerns, saying that he would light matches to enable him to read the instruments. When Borel realised that he was serious, he had lent him a pocket electric torch. Borel and his men watched Bill's plane zig-zag as it took off, as if he was too weary to keep it steady.

Chubbie knew that he should have arrived at Gao long before Thursday evening's newspapers were published. However, the following day was Easter Friday and journalists were having the day off. Everyone was thinking about other things.

Easter Friday was torture. Nothing was open. She couldn't phone the *Daily Express* office to enquire if any further information had come in.

Saturday's newspapers set her stomach churning. 'No news has been received of Captain Lancaster since Wednesday,' revealed *The Times*.

'Our Algiers correspondent reports that he left Reggane, an oasis in the Sahara, at 6.30 on the evening of that day for Gao.' The news account noted that sandstorms were causing bad visibility and that a Transsaharienne car had set off from Reggane to search for him, but had failed to find him.

Bill had been missing for more than two days in the forbidding Sahara Desert, with only two gallons of water to keep him alive.

Chapter Fifty

She had told him she would search for him if he disappeared. She had told him to stay with his plane and she would find him.

That Saturday evening she walked into the office of the *Sunday Express*'s editor and begged for his help. 'I must find Bill!' she told him, adding that she was so worried she had barely eaten for three days. 'There doesn't seem to be anybody but me to find him. I have very little money but I will put my last penny into finding him.' She said that the French were hardly doing anything except sending out a motor-car. 'What good is a motor-car in the desert?' she asked in exasperation.

She told him that she had made Bill promise to stay with his plane because she remembered the story of two RAF men forced down in the desert who had left their plane to walk twenty miles for help. The plane was easily located but the men had died by the time rescuers stumbled across them.

She explained that there were only two or three planes in England that were capable of flying to Bill's rescue. And she begged him for publicity, so she could find a suitable plane, and for financial assistance to mount a rescue operation.

It turned out that the only suitable plane belonged to Dame Mary Russell, the Duchess of Bedford, who three years earlier had flown from Lympne to Cape Town with her pilot, Captain Barnard. Chubbie headed to Gerrards Cross to beg Barnard for his help. He said that he would do anything to assist a fellow pilot in trouble; however, the Duchess's plane was in no condition for such a long flight and he was personally contracted for at least eight flights to Le Touquet. By the time he and the plane were ready, it would be too late.

Meanwhile, the *Daily Express* had interviewed Bill's father who made it clear that he didn't want Chubbie's help. 'It is not our wish that anyone who does not know the terrible flying conditions of the Sahara desert should go out there to try and find our son,' he said deliberately. 'It would be a futile attempt and very much against all our wishes.' He reported that he was in regular contact with the Transsaharienne Company and that they were conducting a thorough search. He wasn't worried and wouldn't worry for at least another week, because Bill had probably come down somewhere south-east of Gao. 'Wherever he is, I am sure that he is quite alright.'

Chubbie was devastated. Edward Lancaster's head-in-the-sand attitude had destroyed any chance of the *Daily Express* funding her rescue mission.

She contacted Colonel Jellicoe, the London manager of the Transsaharienne Company, to find out for herself what was being done. He said that, according to the Paris office, wireless messages had zipped across North Africa, advising desert and military bases to keep an eye out for Bill's plane. A squadron of French military planes had searched the Gao district without success. Another two aeroplanes were heading from Gao to Reggane and would search the terrain for sixty miles either side of the motor track. He assured her that nothing was being left to chance. If Bill had crashed near the motor track, they would find him.

'I am intensely worried about Captain Lancaster,' a haggard Chubbie told the press on Tuesday, 18 April. 'I had a dreadful dream last night that he was lying in the desert and crying for food and water. I live with hopes that he is safe with the natives in some village. I cannot bear to think that he is out there alone. I have walked London endeavouring to secure planes and financial support for a personal search but I have met opposition. If it takes weeks, I shall go and find him alive or dead.' She said that she hoped to get the loan of a plane and the gift of petrol later in the week, but couldn't reveal anything more until she was ready to hop off. In the meantime, she would wait to hear the results of the plane and motor-transport searches.

Information continued to trickle out of Africa. 'We are doing our best,' an African searcher advised, 'but it would be an excellent thing if British pilots would realise the risks they run over the desert.' A dispatch published in the French *Journal des Débats* grumbled that the search operation had already cost £6000, whereas only a fraction of that amount had been demanded as insurance. 'It is high time that these ill-conceived and ill-prepared flights were forbidden.'

On Saturday, 22 April, ten days after Bill had left Reggane, the search organisers reported that they had found no trace of him or his plane and that all hopes of finding him alive had largely been abandoned. 'If Captain Lancaster had succeeded in reaching the belt of vegetation, some 200 miles in depth, which borders the River Niger, there is no reason why he should not be found safe and sound,' said a French major who was an expert on desert flying conditions. 'But if he strayed from the track, with only two gallons of water, his chances are very small.' And if he had strayed from the track, as appeared likely by that time, the potential search area was several times larger than France. No one would even consider conducting such an expensive time-consuming search.

Bill wasn't the only record-attempting aviator to disappear that week. When Chubbie visited him at Lympne, they had chatted to a handsome Italian airman, Captain Leonida Robbiano, who was about to set off in an attempt to beat the England-to-Australia record. As she pored over the newspapers in the days after Bill's disappearance, she read that Robbiano's body and wrecked plane had been discovered near Calcutta.

The mystery of Bill's disappearance continued to generate press coverage in the months that followed. In May, Chubbie read that Bill's parents claimed to know he was dead because they had received messages 'from the other side' via psychic channels. Bill did not suffer, they had been told, which was a source of great relief to his mother.

In October, the *Daily Express* reported that a white pilot had apparently come down in a remote part of the Sahara some months previously and was living with local tribes in the Senegal district. As far back as the previous spring, a plane had been seen to descend over west Mali. A moment later, columns of smoke and flames had risen into the sky. Senegal lay to the west of Mali and both were within range of the *Southern Cross Minor's* fuel tanks. The continent's caravan traffic had been suspended for the summer soon after Bill disappeared so no further news had come out of Africa until it resumed in autumn, bringing reports of the white aviator in Senegal. The man—of medium height and a spare build—didn't speak French and appeared to be of northern European or American origin.

Was it Bill? The general consensus among the aviation experts was that Bill had known he couldn't beat Amy Mollison's record when he left Reggane and that his dash across the Sahara was a form of 'heroicide'. If he had indeed survived a desert crash, had he chosen to remain there rather than face further humiliation upon his return? If it was Bill, perhaps he would later make his way out of the desert and begin life again under a new name.

When no further information surfaced about the white pilot, Chubbie told the world via the *Empire News* that Bill had died as he wished to die: flying. 'Yet it was not aviation that killed him,' she continued, 'but the false accusation of murder.' He had accepted the Cape Town challenge in an endeavour to rehabilitate his reputation, although his plane was unsuitable and the odds of his success were a hundred-to-one against him. Having failed, he had died in that flaming pyre that was the dream of all aviators.

Chapter Fifty-One

Without a body—without an answer—it was hard for Chubbie to move on. 'What if' and 'if only' rattled around in her brain, inevitably coming back to the biggest 'what if' and 'if only' of them all: Haden Clarke. A moment of alcohol-induced libidinous madness had set in motion a chain of events that had now ended in the deaths of two men. And, try as she might, she couldn't lay the blame on anyone but herself.

She had planned to cut her ties with Bill but the forced severance left her feeling adrift, wondering what she was to do with the rest of her life. She decided as a first step to get her British pilot's licence, which she managed after only ten hours of solo flying. She couldn't afford to obtain a commercial licence—not that it would have been of much use, anyway. The airlines wouldn't employ a female pilot and she lacked the knowledge to become a flight instructor. Would she, like Bill, have to resort to death-or-disaster flying—to break a record or travel around the world backwards or do something equally crazy—in order to get the public's attention?

When Colonel Jellicoe of the Transsaharienne Company offered her a job typing and making West African aerial survey maps, she gladly accepted. She had come to know him well while pestering him for information about the search for Bill. And at least the job had something to do with her beloved world of aviation.

One day, a woman named Mary Bruce came into the office and asked the colonel if he would prepare maps for her. She planned to make the first flight to Cape Town in an autogyro—a rotorcraft that flew behind an engine-driven propeller and an unpowered auto-rotating rotor to generate lift. Colonel Jellicoe said that Chubbie prepared his maps and could make Mrs Bruce's as well.

Mary's name was familiar to Chubbie. In 1930 and 1931, she had been the first woman to fly solo 'around the world', solving the problem of crossing the world's oceans by loading her plane onto a ship. In 1932 she had failed in three attempts at breaking the world flight-refuelled endurance record, assisted by a co-pilot, Flight Lieutenant John Barnard Walter Pugh.

The two women soon became friends. One day, Mary asked if she would be interested in accompanying her on her African trip. John Pugh, who was now her business partner, was to escort her across the Sahara in a de Havilland Dragon, accompanied by a wireless operator and engineer. Chubbie could join them as a passenger.

Chubbie had never fulfilled her promise to search for Bill. While the desert was too large for her to have any chance of finding him, she could at least gain a sense of what he had experienced, to feel connected again to her one-time best friend and lover.

They left Lympne aerodrome on 25 November 1934 but didn't travel far. Mary crash-landed in Nîmes, France, and her damaged aircraft had to be shipped back to England for repairs. Chubbie and the three men found themselves fog-bound in Lyons. There, she and John Pugh became friends over evening games of bridge.

After the repairs were completed, Mary asked Chubbie if she would be interested in obtaining a slow plane and accompanying her to

Cape Town. Mary couldn't risk flying her tricky aircraft across Africa's deserts without an escort and John couldn't spare any more time from their businesses.

Chubbie obtained a small two-seat Robinson Redwing biplane and organised finance to pay for maps and extra fuel tanks and all the other costs associated with a long-distance flight. Shortly before their departure though, Mary phoned to say she had a lecture engagement and couldn't make the trip. Chubbie was heartbroken. Not only would she miss out on her opportunity to privately farewell Bill, she had been left with a large debt and a plane so slow it was incapable of setting any records.

She visited all her financiers and said that she could repay some of the money, but would have to earn the rest. All responded, 'Go out by yourself and the best of luck.'

Business-minded as always, she set her mind to working out what she could do with her meagre financial resources—two shillings and threepence halfpenny—and a slow plane. She decided to fly to Cape Town as a commercial traveller. She approached manufacturers and pitched her idea. Some rebuffed her while others were intrigued and supportive. As she wrote in an exclusive for *The Sunday Referee*, which was helping fund her trip, 'After all, why shouldn't there be flying commercial travellers? And flying women commercial travellers at that.'

She set off from Croydon on 4 January 1935 with the names of her sponsor companies emblazoned over the Redwing. Carrying samples of British goods—whisky, wristwatches and other items—she planned to visit lonely trading outposts in central Africa to obtain orders. Fog, rain and snow dogged her across France, forcing her to land in a field, where she was promptly arrested for spying. Mistrals held her up for a week in Marseilles, while strong gusts across the Pyrenees nearly blew her out of the plane.

She took the short Gibraltar-to-Tangier hop across the Mediterranean then flew south-east towards the Transsaharienne Company motor track. She too would follow the track on her own Sahara crossing. At Colomb Béchar, Algeria, where she was to pick up the track, the entire military personnel came out to watch the Redwing land. The looks of astonishment on their faces when she pushed up her goggles and called out, '*Bonjour, messieurs, parlez-vous Anglais?*' left her chuckling.

Treated as if she were royalty, she left Béchar with her plane fully serviced and bearing the squadron's insignia, and with a supply of desert rations including *pâté de foie gras* and a three-gallon container of water. She also had explicit instructions from the commandant: if she lost sight of the track, she must immediately land and go to sleep and he himself would fly out to find her.

Nothing anybody had said had prepared her for the horror of flying for hundreds of miles over flat sand with nothing to break the monotony. And she could understand why the commandant had issued his instructions. Following the motor track sounded easy, but it wasn't. It kept disappearing under the sand.

She thought about Bill as she flew mile after interminable mile. He was out there somewhere, perhaps only a short distance away. Would she ever find out what had happened to him?

When she caught sight of the Niger River, she yelled for joy.

A few days later, everything went belly-up. Huge clouds of billowing smoke blinded her while a strong headwind emptied her fuel tanks. Spotting a deserted road, she touched down safely and was slowing when she saw four locals standing on the road in front of her, gaping at her still-moving plane instead of diving into the bushes. When she swerved into the bushes, the impact broke the Redwing's back. Her marketing trip was over, along with her dream of a commercial travelling business.

Upon her return to England, word spread about her piloting and map-making abilities and she was approached by another aerial survey firm interested in West Africa. After financial issues kept delaying them, Mary Bruce said, 'Those fellows are never going to get anywhere. You'd be much better off working for me. Would you manage my Heston office?' When Chubbie agreed, she found herself office manager for Luxury Air Tours, Air Dispatch, and Commercial Air Hire, the three companies owned by Mary Bruce and John Pugh.

In July 1935, the press caught up with her there, describing her as the woman who had once earned £2000 per year but was now a typist. She said that there were few opportunities for female aviators in England, but that there must be something for her. One way or another she would find it.

There was indeed something, although it wasn't quite what she had expected. The press interviewed her again a year later, when she married John Pugh on 16 May 1936 at the Epsom registry office. 'From now on there will be no more flying stunts for me,' she said, charming everyone again with her sparkling eyes and beaming smile of old. 'My wild days are over. I have had my fun. I'm just going to sit back and let John do the piloting for both of us now.'

And she did.

Epilogue

In 1962, a French motorised patrol was on a reconnaissance mission in Mali, exploring Signal du Tanezrouft, a hundred miles west of Bidon 5 on what is now called the Trans-Saharan track. Tanezrouft, or the 'land of thirst' as the locals called it, was a desert within the Saharan desert, one in which even the desert-dwellers chose not to dwell. Few westerners had ventured into the area. Barren, featureless, waterless, it lay a few hundred miles south of Reggane, where France had exploded its first atomic bomb in 1960.

Finding little but prehistoric tombs, the platoon headed north on a course parallel with the motor track. On 12 February, having found nothing to add to their maps, they decided to return to the motor track. The soft sand proved incapable of supporting a heavy vehicle so they drove north for a further twenty-five miles until the sand firmed enough for them to turn east. The patrol was around forty-five miles from the track when the men spotted something in the distance.

No date palms, no rock outcrops, not even a ripple of a sand dune broke a vista so flat it was almost unnerving. Except for this lump. They steered towards it. The air was so clear the men could identify the object from a mile away: a crashed plane. They looked at it with horror, wondering if one of the four atomic bombs exploded in the Reggane vicinity had downed a lost pilot.

As they drew closer, they saw that it was a small biplane, a model from the 1920s or 1930s. It was so severely damaged it looked little more than a shell and appeared to have been there for decades. Lying near the plane, partly covered with sand, was the mummified corpse of its pilot. His forehead was marked by an ugly gash. His hand was drawn up towards his throat as if to tell them he had died of thirst.

They found a diary and other personal objects attached to the wing. The diary informed them that the pilot's name was Captain William Lancaster and that he had crashed on 12 April 1933. In heartbreaking detail, it described the events that followed.

'Thursday morning, April 13th [1933], 5 am: I have just escaped a miraculous death. Why?' Plopping onto his knees, Bill thanked God he was alive and begged for assistance in his hour of need.

He struggled to remember what had happened. Gradually, it came back to him.

He had left Reggane at 6.30 pm and had followed the motor track until the last of the sun's golden rays disappeared. Above and around him, the sky was filled with pinpricks of light. Below, there was nothing. Pure blackness, as if his eyes were swathed in a thick dark cloth. Until the moon rose, he would be unable to see the motor track or the aerial beacons. He would be flying blind.

Around 8.15 pm, his engine coughed. Five minutes later, it coughed again. Then it missed a beat.

His now struggling engine could no longer keep his plane in the air. Surrounded by impenetrable gloom, he lost all sense of his altitude as he tried to guide the Avian down safely. It slammed into the ground sooner than he had expected. Bouncing into the air, it crashed down again and flipped over.

When he recovered consciousness, he found himself upside down and imprisoned in his cockpit. Blood from a forehead wound had congealed in his eyes, forcing him to prise them open. Petrol fumes filled his nose. He had to get out. Twisting like a corkscrew, scraping sand away with his nails, he extricated himself from the plane.

He thought about walking to the motor track, calculating that it was only about twenty miles away. But he had promised Chubbie he would remain with the plane. And she had promised she would search for him.

He decided instead to ration his water to a pint a day which would enable him to survive for seven days—so long as injuries didn't cause blood poisoning or he didn't go mad with thirst and guzzle the whole lot down in one go.

To pass the time, he began a diary in his logbook. 'I wonder where everyone thinks I am,' he mused. 'I think mostly of my mother and Chubbie. I love them both. Chubbie is my own sweetheart but mother is such a darling. They both were proud of me before I set out.'

Later in the day, he wrote: 'People who haven't been in the desert have no real idea of *thirst*. It's *hell*! Will hold out as long as possible but loss of blood has made me weak. I realise that this period of agony in the Sahara desert is going to be as long to the mind as my whole lifetime. Truly am I atoning for any wrong done on this earth.' He added that he didn't want to die, that he had the love of a good mother and father and a sweetheart he adored.

As the heat gradually eased, he made some rough flares by cutting strips of fabric, rolling them and putting them on the flying wires. He would use the petrol to burn one every twenty minutes throughout the night. Monsieur Borel had promised to send out a rescue car if he hadn't reached Gao by 6 pm. He knew that the rescue cars wouldn't be able to see him but he hoped they might see a fire or a flare. 'Let me *pray* so. The day seems never ending and this is only the first.'

He ignited the fire at 10.30 pm, which helped keep him warm. The temperature had dropped even faster than it had risen until it was near freezing point. Every fifteen to thirty minutes, he put a match to a flare which lit the sky brilliantly for about sixty seconds.

No one came.

Day after day, he calmly noted down his experiences. Four days after his crash, on Monday, 17 April, he wrote: 'Not a breath of air. I am resigned to the end if it has to be. I think I can last until the day after tomorrow—but no longer. Oh for water, water.'

As the sun set that day, he admitted, 'I can see I shall not be rescued unless a miracle happens. Chubbie, remember I kept my word, I "stuck to the ship". I hope it will not be too hard to bear—the end I mean. I have lain gasping with thirst today—but I stuck to my guns and think I can survive two more days. Am getting a bit weak for I have had no food of course. I only feel thirsty.' He asked his mother to kiss his daughters and to tell Kiki that she could now really forget him.

When he woke the following morning, it was a week since he had set off. The air was smotheringly still and flies buzzed around his wounds. He lay there listening for the noise of an engine, thinking it would sound like music to his ears.

No one came.

The next day, Wednesday, 19 April, he wrote: 'My water will give out today. It cannot be made to last longer. It is then just a matter of a few hours and please God a quick end.' Realising that this would be his last diary entry, he had a few final words to say. He told his darling Chubbie to give up flying, to collect any money that was available and pay what was just to his parents. Then she should take a passage to Australia and be with her sweet mother. 'You will always think of old Bill as a good scout. Too bad I had to go like this—think of me occasionally and write your book—I'd like to think it would be dedicated to me.'

It shouldn't have taken so long to find him. The rescue authorities had ordered two planes to search for sixty miles either side of the motor track. In a clear sky, at a height of 1500 feet, a pilot could see nearly fifty miles in either direction. Bill's plane had crashed on flat terrain only forty-five miles from the track. He should have been found alive.

Chubbie was standing in the kitchen of her cottage in Hurley, Berkshire, on the morning of Monday, 19 February 1962, when the telephone rang. A neighbour told her that her name was in the papers again. After twenty-nine years, Chubbie finally had an answer to the mystery of Bill's death.

The press besieged her after the discovery of Bill's remains. Journalists camped outside her house. Her phone rang for days. But Chubbie couldn't bring herself to comment. While the discovery should have closed a door that had long refused to shut, it instead pushed it wide open.

The memories of that terrible period flooded through her again. And they remained strong in the years that followed. Bill had signed a will in her favour before flying to Africa so his diary soon came into her possession. She allowed the press to publish its contents—with Johnny's approval. Her beloved husband had been so moved by Bill's courage and calm acceptance of his dreadful fate, he had urged her to make the diary entries available to the public. In the aftermath, she was interviewed extensively for a book about Bill and the book's publication kept the story alive both in the public's mind and in her own.

Chubbie died in a London hospital in 1972, ten years after the discovery of Bill's remains. Her death went unremarked by the press.

The irony is hard to miss. Chubbie's aviation achievements and popularity had eclipsed Bill's in life but Bill eclipsed her in death.

Author's note

When Mark Twain wrote about his adventures in Australia, he said of his story, 'It is full of surprises, and adventures, and incongruities, and contradictions, and incredibilities; but they are all true, they all happened.' He could have been talking about the life of Chubbie Miller.

I first heard about Chubbie's story early in 2015 when my wonderful publisher at Allen & Unwin, Rebecca Kaiser, told me that Richard Walsh, a prominent member of Australia's publishing industry, had a story he thought I might be interested in. When she sent me the article that had intrigued him, I wasn't just interested—I told them I would sell my soul for the story! They liked my enthusiasm. Soon afterwards, I had a contract for the most extraordinary story I could ever imagine writing.

And it was a story that kept on giving. The four-page article Richard had found devoted only a few paragraphs to the flight of the *Red Rose*. Thanks to the growing availability of online historical newspapers, I stumbled across Chubbie's own ten-part account of the everything-that-could-go-wrong-did-go-wrong flight. Not only did it provide a detailed description of the many dramas she experienced, it documented her thoughts and feelings as well. I felt as though I had been given the key to a goldmine. I also found her own account of her Bahamas misadventure, and of some of her other flights, as well as published transcripts of entries from Bill's diaries. Additionally, Sarah Duncanson—whose father, Ralph Barker, wrote a 1960s book about Bill Lancaster (*Verdict of a Lost Flyer*)—kindly gave me a copy of her father's extensive interviews with Chubbie.

With so much personal information available—thoughts, feelings and conversations—much of *The Fabulous Flying Mrs Miller* reads almost like historical fiction or fictionalised history. Let me stress: it isn't. It is narrative non-fiction—that is, history told as a story. I am making this distinction clear because so many people have mentioned the words 'fiction' and 'fictionalisation' in their remarks to me about my previous books, that it is obvious that the previous author's notes didn't provide enough clarity about the genre. Why is this distinction important? Because writers of fictionalised history can write pretty much anything they want whereas a non-fiction author has extremely limited boundaries.

For example, the dialogue in this book is not made up. It is taken from original records: newspaper accounts, court records and Chubbie's interviews. While some non-fiction authors do make up dialogue, in my opinion made-up dialogue transforms a work of narrative non-fiction into fictionalised history.

Writing non-fiction involves a huge amount of research. My own research trips included visits to Australian, British and American libraries. I also sent requests for help to other libraries and librarians in the United States. Mostly, however, I must thank the internet for my information. When my first book, *An Irresistible Temptation*, was published in 2006, readers regularly asked if I had used the internet to source material. When I said that I'd hardly used it at all, the usual response was, 'So where did you find all your information?' The answer: government record repositories, libraries (public and private), and newspaper originals and microfilms. For *The Fabulous Flying Mrs Miller*, however, much of my original information did indeed come from the internet because so much more information is now available online. The biggest boon was the online historical newspapers. Thanks to the various newspaper digitisation projects, I picked up reports from Australian, British, American, Indian, Chinese and Southeast Asian newspapers and, indirectly, from other international newspapers as well. I spent a lot of money on printer paper and toner.

While I would have liked to travel to every city Chubbie visited in order to undertake research in the local record offices and libraries, it would have cost a fortune. Fortunately, the press included so many different accounts of the various incidents in Chubbie's life that a careful analysis of the similarities and differences made it possible to sift facts from fiction.

This brings us to the troubling 'Did he or didn't he?' question. When history is written as a narrative, it can be difficult to find an appropriate place to include an analysis of the evidence. Since readers might be interested in my thoughts and conclusions, I have analysed the evidence in a series of blog posts on my website: **www.carolbaxter. com/bill-lancaster.html**. Readers can add their own thoughts in the comments section.

Let me begin my acknowledgements by thanking the various governments and commercial enterprises who have invested in the digitisation of historical newspapers. History is being rewritten as a result. And may they continue their investment (only a small proportion of historical newspapers have been digitised to date).

It is now more than a decade since I began working with Rebecca Kaiser. I remember, as I posted my first manuscript, that I yearned with every atom of my being to have it picked up. Little did I realise that a decade later, my sixth work of popular history would be published. So thanks to Rebecca for her ongoing support, insights and friendship.

I had no idea I was even on Richard Walsh's radar when Rebecca mentioned that he had a story for me. Richard later told me that a good book requires the combination of both a good story and a good writer. I am extremely grateful and humbled that he decided I was the right person to write this fabulous story. May we continue our collaboration in the future.

Two other people are key agents in the editorial process. This is the first time I have worked with copyeditor Aziza Kuypers, and my appreciation is shown in the fact that I would be very happy to work with her again. Also, this is my third book with Allen & Unwin editor Angela Handley. Their attention to detail is extraordinary and appreciated. They can both take credit for helping to lift this manuscript to the next level.

It is also a decade since I was picked up by my literary agent, Tara Wynne of Curtis Brown. Thanks again for your terrific support. May this be the one!

My heartfelt thanks to Sarah Duncanson for providing a copy of Chubbie's interviews along with other material including photocopies from Miami newspapers (which are not available online). Sarah was travelling there on holiday and kindly offered to obtain copies of some newspaper trial reports I hadn't been able to access. I am so very, very grateful. Her father's book about Bill was republished under the title *Bill Lancaster: The final verdict—The life and death of an aviation pioneer* in 2015.

I also wish to thank Bill Lancaster's granddaughter, Debbie Squires, and documentary film-makers Andrew Lancaster and Noni Couell (*The Lost Aviator: The true story of Bill Lancaster*) for their help and support. Debbie, I hope you feel that I have done justice to your grandfather's story.

All writers need a group of trusted readers who are willing to spend hours and hours reading an early draft and offering criticisms and suggestions to improve it. I am blessed with my own group: Mike Elliott, from Stoke Poges, England, who also devoted hundreds of hours to helping me with internet and British library research for this book and who found most of the published pictures; Kate Wingrove (you are still always right); Meredith Jaffé (whose debut novel, *The Fence*, has just been published to critical acclaim); and my pilot and engineer brother, Peter Baxter, for helping me with aviation technicalities that were leaving me stumped.

To Natasha Duwin, Tobias Franoszek and their sons Ivo and Kai, who welcomed me to an Argentine barbecue in what was once Chubbie's Miami home, thank you! To see that room, to imagine it in the early hours of 21 April 1932, was a surreal experience.

To the many others who provided assistance with the book: Hamish Allen, aviation writer; Dave Batchelor, archivist, Craighead Diocesan School, Timaru, New Zealand; Scott Brener, aviation historian of Apple River, Illinois; Jim Eames, aviation expert; David Howells, aviation expert; Jenny Johnson, archivist, Stanford University; Sarah Keen, Head of Special Collections, Colgate University; Dan Lewis, Public Relations Manager, Stanfords, London; Christopher Manvell, seller of *Popular Flying* magazines; Terry Metter, librarian, Cleveland Public Library; Blake Robinson, librarian, Florida Collection, State Library of Florida; Dave Robinson, Aviation Ancestry, UK; Sheila Sanders, researcher, Sacramento Genealogical Association; Michael Sheraba, Collections Manager, International Women's Air and Space Museum, USA; John Shipley, librarian, Miami-Dade Public Library; Clive Small, former Assistant Police Commissioner of New South Wales; Drew Smith, librarian, Academic Services Department, University of

South Florida; Robert Tucker, librarian, Wichita Public Library; Colin Wells, author, of New York, and Andrew Wright, editor, *Aircrew Book Review*, who proofread the book and checked technical details. Thank you all.

As ever, to my wonderfully supportive and forbearing family: my husband, Allan Ashmore, who was so intrigued by all the stories I kept telling him about Chubbie's adventures ('You're not going to believe what I've found *now* . . .!') that he insisted on reading the manuscript rather than waiting for the published book; my snake-phobic daughter, Camillie Ashmore, who raced from the room every time I mentioned the snake-in-the-plane incident (sorry about that!); my son, Jaiden Ashmore, for putting up with my constant talk about Chubbie; and my mother, Jill Baxter, who is my best-ever publicist. Also to my daughter's boyfriend, Chris Holliday-Smith, for his suggestion regarding a title: *The Girl on the Plane*. Somehow I will manage to slip that into my author talks.

And finally, to Chubbie herself. It is a strange experience to have another person take over one's life for two years—even more so, I suspect, when that person was real. For the first time ever, I am a little bit in love with my protagonist—particularly after seeing the film footage of her (look at the eight-minute mark on http://mirc.sc.edu/islandora/object/usc%3A28623). She is just gorgeous. It's going to be extremely hard to cut her out of my life and to embrace another historical character. So, Chubbie, this is for you. I hope you would have loved what I have written as much as I loved writing about you.

Notes

Page 19: *He had just turned sixteen when his parents dispatched him to Australia to gain experience on the land*: Previous publications have noted that Bill and Jack went to Australia with the Dominions Royal Commission; however, original sources indicate that this information is not correct. The Dominions Royal Commission visited Australia in 1913 with Sir Rider Haggard in attendance. Bill sailed for Australia in February 1914 and Jack two years later. When Bill was later interviewed by Chubbie's husband, he said that his father, acting on the advice of Sir Rider Haggard, had sent his boys to Australia to gain experience on the land. This explains why the boys were in the Riverina district (although working as electricians by then) when they enlisted. It is possible Haggard's advice was generic—from the stage during a seminar—rather than as the result of a personal conversation with Bill's father.

Page 117: During the *Red Rose* flight, the press referred to Chubbie either as Mrs Keith Miller or Mrs Miller. In America, Chubbie referred to herself as Mrs Keith Miller. The press often treated the two components as a hyphenated surname: Mrs Keith-Miller. After her divorce, she called herself Mrs J.M. Keith Miller or Mrs Jessie M. Keith Miller, as if she had a double-barrelled surname. However, the press often treated it as a hyphenated surname: Mrs Keith-Miller. For consistency purposes, this publication uses Mrs Miller unless the reference to her name is in a quote.

Page 141: *Only nineteen of the twenty registered planes were lined up.* The twenty participants in the Powder Puff Derby of 1929 were Pancho Barnes, Marvel Crosson, Amelia Earhart, Ruth Elder, Claire Fahy, Edith Foltz, Mary Haizlip (who arrived late), Opal Kunz, Mary von Mach, Chubbie Miller, Ruth Nichols,

Blanche Noyes, Gladys O'Donnell, Phoebe Omlie, Neva Paris, Margaret Perry, Thea Rasche, Louise Thaden, Bobbi Trout and Vera Walker. Marjorie Crawford, Peggy Hall, Gladys Poole and Patty Willis registered but withdrew before the race began.

Page 187: The National Air Tour destinations (5–21 October 1929) were: Detroit (Michigan), Windsor (Ontario, Canada), Toronto, Ottawa, Montreal (all in Canada), Portland (Maine), Springfield (Massachusetts), New York, Philadelphia (Pennsylvania), Baltimore, Richmond (Virginia), Winston-Salem (North Carolina), Greenville (South Carolina), Augusta (Georgia), Jacksonville (Florida), Macon (Georgia), Atlanta (Georgia), Nashville (Tennessee), Cincinnati (Ohio), Louisville (Kentucky), St Louis (Missouri), Springfield (Missouri), Wichita (Kansas), St Joseph (Iowa), Des Moines (Iowa), Cedar Rapids (Iowa), St Paul (Minnesota), Wausau (Wisconsin), Milwaukee (Wisconsin), Moline (Illinois), Chicago (Illinois), Kalamazoo (Michigan), Detroit.

Bibliography

Primary sources (selected)

Australian Electoral Rolls, 1903–1980: Charles Stanley Beveridge, Ethelwyn Maude Beveridge, George Keith Miller, Jessie Maude Miller,

British Royal Air Force, Officers' Service Records, 1912–1920: Jack Kelvin Lancaster; William Newton Lancaster,

California Passengers and Crew Lists, 1882–1959: Jessie Miller and William Newton Lancaster per *Malolo*, arrived from Honolulu, 11 July 1929,

Death Certificate, Jessie Maude Pugh, 1972: General Register Office, UK, Hammersmith Registration District, Vol. 5b, p. 1987.

Death Certificate, Thomas Charles Beveridge, 1926: Queensland Department of Justice and Attorney General, 1926/B49874.

England & Wales, National Probate Calender (Index of Wills and Administrations), 1858–1966: William Newton Lancaster, probate, 22 November 1933,

Florida Passenger Lists, 1898–1964: William Newton Lancaster and Jessie Maude Miller, 5 December 1930; William Newton Lancaster, 6 December 1930; Jessie Maude Miller, 26 May 1931,

Great Britain Royal Aero Club Aviators' Certificates, 1910–1950, Album 25, Certificate No. 8819: William Newton Lancaster, 1 November 1917, <www.ancestry.com.au>

Honolulu, Hawaii, Passenger and Crew Lists, 1900–1959: William Lancaster and Jessie Miller, 6 July 1928,

Index to Alien Arrivals by Airplane at Miami, Florida, 1930–1942: Jessie Maude Miller, 6 December 1930,

Marriage Certificate, Jessie Beveridge: Births, Deaths & Marriages, Victoria: 1919/9161

War Service Records, Jack Kelvin Lancaster: National Archives of Australia, <http://recordsearch.naa.gov.au>

War Service Records, William Newton Lancaster: National Archives of Australia, <http://recordsearch.naa.gov.au>

New York City Passenger Lists, 1820–1957: William N. Lancaster per *Vauban* arrived from Trinidad (departed 13 April 1929),

New York Passenger Lists, 1820–1957: William N. Lancaster per *Vauban* from Trinidad arrived 20 April 1929,

New York Passenger Lists, 1820–1957: Ethelwyn M.L. Beveridge per *Berengaria* arrived from Southampton, England, on 1 August 1930,

Passenger Lists leaving UK, 1890–1960: Jack K. Lancaster per *Orontes* departed London 27 January 1916,

UK Incoming Passenger Lists, 1878–1960: Jessie Miller per *American Banker* from New York to London arriving 24 October 1932; William N. Lancaster per *Scythia* from New York to Liverpool, England, arriving 24 October 1932,

UK Outward Passenger Lists, 1890–1960: William N. Lancaster departed London on 26 February 1914 per *Benalla* for Sydney,

Victoria, Australia, Assisted and Unassisted Passenger Lists, 1839–1923: William N. Lancaster per *Benalla* from London arrived 10 April 1914,

Victoria Inward Passenger Lists, 1839–1923: William N. Lancaster per *Benalla* from Britain arrived April 1914,

Film footage

'National Air Race—Outtakes', filmed 27 August 1929, Moving Image Research Collections, <http://mirc.sc.edu/islandora/object/usc%3A28623>

Newspaper and journal digitisation services

Aero Digest, <https://archive.org/details/aerodigest1919unse?>

British Library Newspapers, 1741–1950 (UK)—accessed via State Library of New South Wales

Californian Digital Newspaper Collection (USA), <http://cdnc.ucr.edu/cgi-bin/cdnc>

Daily Mail Historical Archive, 1896–2004 (UK)—accessed via State Library of New South Wales

Flightglobal: Archive (UK), <www.flightglobal.com/pdfarchive/index.html>

Google Newspapers (USA), <https://news.google.com/newspapers>

Newspaper.com (USA), <https://www.newspapers.com/>

Newspaper Archive.com (USA), <http://newspaperarchive.com/>

NewspaperSG (Singapore), <http://eresources.nlb.gov.sg/newspapers/default.aspx>

Pittsburgh Post-Gazette (USA), <https://archives.post-gazette.com/>

Pro Quest Historical Newspapers (International)—accessed via State Library of New South Wales

Red Bank Register Newspaper Archives (USA), <http://209.212.22.88/>

The British Newspaper Archive (UK),

The Illustrated London News Historical Archive, 1842–2003—accessed via State Library of New South Wales

The Telegraph Historical Archive (UK)—accessed via State Library of New South Wales

The Times Digital Archive, 1785–2010 (UK)—accessed via State Library of
    New South Wales
Trove (Australia), <http://trove.nla.gov.au/newspaper/>
UK Press Online (UK), <www.ukpressonline.co.uk/ukpressonline/open/userLogin.
    jsp;jsessionid=01605911D6BF7EBBA48C69CE4EF79E55>

Newspapers and magazines

AUSTRALIA
The Advertiser (Adelaide, SA)
Advocate (Burnie, TAS)
The Argus (Melbourne, VIC)
The Australasian (Melbourne, VIC)
Barrier Miner (Broken Hill, NSW)
The Brisbane Courier (QLD)
Call News-Pictorial (Perth, WA)
The Church of England Messenger
    (Melbourne, VIC)
Daily Mercury (Mackay, QLD)
The Daily News (Perth, WA)
Daily Standard (Brisbane, QLD)
Daily Telegraph (Launceston, TAS)
*The Dubbo Liberal and Macquarie
    Advocate* (NSW)
Evening News (Sydney, NSW)
Examiner (Launceston, TAS)
Gippsland Times (VIC)
Kalgoorlie Miner (WA)
The Mail (Adelaide, SA)
Maitland Daily Mercury (NSW)
The Maitland Mercury (NSW)
The Mercury (Hobart, TAS)
Morning Bulletin (Rockhampton, QLD)
*Newcastle Morning Herald and Miners'
    Advocate* (NSW)
The Newcastle Sun (NSW)
News (Adelaide, SA)
Northern Herald (Cairns, QLD)
Northern Standard (Darwin, NT)
Northern Star (Lismore, NSW)
Northern Territory Times (Darwin, NT)
Observer (Adelaide, SA)
Queensland Times (Ipswich, QLD)
The Register (Adelaide, SA)
The Riverine Grazier (Hay, NSW)

The Southern Cross Times (WA)
The Sun (Sydney, NSW)
Sunday Times (Perth, WA)
The Sydney Morning Herald (NSW)
The Telegraph (Brisbane, QLD)
Townsville Daily Bulletin (QLD)
The West Australian (Perth, WA)
Western Champion (Parkes, NSW)
Western Mail (Perth, WA)

INDIA, ASIA AND THE PACIFIC
China Press
Malayan Saturday Post
*The North China Herald and Supreme
    Court and Consular Gazette*
The Rangoon Times
*The Singapore Free Press and Mercantile
    Advertiser*
The Straits Times (Malaya)
The Times of India

NEW ZEALAND
Auckland Star
Press (Christchurch)
Southland Star (Invercargill)
Timaru Herald

UNITED KINGDOM
The Aeroplane (London, UK)
Army, Navy and Air Force Gazette
    (London, UK)
Daily Express (London, UK)
Daily Herald (London, UK)
Daily Mirror (London, UK)
Daily Worker (London, UK)
Flight (London, UK)
Grantham Journal (Lincolnshire, UK)

The London Gazette (UK)
Manchester Guardian (UK)
The Observer (London, UK)
Popular Flying (Boreham Wood, UK)
Sunday Express (London, UK)
The Sunday Referee (London, UK)
The Scotsman (Edinburgh, UK)
The Times (London, UK)
Yorkshire Post (UK)

**UNITED STATES OF AMERICA
AND CANADA**
Abilene Reporter-News (TX)
Aero Digest (New York, USA)
Alton Evening Telegraph (IL)
The Altoona Mirror (PA)
Altoona Tribune (PA)
The Amarillo Globe-Times (TX)
Ames Daily Tribune (IA)
The Anniston Star (AL)
The Bee (Danville, VA)
Belvidere Daily Republican (IL)
The Billings Gazette (MT)
*Bradford Evening Star and the Bradford
    Daily Record* (PA)
The Brainerd Daily Dispatch (MN)
The Brooklyn Daily Eagle (NY)
Calexico Chronicle (CA)
The Charleston Daily Mail (WV)
The Chicago Tribune (IL)
The Columbus Dispatch (OH)
Daily Capital Journal (Salem, OR)
The Daily Courier (Connellsville, PA)
The Daily Journal-Gazette (Mattoon, IL)
The Daily Notes (Canonsburg, PA)
The Daily Republican (Monongahela, PA)
The Decatur Herald (IL)
Dunkirk Evening Observer (NY)
El Paso Herald (TX)
The Eugene Guard (OR)
Eugene Register (OR)
The Evening Standard (Uniontown, PA)
Florence Morning News (SC)
The Gettysburg Times (PA)
Greenfield Daily Reporter (IN)
The Havre Daily News (MT)

The Hutchinson News (KS)
The Independent Record (Helena, MT)
The Index-Journal (Greenwood, SC)
The Indiana Evening Gazette (PA)
The Indiana Gazette (PA)
The Indianapolis News (IN)
Ironwood Daily Globe (MI)
Jefferson City Post-Tribune (MO)
Joplin Globe (MO)
The Journal News (Hamilton, OH)
Key West Citizen (FL)
Kingsport Times (TN)
The Klamath News (Klamath Falls, OR)
The Lasso (Denton, TX)
Lincoln Evening Journal (NE)
The Lincoln Star (NE)
The Los Angeles Times (CA)
Lubbock Morning Avalanche (TX)
Mail Tribune (Medford, OR)
Manitowoc Herald-Times (WI)
The Mason City Globe-Gazette (IA)
Miami Daily News-Record (OK)
Miami Daily News (FL)
Miami Herald (FL)
Midland Reporter Telegram (TX)
New Castle News (PA)
The News-Herald (Franklin, PA)
The New York Times (NY)
Oakland Tribune (CA)
The Oregon Statesman (Salem, OR)
Oshkosh Daily Northwestern (WI)
The Ottawa Journal (Canada)
Pittsburgh Post-Gazette (PA)
Pittsburgh Press (PA)
Pittston Gazette (PA)
Plain Dealer (Cleveland, OH)
Popular Aviation (Chicago, USA)
Portsmouth Daily Times (TX)
The Rhinelander Daily News (WI)
Richmond Times Dispatch (VA)
The San Bernardino County Sun (CA)
San Bernardino Evening Telegram (CA)
Santa Monica Evening Outlook (CA)
Sarasota Herald (FL)
The Scranton Republican (PA)
Shamokin News-Dispatch (PA)

Simpson's Leader-Times (Kittanning, PA)   Tyrone Daily Herald (PA)
The Springfield Leader (MO)   The Washington Post (DC)
Sterling Daily Gazette (IL)   Wichita Eagle (KS)
The Times-Herald (Olean, NY)   The Wilkes-Barre Record (PA)
The Times Recorder (Zanesville, OH)   The Winnipeg Tribune (Canada)

Online databases
Ancestry.com,
FamilySearch, <https://familysearch.org/>
Findmypast,
GenesReunited,

Books, articles, journals and websites
'31 Squadron History', Royal Air Force: RAF Marham, <www.raf.mod.uk/
    rafmarham/aboutus/31sqnhistory.cfm>
'Abbeville', Through These Lines, <http://throughtheselines.com.au/research/Abbeville>
Aeronautical Chamber of Commerce of America, Aircraft Yearbook for 1931, Vol. 13,
    D. Van Nostrand Company, 1931, pp. 232 & 459
'Air Racing', Smithsonian National Air and Space Museum: Pioneers of Flight,
    <http://pioneersofflight.si.edu/culture/air_racing>
'Alexander Aircraft Company', Wikipedia entry, <https://en.wikipedia.org/wiki/
    Alexander_Aircraft_Company>
'Ambulance Service of New South Wales', NSW Government: Health, <www.
    ambulance.nsw.gov.au/about-us/History/History-of-the-Maltese-Cross.html>
The Americana Annual, Americana Corporation, 1931, p. 8
'Aviation humour', Pilot Friend, <www.pilotfriend.com/humour/jokes/cliches.htm>
'Bill Lancaster, aviator', Wikipedia entry, <https://en.wikipedia.org/wiki/
    Bill_Lancaster_(aviator)>
'Biplane', Wikipedia entry, <http://en.wikipedia.org/wiki/Biplane>
Barker, Ralph, Verdict on a Lost Flyer: The story of Bill Lancaster and Chubbie Miller,
    Fontana, [1969] 1986 (republished as Bill Lancaster: The Final Verdict—The life
    and death of an aviation pioneer, Pen & Sword Aviation, 2015)
'Bill Lancaster: Lost in the Sahara after attempting to break the England–
    Cape Town Flight Speed Record', HistoryNet, <www.historynet.com/
    bill-lancaster-lost-in-the-sahara-after-attempting-to-break-the-england-cape-
    town-flight-speed-record.htm>
'Biplane', Wikipedia entry, <http://en.wikipedia.org/wiki/Biplane>
Brazil, Eddie, Bloody British History: Buckinghamshire, History Press, 2014
'Brief history', FloridaJuryDuty.com, <www.floridajuryduty.com/brief-history.php>
Bryson, Bill, One Summer: America 1927, Doubleday, 2013
Buckrich, Judith, 'Collins Street Clubs', <www.judithbuckrich.com/pdfs/Collins.pdf>
Butler, C. Arthur, Flying Start: The history of the first five decades of civil aviation in
    Australia, Edwards & Shaw, 1971
'Caterpillar Club', Wikipedia entry, <https://en.wikipedia.org/wiki/Caterpillar_Club>
'Cavill, Frederick', Australian Dictionary of Biography, <http://adb.anu.edu.au/
    biography/cavill-frederick-5536>

Çelik, Zeynep, Favro, Diane & Ingersoll, Richard, *Streets: Political perspectives on public space*, University of California, 1994

Chronicling America: Historic American Newspapers, < http://chroniclingamerica. loc.gov/>

Clark, Sarah (ed.), *Insight Guide: Myanmar (Burma)*, APA Publications, 2015

Cohen, Isidor, Historical sketches and sidelights of Miami, Florida, 1925, <http://files.usgwarchives.net/fl/dade/history/1925/historic/pioneers55nms.txt>

'Compagnie générale transsaharienne', Wikipedia entry, <https://en.wikipedia.org/ wiki/Compagnie_g%C3%A9n%C3%A9rale_transsaharienn>

Courtney, Captain Frank T., 'Riding the Wind', *Popular Science*, February 1932, pp. 38–9, 123–5

'The Crown building (formerly the Heckscher building)', The Midtown Book, <www.thecityreview.com/crown.html>

Croydon Advertiser: 1869–1969, Croydon Advertiser, 1969

'Cubana de Aviacion', Wikipedia entry, <https://en.wikipedia.org/wiki/Cubana_de_ Aviaci%C3%B3n>

Davis, Pedr, *Charles Kingsford Smith: The world's greatest aviator*, Summit Books, 1977

Dawson, Virginia P. & Bowles, Mark D., 'Realizing the Dream of Flight', Biographical Essays in Honor of the Centennial of Flight, 1903–2003, <http://history.nasa. gov/sp4112.pdf>

Degremont, Cecile, 'In Pictures: Libya's Roman Ruins', *Al Jazeera*, <www.aljazeera. com/indepth/inpictures/2013/06/2013619141153737358.html>

De Leeuw, Hendrick, *Conquest of the Air: The history and future of aviation*, Vantage Press, 1960

Dymock, D.R., *Hustling Hinkler: The short tumultuous life of a trailblazing Australian aviator*, Hachette, 2013

'Early Airlines: Maddux Air Lines', *Flying Magazine*, November 1963, 73(5): 76

Earhart, Amelia, *The Fun of It: Random records of my own flying and of women in aviation*, Academy Chicago Publishers, [1932] 2006

Fisher, Jim, 'Firearms identification in the Sacco-Vanzetti Case: Part 2. Dr Calvin Goddard: A real expert', <http://jimfisher.edinboro.edu/forensics/sacco2_1. html>

Florida Online Genealogy Records, <https://familysearch.org/wiki/en/ Florida_Online_Genealogy_Records>

'Florida First Degree Murder Laws', FindLaw, <http://statelaws.findlaw.com/ florida-law/florida-first-degree-murder-laws.html>

Fortgang, Laura B., 'The Hero Syndrome', *Innovative Leader*, May 1999, 8(5), <www.winstonbrill.com/bril001/html/article_index/articles/401-450/article401_ body.html>

Free Map Tools (distance calculator), <www.freemaptools.com/how-far-is-it- between.htm>

Goldsborough, Frank, Davis-Monthan Aviation Field Register, <http://dmairfield. com/register_detail.php?CardinalOrder=2289> and <http://dmairfield.com/ Slice_Full.php?image_url=136137.jpg>

Goldsborough, Frank, Wikipedia entry, <https://en.wikipedia.org/wiki/Frank_ Goldsborough>

Goldschmidt, Arthur, *Modern Egypt: The formation of a nation-state*, Westview Press, 1988

Gott, Richard, *Cuba: A new history*, Yale University Press, 2004

Gragert, S.K. & Johansson, M.J. (eds), *The Papers of Will Rogers: The final years, Aug 1928 – Aug 1935*, University of Oklahoma Press, 2006

'The Great Depression and Dow Jones Industrial Average', Generational Dynamics: Forecasting America's Destiny . . . and the World's, <www.generationaldynamics.com/pg/ww2010.i.djia.htm>

Gwynn-Jones, Terry, *Wings Across the Pacific: The courageous aviators who challenged and conquered the greatest ocean*, Allen & Unwin, 1991

Ham, Anthony, *Libya*, Lonely Planet, 2002

Harris, Lillian Craig, *Libya: Qadhafi's revolution and the modern state*, Westview Press, 1986

'The history of air racing: 1929 National Air Races and Aeronautical Exposition', Society of Air Racing Historians, <www.airrace.com/1929NAR-rs.htm>

Hinkler, Bert, 'Hinkler's story: How I flew from London to Melbourne', *Examiner*, 21–31 March 1928

'Jessie Maude "Chubbie" Keith-Miller', Parks Airport, East St Louis, Illinois, <http://parksfield.org/people/keithmiller_jm/index.php>

'Jessie Maude "Chubbie" Miller, 1901–1972', The Pioneers: Aviation and Aeromodelling: Interdependent Evolutions and Histories, <www.ctie.monash.edu.au/hargrave/miller.html>

'Jessie Miller', Wikipedia entry, <https://en.wikipedia.org/wiki/Jessie_Miller>

Jessen, Gene Nora, *The Powder Puff Derby of 1929: The first all-women's transcontinental air race*, Sourcebook, 2002

Johnson, Ben, 'Bright Young Things', Historic UK, <www.historic-uk.com/CultureUK/Bright-Young-Things/>

Karlin, Adam, *Miami and the Keys*, Lonely Planet, 2015

Klaas, Joe, *Amelia Earhart Lives: A trip through intrigue to find America's First Lady of mystery*, McGraw-Hill Book Company, 1970

'L'aérodrome d'Abbeville-Buigny-Saint-Maclou', CCI Littoral Normand-Picard, <www.littoral-normand-picard.cci.fr/Implantation-territoire-equipements/L-aerodrome-d-Abbeville-Buigny-Saint-Maclou>

'Larry Bell: Aviation's super salesman', *Airport Journals*, <http://airportjournals.com/larry-bell-aviations-super-salesman-2/>

Learmonth, Bob, Nash, Joanna & Cluett, Douglas, *The First Croydon Airport, 1915–1928*, Sutton Libraries and Art Services, 1977

Lewis, David L., *The Public Image of Henry Ford: An American folk hero and his company*, Wayne State University Press, 1976

'Libya: Ancient Ruins in African City', *Telegraph*, <www.telegraph.co.uk/travel/activityandadventure/2043044/Libya-Ancient-ruins-in-African-sand.html>

'Love is in the air', *The Sunday Times*, 29 February 2004

McDonald, Ann, 'Henry Lyon Jr: An old sea dog takes to the air', Maine Memory Network, <www.mainememory.net/sitebuilder/site/272/page/531/display?use_mmn=1>

The Fabulous Flying Mrs Miller

Mann, Sheila, *The Girls Were Up There Too: Australian women in aviation*,
Department of Aviation, 1986

Mann, T. & Ward, A., 'Forbidden Fruit: Does thinking about a prohibited food
lead to its consumption', *International Journal of Eating Disorders*, April 2001,
29(3): 319–27

'Marvel Crosson', *20th Century Aviation Magazine*, <http://20thcenturyaviation
magazine.com/o-capt-nancy-aldrich/marvel-crosson>

Matowitz, Thomas G., *Cleveland's National Air Races*, Arcadia Publishing, 2005

Mellon, Steve, 'Pittsburgh: The dark years', *Pittsburgh Post-Gazette*, <http://news
interactive.post-gazette.com/prohibition/>

Miller, G. Keith, 'Lancaster, Captain William Newton: Adventurous life from
boyhood', *Examiner*, 26 April 1929

Miller, Jessie, 'Down in the forest: The true story of my adventures while flying in
Africa', *Popular Flying*, August 1935, 4(5): 268–71

Miller, Jessie, 'Mrs Keith Miller's story', *The Register*, 19–30 April 1928

Miller, Jessie, 'Mrs Keith-Miller tells own story of air adventures', *Pittsburgh
Post-Gazette*, 3 December 1930

Miller, Jessie, 'Willing to sacrifice reputation to save life of man she admires',
The Indiana Gazette, 3 August 1932

Miller-Pugh, Jessie, correspondence with Ralph Barker (provided by Sarah
Duncanson, daughter of Ralph Barker)

Miller-Pugh, Jessie, transcript of interviews with Ralph Barker (provided by Sarah
Duncanson and Debbie Squires, granddaughter of Captain W.N. Lancaster)

Mostyn, Trevor, *Egypt's Belle Epoque: Cairo 1869–1952*, Quartet Books, 1989

Munger, Sean, 'Spiritualism: The 1920s obsession with the dead', <http://
seanmunger.com/2014/03/16/spiritualism-the-1920s-obsession-with-the-dead/>

'Murray Night Club', *Jazz Age Club*, <www.jazzageclub.com/venues/murrays-night-
club/>

Nijman, Jan, *Miami: Mistress of the Americas*, University of Pennsylvania Press, 2011

'Open cockpit flying', *Pilot*, <www.pilotweb.aero/features/
open_cockpit_flying_1_1690514>

'The origin of free style: The Australian Crawl', Swim Swam, <http://swimswam.
com/the-origin-of-freestyle-the-australian-crawl/>

Parnell, Neville & Boughton, Trevor, *Flypast: A record of aviation in Australia*,
Civil Aviation Authority, Canberra

Payne, Vernon W., 'How to locate the wings', *Popular Aviation*, October 1933, 13:
249–51

Parsons, Elsie Clews, *Folk-Tales of Andros Island, Bahamas*, [1918], Google Books,
2009

Pearce, Carol A., *Amelia Earhart*, Facts on File Publications, 1988

Perez-Stable, Marifeli, *The Cuban Revolution: Origins, course and legacy*, Oxford
University Press, 1999

'Postcard: Cubana Ford Tri-Motor', Airline Artifacts from the Past, <https://
airlineartifacts.wordpress.com/2015/04/04/postcard-cubana-ford-tri-motor/>

'Prohibition', 'It's the booze talking: Prohibition and the gangster film', <http://xroads.
virginia.edu/~ma03/holmgren/prohib/prohib.html>

408

Reilly, Rachel, 'Carbon monoxide: The deadly gas which kills in minutes', *Daily Mail*, <www.dailymail.co.uk/health/article-1356290/Carbon-monoxide-The-deadly-gas-kills-minutes-turns-brain-red.html>

'Rollover', Wikipedia entry, <https://en.wikipedia.org/wiki/Rollover>

'Royal Flying Corps: Research data', <www.airhistory.org.uk/rfc/home.html>

'The Schenley Hotel and Apartments', The Brookline Connection, <www.brooklineconnection.com/history/Facts/Schenley.html>

Shannon, David A., *Between the Wars: America, 1919–1941*, Houghton Mifflin Company, 1979

Sharman, Janann, *Walking on Air: The aerial adventures of Phoebe Omlie*, University Press of Mississippi, 2011

Shiles, Jerry E., 'Chautauqua: A chronology', <www.brownlaw-ok.com/enidhistory/chart1.html>

Simundson, Lisa, *Miami and the Florida Keys Alive!*, Hunter Publishing, 2008

Singerman, Diane & Amar, Paul (eds), *Cairo cosmopolitan: Politics, culture, and urban space in the new globalized Middle East*, The American University in Cairo Press, 2009

Spicer, Chrystopher J., *Great Australian World Firsts: The things we made, the things we did*, Allen & Unwin, 2012

'Stinson Junior', Wikipedia entry, <https://en.wikipedia.org/wiki/Stinson_Junior>

Styles, Ruth, 'The female Top Guns of World War II: Inside the RAF squadron who rubbed shoulders with the men—and flew their Spitfires', *Daily Mail*, <www.dailymail.co.uk/femail/article-3194754/The-female-Guns-World-War-II-Inside-RAF-s-woman-ferry-squadron-rubbed-shoulders-men-flew-Spitfires.html#ixzz44FxZSqxc>

Staten, Clifford L., *The History of Cuba*, Palgrave MacMillan, 2005

'Tanezrouft', Wikipedia entry, <https://en.wikipedia.org/wiki/Tanezrouft>

Taylor, Heather, 'Breaking through the clouds: The first women's National Air Derby', <www.breakingthroughtheclouds.com/pdf/skywaysmagazine1.pdf>

'Test pilot', Wikipedia entry, <https://en.wikipedia.org/wiki/Test_pilot>

Thaden, Louise (McPhetridge), *High, Wide and Frightened*, University of Arkansas Press, 2004

Thaden, Louise (McPhetridge), 'The Women's Air Derby', *Aero Digest*, October 1929, 15(4): 62, 299

'Timetable history of Cuba', historyofcuba.com, <www.historyofcuba.com/history/time/timetbl3.htm>

Trenckmann, Clara, 'Three more women's flying clubs', *Women and Aviation*, January 1930, 18, <www.ninety-nines.org/pdf/newsmagazine/19300112000000.pdf>

Vandewalle, Dirk, *A History of Modern Libya*, Cambridge University Press, 2006

'Venereal disease and treatment during WW2', WW2 US Medical Research Centre, <www.med-dept.com/articles/venereal-disease-and-treatment-during-ww2/>

Walker, Mike, *Powder Puff Derby: Petticoat pilots and flying flappers*, John Wiley & Sons, 2003

Welch, Rosanne, *Encyclopedia of Women in Aviation and Space*, ABC-CLIO, 1998

'William Lancaster and the Red Rose Garage', *Wendover News*, 6 April 2014,
    <www.wendovernews.co.uk/news/william-lancaster-red-rose-garage>

Wright, Arnold (ed.), *Twentieth Century Impressions of Burma: Its history, people, commerce, industry and resources*, Lloyds Greater Britain Publishing Company, 1910

Wright, John, *Libya: A modern history*, John Hopkins University Press, 1982

Southern Cross Railway Station: at the end of nowhere. The photo dates from around the time Chubbie was growing up in the Western Australian town.
(E.L. Mitchell / State Library of Western Australia, b2940835_3)

Chubbie, Bill and the *Red Rose* on 14 October 1927, as they prepared for their 12,000-mile journey.

Chubbie packing her bags: 'The smallest amount of luggage ever taken by a woman on a journey of this length.'

Running to catch her flight. (George Rinhart / Getty Images)

The 1928 AVIAN

NOT only does the 1928 AVIAN represent the accumulated experience resulting from the design and construction of a wide range of aeroplanes having engines of from 3¼ h.p. to 1,000 h.p. in a single unit, but it is the outcome of several years' research devoted particularly to light aeroplanes, commencing with the Avro "BABY" of 1919.

The AVIAN definitely leads in SAFETY, ECONOMY, RELIABILITY, EASE OF HANDLING, EASE OF MAINTENANCE and COMFORT.

PRICE:

£730

Ex aerodrome, with complete standard equipment, ready to fly. Air Ministry fees for Certificates of Airworthiness and Registration are included.

Illustrated folder sent on request.

A. V. ROE & CO., LTD., MANCHESTER.

London Office & Export Dept.: 166, Piccadilly, W.1.   Experimental Works: Hamble, Southampton.

The 'ship' that was to carry Chubbie and Bill halfway around the globe.

(*Flight* magazine, courtesy Dave Robinson, Aviation Ancestry)

A personal farewell between Bill and his wife, Kiki.

Rutbah Wells: wind and rain in the sands of Iraq.

The *Red Rose* survives the flight to Darwin. (Peter Spillett Collection / Northern Territory Library)

Flying across New South Wales. (Fairfax, FXT288665)

An unceremonious arrival at Sydney's Mascot aerodrome. Chubbie's husband (standing behind Chubbie) was there to greet her. (Fairfax, FXT165646)

A 100,000-strong crowd at the Australian Air Derby at Mascot on the day of the *Red Rose*'s arrival.

Chubbie and Bill considering their options. (Fairfax, FXT283256)

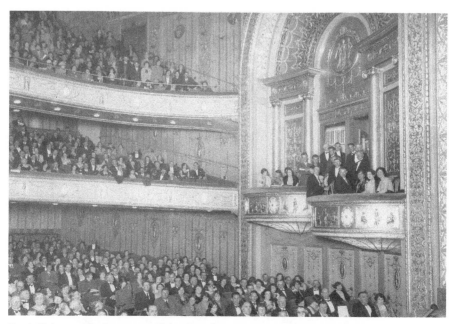

Socialising with the crew of the *Southern Cross* at St James' Theatre, Sydney. Chubbie is at the far left of the box; Kingsford Smith is leaning on the pillar. (National Library of Australia)

An advertisement for Bill and Chubbie's speaking tour of the eastern states of Australia. (*Hobart Mercury*)

Below: Standing on the deck of the *Sonoma* before their departure from Australia: (front row, from left) Bill Lancaster, Charles Kingsford Smith, Harry Lyon, Chubbie Miller, Charles Ulm and James Warner. (*Call-News Pictorial*, National Library of Australia)

Ten of the competitors in the National Women's Air Race (the Powder Puff Derby), 1929: (from left) Mary von Mach, Chubbie Miller, Gladys O'Donnell, Thea Rasche, Phoebe Omlie, Louise Thaden, Amelia Earhart, Blanche Noyes, Ruth Elder and Vera Walker. (Courtesy of the Women's International Air and Space Museum, Cleveland, Ohio)

One of the rudimentary landing fields on the route of the Powder Puff Derby. (Courtesy of the Women's International Air and Space Museum, Cleveland, Ohio)

After each leg of the derby, the aviators were driven to a function. Chubbie (far right) wears her usual high-heeled shoes. (Courtesy of the Women's International Air and Space Museum, Cleveland, Ohio)

Competitors in the Powder Puff Derby. The all-female event was followed with interest by every major US newspaper. Pancho Barnes, the stunt pilot, is second from left in the central row.

Marvel Crosson, one of the youngest but most experienced competitors in the race, posing with her new Travel Air.

Chubbie was thrilled to land at Cleveland, Ohio, at the finish of the Powder Puff Derby. (Fox Movietone News Story 3-485); (inset) The bracelet presented to each participant in the first ever women's air race. (Courtesy of the Women's International Air and Space Museum, Cleveland, Ohio)

A delighted Chubbie is announced as the winner of the first women's pylon race at the National Air Races, 1929.

The White Fleet, with Chubbie flying the lead plane, participates in the Ford Reliability Tour in October 1929. (City of Toronto Archives)

(From left) Chubbie, Blanche Noyes and Amelia Earhart flying kites at a promotional shoot for the 1930 Women's Powder Puff Derby.

At the rules meeting, the female aviators discovered the new conditions that were to be imposed on them for the 1930 race. (From left) Chubbie, Blanche Noyes and Amelia Earhart with race organisers.

The Eaglerock Bullet was rapidly dubbed the 'Killer Bullet' after several test pilots died. (*Aeronautics* magazine, June 1929)

The happy couple in 1932. Contrary to appearances, tensions were growing in the relationship.

Charles Haden Clarke
(*St Louis Post-Dispatch*)

Ida Clyde Clarke and her son, Dr Beverly
Clarke, at the trial. (*Kane Republican*)

Bill shaking hands with the jury foreman after the ordeal was over.

Bill and the *Southern Cross Minor*, another Avro Avian, before setting off for North Africa in 1932.

Chubbie's office job: so close to the aviation world yet so far from the cockpit.

CPSIA information can be obtained
at www.ICGtesting.com
Printed in the USA
LVHW090330230919
631917LV00001B/1/P